JANE BARNES • DREW HYDE • NICK KENNY • JACKY NEWBROOK

advanced expert

STUDENT'S RESOURCE BOOK

WITH KEY

with audio cd set

PEARSON
Longman

Contents

Module	Section	Reading/Vocabulary	Listening	English in Use	Language development	Writing
4 Life's rich tapestry (pp. 39–49)	**A** **Making choices**		**Paper 4 Part 3** Multiple-choice questions: Five people talk about difficult decisions (p. 42)	**Paper 3 Part 1** Lexical cloze: *A successful working relationship* (p. 39) **Paper 3 Part 4** Word formation: *Find your ideal job-share partner, Working as a team* (p. 41)	Spelling. Negative prefixes. Word families. (p. 40)	
	B **Human nature**	**Vocabulary** Relationships (p. 43) **Reading: Paper 1 Part 4** Multiple matching: *Mirror images* (pp. 48–49)		**Paper 3 Part 2** Open cloze: *Give the brain a breather* (p. 46)	*that*-clauses. Clauses beginning with a question word. *to*-infinitive and -*ing*-clauses. (pp. 44–45)	**Paper 2 Part 2** Competition entry: *Why the family is an influential part of a young person's life* (p. 47)
5 Global issues (pp. 50–60)	**A** **In the slow lane**		**Paper 4 Part 3** Multiple-choice questions: Environmentally friendly walking tours. (p. 54)	**Paper 3 Part 4** Word formation: *The pleasures of slow food, Fast food slows to a stop* (p. 50) **Paper 3 Part 5** Register transfer: email ➤ hotel leaflet (hotel facilities) (pp. 52–53)	Gradable and ungradable adjectives. Confusing adjectives/adverbs. (pp. 51–52)	
	B **A fight for survival**	**Vocabulary** The environment (p. 55) **Reading: Paper 1 Part 3** Multiple-choice questions: *Garbage guru* (pp. 58–59)		**Paper 3 Part 3** Error correction (spelling and punctuation): *Useless things, umbrellas* (p. 57)	Review of conditionals. Mixed conditionals. Alternatives to *if*. (p. 56)	**Paper 2 Part 1** Notes and emails: clean-up campaign (p. 60)
6 Looking forward, looking back (pp.61–71)	**A** **Health and fitness**		**Paper 4 Part 1** Sentence completion: *Complementary therapist* (p. 66)	**Paper 3 Part 4** Word formation: *No cosmetic surgery for Catwoman, Science matters* (p. 61) **Paper 3 Part 6** Gapped text: *Maintaining a youthful appearance* (p. 63)	Emphasis with *what, the thing that*, etc. Emphasis with *It + be*. (p. 62)	Cohesion. Substitution and omission. Linking devices. (pp. 64–65)
	B **Unveiling the past**	**Reading: Paper 1 Part 2** Gapped text: *Digging for dinosaurs* (pp. 70–71)		**Paper 3 Part 5** Register transfer: information sheet ➤ email (Museum of Natural History guide) (p. 68)	Verbs + -*ing*, *to*-infinitive or infinitive without *to*. Verb + -*ing* form/ *to*-infinitive with a change in meaning. (p. 67)	**Paper 2 Part 2** Guidebook entry: *Come to sunny Compton* (p. 69)

3

A Learning experiences

English in Use
Lexical cloze (Paper 3 Part 1)

▶ CB page 10, ER page 169

Exam strategy

For this task, you need a good knowledge of fixed expressions, phrasal verbs and collocations. Add any new expressions you come across to your vocabulary notebook. Remember to review them regularly, and try to use them in your speaking and writing.

1 a Read the title of the text. What do you think it is going to be about?

   b Read the whole text quickly for general understanding, ignoring the gaps for the moment.

2 a Read the text again carefully and think about the type of word which will fit in each gap. Try to predict what the answer will be.

   b Look at the options A–D and choose the option which you feel fits best in each gap. Use the Help clues if necessary.

3 Read through the text again when you've finished and check that the options you've chosen fit in with the overall meaning of the text.

HELP

➤ Question 1
All of these words express the idea of *continue*, but only one of them collocates with *impression*.

➤ Question 2
Each of these words is used to link two ideas. Read the whole sentence carefully to decide which one fits the meaning here.

➤ Question 13
Only one of these words can follow the preposition *by*.

For questions **1–15**, read the article below and then decide which answer **A**, **B**, **C** or **D** best fits each space. The exercise begins with an example **(0)**.

The Earth from the air

Around ten million people worldwide have been to see Yann Arthus-Bertrand's exhibition of aerial photos **(0)** A *The Earth from the Air*. The exhibition features shots taken in over 100 different countries and never fails to make a **(1)**...... impression on those who come to see it. **(2)**...... part of the fascination probably comes from the fact that Bertrand is **(3)**...... on record things that the public could not otherwise see, this alone cannot explain why people are so **(4)**...... affected by the photographs themselves. The exhibition **(5)**...... people feeling enriched, with a more positive **(6)**...... on life, and many return with their friends. It's almost as if the exhibition was communicating something of the spiritual and educational **(7)**...... of travel itself.

Bertrand was living in Kenya, studying lions, when he began taking the photographs. 'It's hard to get a **(8)**...... idea of that sort of territory from the ground,' he explains, so when a friend offered to take him up in her plane, he **(9)**...... . 'Suddenly I could really see the beauty of the landscape in a new way,' he **(10)**...... . 'I was captivated.'

Since that day, Bertrand has been taking aerial photographs on a world-wide **(11)**...... . For some shots, he **(12)**...... with a specific place in mind, but around 80% of the destinations were found by **(13)**...... . What's more, he never **(14)**...... of searching for new places, always believing that he'll **(15)**...... something tomorrow that will be even more impressive than what he has seen today.

0 **A** called	**B** known	**C** labelled	**D** termed
1 **A** persisting	**B** keeping	**C** lasting	**D** remaining
2 **A** Because	**B** Since	**C** Once	**D** Although
3 **A** giving	**B** holding	**C** catching	**D** putting
4 **A** widely	**B** deeply	**C** largely	**D** wholly
5 **A** leaves	**B** sends	**C** makes	**D** lets
6 **A** feeling	**B** attitude	**C** outlook	**D** approach
7 **A** value	**B** profit	**C** gain	**D** credit
8 **A** clear	**B** sure	**C** plain	**D** pure
9 **A** complied	**B** approved	**C** accepted	**D** consented
10 **A** replies	**B** recalls	**C** repeats	**D** retains
11 **A** extent	**B** spread	**C** degree	**D** scale
12 **A** comes up	**B** gets on	**C** sets out	**D** does away
13 **A** luck	**B** chance	**C** fate	**D** fortune
14 **A** exhausts	**B** weakens	**C** tires	**D** bores
15 **A** spot	**B** note	**C** meet	**D** grasp

Language development

Tense forms

▶ CB page 13, GR page 173

Past to present tenses

1 Complete each pair of sentences using one verb from the list.
   Put the verb into the present perfect simple or continuous.

   cook   eat   hear   live   take   tell   steal   wear

   1 a I .... you everything I know already.
      b Cal .... everyone about his promotion.
   2 a Simon .... that jacket for years; it's the only one he's got.
      b I'm sure Keith .... that jacket before; it looks familiar.
   3 a We .... in that restaurant before. It wasn't bad.
      b We .... in that restaurant for years. It's great.
   4 a I've still got a headache and I .... aspirins all day.
      b I've still got a headache and I .... six aspirins today.
   5 a I .... always .... in the same house.
      b I .... only .... in this house for two months.
   6 a I .... this song everywhere I go recently. It's really annoying me.
      b I am sure I .... your name mentioned in a meeting.
   7 a I .... dinner for 20 before, but it wasn't great.
      b I haven't had time to check the car because I .... dinner.
   8 a Someone .... my CDs; they've all suddenly disappeared.
      b Someone .... my CDs; they keep disappearing.

2 a Complete the biography of the musician Norah Jones below by putting
      the verbs in brackets into the past simple or present perfect simple or
      continuous.

   b In your notebook, write a short
      biography of someone you
      admire.

Past tenses

3 Correct the mistakes with past
   tenses. There are either one or two
   mistakes in each sentence.

   1 I lived at home when I passed my
      driving test, but after that I
      moved out.
   2 When the accident happened,
      John drove, but it wasn't his fault.
   3 He said he was feeling sick and
      he was apologising for not
      coming.
   4 My tooth was hurting again, so I
      was deciding to visit the dentist
      that afternoon.
   5 I had already been hearing the
      news when the director told me.
   6 When I arrived, I saw that 20
      people waited; some were already
      waiting for over three hours.
   7 When my exam results were
      coming, I got exactly the grades
      that I had hoped for.
   8 I think my boss was sleeping
      badly the night before, as he was
      being very critical that day.

Norah Jones **(1)**.................. (*be*) born in March 1979 in New
York, but her family **(2)**.................. (*move*) to Texas four years
later. She **(3)**.................. (*start*) singing when she **(4)**..................
(*be*) five years old and **(5)**.................. (*play*) the piano since she
was seven. She **(6)**.................. (*study*) music at North Texas
University, where she **(7)**.................. (*graduate*) in jazz piano.
Her mother and father, who are both in the music business,
(8).................. (*influence*) her greatly. She **(9)**.................. (*learn*)
to mix diverse styles such as jazz, pop and country to
develop her distinct style.

   Five years ago, she **(10)**.................. (*move*) back to New York
and **(11)**.................. (*live*) there ever since. In 2001, she
(12).................. (*become*) an overnight sensation when she
(13).................. (*release*) her first album *Come Away With
Me*, which **(14)**.................. (*sell*) over 15 million copies and is
still very popular. Since then, she **(15)**.................. (*release*) a
second album, and continues to tour widely with her
band.

4 Put the verbs in brackets into the correct past tense form.

Traditionally, it was students who took a 'gap year' (a year off to travel or gain experience), but last year 60% of 'gappers' (**1**)............................ (*be*) people taking a career break. Many of them (**2**)........................... (*give up*) their job before setting off around the world. Others (**3**)........................... (*work*) for companies that (**4**)........................... (*agree*) to give them unpaid leave in order to travel.

Why did they decide to take a gap year? Many (**5**)........................... (*work*) hard for years and simply (**6**)........................... (*feel*) they needed a break. Others (**7**)........................... (*want*) to 'give something back' by doing volunteer work abroad.

Fran Hodges is one of these people. Although she (**8**)........................... (*plan*) to be away for only six months, she (**9**)........................... (*end up*) staying away for a year. She (**10**)........................... (*celebrate*) her 40th birthday while she (**11**)........................... (*work*) at an elephant sanctuary in Sri Lanka.

Fran (**12**)........................... (*be*) a researcher, but she (**13**)........................... (*quit*) her job in order to go off travelling. She (**14**)........................... (*buy*) her ticket two days before she (**15**)........................... (*give in*) her notice so she couldn't be talked out of it. She (**16**)........................... (*never/travel*) alone before, but (**17**)........................... (*be*) surprised how easy it was and how much fun she had.

Referring to the future

5 Underline the most appropriate verb forms in italics.

By next month (**1**) we'll be living / we'll have been living in this house for 11 years! But (**2**) we're moving / we will move to a bigger place very soon. (**3**) We're buying / We will be buying a house just outside of town – the owners have accepted our offer.

It's a nice house, but it needs updating, so (**4**) we're going to plan / we plan to make quite a few changes. We estimate the work (**5**) is going to take / is taking two or three months, so we'll have to stay with friends until the builders (**6**) will finish / have finished. We'll move in as soon as the house (**7**) is / will be ready. You must come and visit us.

On 12 September, (**8**) I'll start / I'll be starting a new job. I reckon it (**9**) takes / will take me a little longer to get to work in the mornings.

6 Complete each gap with a suitable word from the list.

about are bound due expect not unlikely verge

A: Hurry up! The train is just (**1**)................... to leave.
B: Don't worry, it's (**2**)........................... to leave on time.
A: I am worried. They're on the (**3**)........................... of closing the platform barrier.
B: We have plenty of time. They (**4**)........................... people to be late.
A: The ticket says that passengers (**5**)........................... to board the train five minutes before departure.
B: But the doctor said you are (**6**)........................... to get stressed out on this trip. If we miss this train, there's (**7**)........................... to be another one soon.
A: No, the next one isn't (**8**)........................... to leave for another three hours.

7 Complete the sentences using an appropriate structure in the correct form: *be going to, be due to, be about to.*

1 I could tell from the expression on his face that he .... refuse the job.
2 We were sure the builders .... finished by now, but they say they need another two weeks.
3 We thought we .... moving house next week, but now it will be next month.
4 Petra .... graduated this year, but she's had a lot of illness, so now it won't be until next year.
5 Anna .... have the baby in May, but it was four weeks premature.
6 We were just .... leave when Peter arrived.

8 Complete the text, using an appropriate future form of the verbs in brackets.

By this time next week, I (**1**)........................... (*finish*) school. I'm looking forward to the holidays, as you can imagine. First, I (**2**)........................... (*spend*) some time just relaxing – I (**3**)........................... (*probably/stay*) at home. Then my boyfriend and I (**4**)........................... (*start*) work at a new hotel on the coast. It's not quite finished yet, but it's (**5**)........................... (*open*) in two weeks' time. George and I (**6**)........................... (*serve*) meals in the restaurant all day. It (**7**)........................... (*be*) quite a laugh. We (**8**)........................... (*work*) for my uncle, but had to cancel that as he (**9**)........................... (*plan*) to be away for the summer. After six weeks in the hotel, I think I (**10**)........................... (*need*) a holiday before my university course (**11**)........................... (*start*) in September!

English in Use
Error correction (extra word) (Paper 3 Part 3)

▶ ER page 169

1 Read the title of the text below to identify the topic. Why do you think carpentry might be 'a disappearing art'?

2 Read the whole text quickly for general understanding, ignoring the mistakes for the moment.
   1 How does the writer feel about the workshop he describes?
   2 What explanation does he give for what he describes there?

3 Read the text again, sentence by sentence, and complete the task. Use the Help clues if necessary. Remember that:
   • most of the errors are grammatical
   • some of the lines will be correct.

4 When you've finished, read the whole text again to check it makes complete sense.

In **most** lines of the following text, there is **one** unnecessary word. It is either grammatically incorrect or does not fit in with the sense of the text. For each numbered line (1–16), find this word and write it in the box. **Some** lines are correct. Indicate these lines with a tick (✓) in the box. The exercise begins with two examples (0) and (00).

The disappearing art of carpentry

In a little carpentry workshop deep in the English countryside, joiners have	**0**	✓
been making hand-crafted furniture for the generations. Today, there's also	**00**	the
a visitors' showroom, a gift shop and, if you want to watch out the craftsmen	**1**	
at work, a viewing gallery from where you find yourself behind a glass panel,	**2**	
nose-to-nose with some joiners been working at their benches. They are	**3**	
cutting timber, making joints and carving wood – the sort of same operations	**4**	
that carpenters have been carrying out for centuries. It may seem odd,	**5**	
therefore, that tourists should be interested in observing of them. But many	**6**	
clearly are, probably because they will rarely, if ever, have seen a chair or	**7**	
table being made before. These simple processes, which were not so long	**8**	
ago could be witnessed in workshops up and down the country, are now	**9**	
become so unusual that skilled joiners are an endangered species, and	**10**	
watching them at work has become a spectator sport. One reason for this is	**11**	
the trend towards mass-production of furniture, but there has also been seeing	**12**	
a change in values. Becoming a craftsperson get used to be a worthwhile	**13**	
ambition for a teenager. But sadly, now that education has become and	**14**	
more widely available, skilled manual work is thought as suitable only for	**15**	
those youngsters not bright enough nor to get on computer-studies courses.	**16**	

HELP

➤ Question 1
Check the phrasal verb in this line. Is one needed in this sentence?

➤ Question 2
There are three prepositions in this line. Are they all needed?

➤ Question 3
Check the verb forms in this line. Are the tenses correct?

➤ Question 4
Check the word order in this line – there's a word that fits the sense, but it's in the wrong place.

➤ Question 5–10
Three of these lines are correct. Do you know which ones?

Language development

Look at all the verbs in the text. Which ones are in the present perfect? Underline them. Are any of them continuous tenses?

Listening

Note completion (Paper 4 Part 1)

▶ ER pages 170–171

1 a Read the instructions for the task.
   1 What kind of text are you going to hear?
   2 What is the topic?

 b Read through the notes. Think about the topic and what you expect to hear. How much do you find out about the course from the notes?

 c Can you predict the type of information you will be listening for? For example:
   1 What type of information are you listening for in question 1?
   2 In which questions are you looking for the name of a session?
   3 Which answer is the name of a profession? Can you predict the type of profession it's likely to be?

2 ⌒ Listen to the recording once and complete the notes. Use the Help clues if necessary. Remember that:
   • the information comes in the same order as the notes on the page
   • the words you need to write in the gaps are in the recording
   • the answers are single words or short phrases
   • you shouldn't repeat words or information that are already in the notes.

HELP
➤ Question 1
You're listening for the name of an organisation. There are two in the recording, but only one is actually organising the seminars.
➤ Question 3
The notes say *what's called a* – so you need to write the name of something. Listen for a similar phrase in the recording.
➤ Question 7
The name of this session includes a verb. Look at the other headings to predict what form the verb will take.

3 Listen again to check and complete your answers. Remember to check your spelling.

4 Look at the following wrong answers that students gave to some of the questions. Listen again and decide why they are not correct.
   1 City's Commerce
   2 sales company
   5 money
   6 Leadership says it all
   8 being a head
   10 eight Novembre

You will hear part of a radio programme describing a course designed to help young people who want to start their own business. For questions **1–10**, complete the notes.

DAWN OF OPPORTUNITY
Five-week seminar programme

Organised by: [1] in the city

Sessions led by: Vimmi Singh, a qualified [2]

Session 1: Envisioning your Business
• defines basic idea
• participants develop what's called a '[3]'

Session 2: Dynamics
• covers the main [4] needed for the business

Session 3: Fuelling the Business
• getting the best type of [5]

Session 4: [6]
• team-building skills
• motivating staff

Session 5: [7]
• 'Route Plan' sets personal objectives and business agenda, e.g. getting started, [8] and dealing with setbacks

Price of course: £200

Participants must:
• be under 25
• have a minimum of three years' [9]
• have a business idea

Dates: Weekly sessions from October 4th to [10]

B A job for life?

Language development
Passive forms
▶ CB page 19, GR page 174

The passive in different tenses

1 a Rewrite the sentences using passive forms. Only include the agent where necessary.
   1 The company requires a new training manager.
   ....
   2 The Human Resources Department has advertised the post in all national newspapers.
   ....
   3 The company is seeking a highly motivated individual.
   ....
   4 We were training someone for the role, but she left.
   ....
   5 The company has received 45 applications so far.
   ....
   6 We will not contact unsuccessful candidates.
   ....
   7 We are only going to interview the five best candidates.
   ....
   8 The Director will have completed the interviews by the end of next week.
   ....

b Do the same with these sentences containing modal verbs.
   1 Each candidate must complete an aptitude test.
   ....
   2 You should have warned me that the interview room was unavailable.
   ....
   3 We will have to rearrange the interviews.
   ....
   4 People must tell me about any changes to the schedule.
   ....
   5 The company has to do something about the lack of space.
   ....
   6 The company could have improved its interview procedure.
   ....

2 Decide which of these sentences **can't** be rewritten in the passive. Then rewrite the rest. Only include the agent where necessary.
   1 Jenny told the police officer a lie.
   ....
   2 Louis hates people telling him what to do.
   ....
   3 I hate you looking like that.
   ....
   4 I don't like people checking up on me.
   ....
   5 We encourage our customers to give us their opinions.
   ....
   6 I walked into the restaurant and sat down at a table.
   ....
   7 I think he has broken his arm.
   ....
   8 The police are looking into the cause of the accident.
   ....

Passive -*ing* forms and infinitives

3 Decide whether the -*ing* or *to*-infinitive form fits the sentence. Underline the correct verb form.
   1 The children remember *being* / *to be* taken to the museum.
   2 Some people seem to enjoy *being* / *to be* frightened.
   3 She wanted *being* / *to be* told the truth.
   4 Harry deserves *being* / *to be* given a promotion.
   5 Young children resent *being* / *to be* bossed around by older children.
   6 Gary is hoping *being* / *to be* released from prison in a few weeks.
   7 The manager insisted on *being* / *to be* kept informed of new developments.
   8 I didn't expect *being* / *to be* invited to the party.

4 Rewrite the sentences using a passive -*ing* form or infinitive.
   0 No one enjoys it when other people tell them what to do.
   No one enjoys being told what to do.
   1 I wanted someone to offer me the opportunity to travel.
   ....
   2 She could remember someone carrying her out of the burning building.
   ....

11

3 He didn't expect the company to make him redundant.

....

4 She is hoping that voters will elect her as mayor.

....

5 My father insisted that we should call him 'Sir'.

....

6 I hate it when people let me down at the last minute.

....

have/get + object + past participle

5 **Complete the sentences using the correct form of the verbs in the list.**

*alter   build   check   cut   enlarge   launder
redecorate   ~~replace~~*

1 She has found a dress she likes, but she will need .... it .... before the wedding.
2 The price includes the cost of .... your hair washed, ... and dried.
3 I'd rather pay .... my shirts .... than spend the time doing it myself.
4 I took some great photos of the landscape and .... a couple of them .... and framed.
5 Look at the state of this room! Let's .... it .... before the holidays.
6 You should .... all electrical equipment .... regularly to make sure it is safe.

6 **Read the text and complete each gap with one suitable word. In some cases, there is more than one correct answer.**

Ever since I first heard that I (1)..................... had my paper accepted at the conference, I've been worrying about everything that I need to (2)..................... done.
First of all, I had to work out what to wear when I give my talk. In the end, I've just decided to (3)..................... my best suit cleaned rather than have all the hassle of finding a new one or (4)..................... one made.
Next, my hair (5)..................... cutting. I'm thinking of (6)..................... it drastically restyled for a smarter, more professional look. I'll get Tony (7)..................... give me a few ideas on what will look best.
As I (8)..................... my laptop stolen when my car (9)..................... broken into, I've borrowed one and I'll get one of the IT guys at the university (10)..................... transfer my presentation onto it.
I'll (11)..................... a taxi to pick me up from home, so I won't (12)..................... taking to the airport, but thanks for asking!

English in Use

Register transfer (Paper 3 Part 5)

▶ CB page 18, ER page 170

1 a **Read the publicity leaflet on page 13 quickly for general understanding. Answer these questions.**
   1 What type of person would attend such a course?
      a) People interested in local history
      b) Bookshop owners wanting to increase sales
      c) People interested in learning to write books
   2 Is the leaflet relatively formal or informal in style?

  b **Now read the letter on page 13.**
   1 Why is Mark writing to Andrea?
   2 How is the style of the letter different from that of the leaflet?

2 a **Look at the words and phrases in bold in the leaflet. Find and mark related parts of the letter.**

  b **Now answer these questions to help you complete gaps 1–3 and 6.**
   1 Look at question 1. The correct answer completes an informal phrase with the same meaning as *is easily accessed*. Which word does this best?
      a) proceed   b) get   c) arrive
   2 Look at question 2. The correct answer completes an informal phrase with the same meaning as *wide range*. Which is it?
      a) many   b) lots   c) lot
   3 Look at question 3. The correct answer has the same meaning as *the size of each group is strictly limited*. Which is it?
      a) limited numbers   b) small   c) a few people
   4 Look at question 6. Underline the passive verb in the leaflet which relates to this gap. The answer to question 6 is a less formal expression which is not in the passive.

3 **Now complete the task using the same techniques. Remember that:**
   - the correct word must fit in with the style of the text
   - you should think carefully about the words before and after the gap – the correct answer must fit grammatically
   - the words you need do not occur in the first text
   - you must use no more than two words in each gap
   - you should read the text through to make sure your answers fit in grammatically and the text makes complete sense.

For questions **1–14**, read the publicity leaflet. Use the information in it to complete the numbered gaps in the informal letter. The words you need **do not occur** in the publicity leaflet. **Use no more than two words for each gap.** The exercise begins with an example (**0**).

PUBLICITY LEAFLET

WEEKEND WRITING COURSE

Looking for a new career? Learn the skills you need to become a writer by attending our weekend residential course held in the inspirational location of historic Hanbury Hall. This lovely mansion is in a rural location, yet **is easily accessed** from the nearby railway station.

Course Details
- Seminars are available on a **wide range** of literary topics. The **size of each group is strictly limited**, so early registration is recommended.
- Benefit from the experience of best-selling authors. **Individual tuition** is available at an additional fee.
- A **compulsory** pre-course reading list is supplied on registration.
- Participants are requested to prepare a review (maximum 1,000 words) of a novel selected from the enclosed list. This should be submitted at least two weeks prior to the start of the course.
- A complimentary copy of the book you review, signed by the author, is presented to you on completion of the course.

Course Fees
- Prices inclusive of half-board accommodation (lunch extra). Please notify us of any special dietary requirements in advance.
- Reductions available for students and senior citizens.

INFORMAL LETTER

Dear Andrea,

You know you want to be an author? Well, I've just heard about a weekend writing course you can go on – it sounds perfect! It's at Hanbury Hall, a lovely old country house where you can (**0**) stay for the weekend! It's quite convenient because you can (**1**)_____ there easily by train.

They have seminars on a (**2**)_____ of different subjects, all connected with literature. But as the groups are only (**3**)_____ , you should book soon if you want to go. There will be talks by well-known authors, and you can have a (**4**)_____ with one if you pay extra. They give you a list of the books that you (**5**)_____ read before you go, and they (**6**)_____ to write a 1,000-word book review. You can (**7**)_____ from the list. You've got to (**8**)_____ the review two weeks (**9**)_____ the course begins. You even get a (**10**)_____ signed copy of the book at the (**11**)_____ the course.

The price includes bed, breakfast and (**12**)_____ , but you should (**13**)_____ know that you're vegetarian before you arrive. As you're a student, you can get a (**14**)_____ the price of the course. If you want to give them a ring, the number is 01234 567891.

Let me know how you get on.

Cheers

Mark

Language development
Look at all the verbs in the leaflet. Which of them are in the passive? What is the tense of the passive verb in each case?

Reading

Multiple matching (Paper 1 Parts 1 and 4)

▶ ER page 168

1 Read the title of the text and the subheading. Make a list of jobs that you would describe as 'glamorous'.

2 a Read the instructions for the exam task. The text is about the four people in the options A, B, C and D.

   b Scan the article to find their names and write the letters A, B, C and D beside the paragraph relating to the person.

   c Now skim those paragraphs to find out what job each person does. Are any of their jobs on your list in Exercise 1?

3 a Read all the questions and highlight the key words in each question. The first four have been done for you.

   b Read the first section of the text about Kieran O'Rourke carefully. Look back at the questions and mark any parts of the text which mention similar information or ideas. For example:
   1 Look at question 1 and find the sentence in the paragraph which seems to have the same meaning. Mark the parts that mean *a team of colleagues* and *appreciates the value*.
   2 Look at question 4 and find the phrases in the paragraph that are similar in meaning to the highlighted key words.

   You have now found two questions which match option A. There are two more. Can you find them?

   c Look at question 9. Scan the whole text quickly to find the three places where stress is mentioned. These are marked for you. Which person *enjoys helping clients cope with stress*?

4 Now continue to match the rest of the questions to the text. Always read the section of text carefully, to check it has exactly the same meaning as the question. There may be several sections of text that are similar in meaning to the questions, but there is only one that matches exactly.

TIP

When you have found a match for the question in the text, write the question number in the margin next to the relevant piece of text – you will need to go back and check it later.

Answer questions **1–15** by referring to the magazine article opposite about four people with glamorous jobs. Choose your answers from the people listed **A–D**. Some of the choices may be required more than once.

A Kieran O'Rourke   **C** Sankha Guha
B Christina Booth   **D** Becky Regan

Which person

appreciates the value of working with a team of colleagues?	**1** ....
believes you need individuality to succeed in the job?	**2** ....
insists on working independently in the job?	**3** ....
accepts that immaturity can be a disadvantage in their job?	**4** ....
enjoys the fact that the job offers so much variety?	**5** ....
assists colleagues in the development of their career prospects?	**6** ....
has the confidence to make decisions which are unpopular with colleagues?	**7** ....
applied for a job about which there was little information?	**8** ....
enjoys helping clients cope with stress?	**9** ....
is able to achieve personal goals in the course of the job?	**10** ....
was keen to escape from a sheltered upbringing?	**11** ....
gained the experience for their present job through being assertive?	**12** ....
found a lack of experience in the job to be an advantage?	**13** ....
failed to achieve a childhood ambition?	**14** ....
feels that single-mindedness is necessary for success in the job?	**15** ....

'That's the kind of job I've always wanted.'

Katrina Bentley interviews four people who have very glamorous jobs.
How did they get these jobs and are they as good as they sound?

I was standing on a breezy mountainside in Scotland, watching the filming of a historical drama. I was waiting to interview the producer, Kieran O'Rourke, and I knew I'd have to be patient. As I watched him talking animatedly to two of the actors in the gateway to the ancient castle, I wondered how, at the surprisingly young age of 35, he came to be producing films for a leading film company. When an ill-timed rain shower stopped the filming, I asked him if this career had been his life-long dream. 'Not really,' he told me. 'I'd always wanted to act, but after years of playing really minor roles I realised I'd never make the big time. So I got a job working on the production side of films and found it fascinating. One evening at a party I was introduced to one of the top producers, and I plucked up the courage to ask him for a job.' Kieran's cheek paid off, and he began working amongst some of the best production teams in the film industry. He learned quickly, talking his way into key jobs by correctly assessing the techniques necessary to create a box-office success. Dealing with actresses who are notoriously temperamental was a new challenge for Kieran. 'My age does count against me at times, but I've learned to be diplomatic,' he says, with a rueful grin. 'I let their temper tantrums just bounce off me. After all, acting is very stressful. To make a successful film, a huge number of people are involved, and it's important that we're all pulling in the same direction.'

Another young person who has close contact with well-known celebrities in the course of her job is Christina Booth who, at only 26, works as the manager of the health spa in one of London's most luxurious hotels. 'I left school at 16 to begin my training as a beauty therapist at a salon in the town where I was brought up. My parents would've liked me to stay close to home where they could keep an eye on me, but I knew there was a far bigger world out there to explore. I soon realised that to achieve a lot in this business, you have to concentrate totally on your personal objectives. Now, I can hardly believe the kind of people I'm dealing with every day – I'll often see them on the front page of the newspapers!' Christina sees each day as a new challenge. 'But the most satisfying part of the job is helping my clients to relax,' she says. 'They come into the spa exhausted after living life in the spotlight and they literally leave as different people.' Christina loves having a team of therapists whom she is responsible for training. 'I enjoy the management side of the job and helping my team to develop skills that will help them when it comes to thinking about promotion.'

As a child, Sankha Guha had no burning ambitions to work in TV. The fact that he was born in India, however, and travelled extensively with his family, equipped him very well to present one of TV's most successful travel programmes. After working in local radio, Sankha felt ready for new challenges, so when he came across a job advert for a researcher on a TV programme, he decided to go for it. 'There was no explanation for what the programme was,' he told me, 'but the next thing I knew, I was fronting a live show.' Being in front of a camera was a shock for Sankha. 'It was a totally new environment for me, and I was always searching for the right words,' he says. But he didn't have to worry, viewers perceived his chatty presentation as a fresh, irreverent style of journalism, and he was soon offered a range of travel and documentary programmes. A journalist by nature, he refuses to be told what to say and likes to do his own research. His most recent project is a documentary on the life of the Sherpa porters who provide the support for people on trekking expeditions in Nepal. Sankha was keen to film this, as he is full of admiration for the courage and stamina of the Sherpa guides in that mountainous country. Television, he says, has given him a lot. 'I've had fantastic opportunities to go places I've always wanted to see. My next programme is about polar bears in the north of Canada.'

After university, Becky Regan, who's in her twenties, had no burning career ambitions, so she drifted into the world of journalism and spent three years working for various business magazines. 'I got valuable experience, working in the editing department, but I decided it was fashion magazines that really appealed to me and after countless job applications I finally landed the job of features editor at *Lady Jane* magazine.' It took another three years before she achieved her current position as editor. I asked her what the secret was to getting the top job in one of the UK's most prestigious women's glossy magazines. 'This is a very high-pressure business,' she replied. 'You have to show yourself to be a bit ahead of the rest, so you stand out from the crowd.' As editor, Becky takes on new staff and directs the whole *Lady Jane* team. She also selects the cover design of the magazine. One of her most memorable choices was the footballer David Beckham. 'The editorial team thought I was crazy, breaking away from the normal cover format, but being me I stuck to my guns. Why shouldn't a man be on the front of a women's magazine? And that issue was a sell-out!' Becky feels that she has 'the perfect job' because it has so many different elements. 'This job has such scope, I see it as a long-term project.'

> **This is a very high-pressure business. You have to show yourself to be a bit ahead of the rest, so you stand out from the crowd.**

Writing

Article (Paper 2, Part 2)

▶ CB pages 20–21, WR page 192

Exam strategy

For any piece of writing, you should use a style that is appropriate for the target reader. Read the task carefully to identify who that is, then decide on the appropriate style. Make sure you use that style consistently.

1 Read the task below and answer these questions.
   1 Who is the target reader?
   2 Will your answer be:
      a) formal or neutral? b) friendly and informal?
   3 What points should you include in your article? Mark them.

You have seen the following competition advertised in an international student travel magazine.

Win a holiday for you and your friend!
We are looking for the winner of this year's 'Best Friend' award and are offering a three-week all-inclusive holiday in the Caribbean. Write an article explaining why you are nominating your friend and saying how your friend would benefit from the holiday.

Write your **article** in approximately 250 words.

2 a Decide in what order you would deal with the following topics.

Reason for nomination	Paragraph ....
Final recommendation	Paragraph ....
Name of nominee	Paragraph ....1....
Benefits of winning	Paragraph ....
Specific example	Paragraph ....

   b Read a student's answer opposite and compare your ideas.

3 Some of the student's writing is too formal. Find and replace the formal expressions in the answer with the informal expressions below:
   1 turn to (paragraph 2)
   2 a bit down (paragraph 2)
   3 nothing is ever too much trouble for him (paragraph 2)
   4 let me (paragraph 3)
   5 with flying colours (paragraph 3)
   6 a real plus (paragraph 3)
   7 plus (paragraph 4)
   8 get so much out of (paragraph 5)

My best friend

①The moment I saw the advert for the 'Best friend' award I knew who I wanted to nominate – my oldest and best friend, Julio.

②I <u>know</u> Julio since we were four years old, when we started school together. The teacher put us next to each other in class, and we've been inseparable ever since. I can always rely on him in a crisis, or when I'm feeling a little depressed. He is always willing to help. **T**

③Allow me to give you an example. Last summer I was working for an important exam, but it was very difficult. Julio gave up all his evenings to help me study, and never <u>complained to</u> the time he could have been spending on something else. I managed to pass with an excellent mark – and it was <u>intirely</u> thanks to him. Having his help was a valuable benefit. **Gr** **Sp**

④This holiday would be perfect for Julio for two reasons. First, he has given up so much time for me, I wish I could find a way to repay him. Second, <u>he never has</u> been abroad, but he would love to see new things and <u>experiment</u> different cultures at the same time. The Caribbean would be the perfect destination for him to do this. Moreover, he is a fantastic photographer, so we could send in some pictures from our trip to the magazine. **Wo** **Ww**

⑤So, for being the best friend anyone could ask for and a person who would benefit greatly from this holiday, I nominate Julio.

Key to correction symbols

P = punctuation
Sp = spelling
Gr = grammar
T = verb tense
Ww = wrong word
Wo = word order
St = style

---

4 Correct the grammatical and spelling mistakes marked. Look at the key to see what the correction symbols mean.

5 Write your own answer to the task in your notebook.

A The inexplicable

English in Use
Lexical cloze (Paper 3 Part 1)
▶ CB page 26

1 a Read the title of the text and think about what you are going to read. What is hypnosis generally used for?

 b Read the whole text quickly for general understanding, ignoring the gaps for the moment. What is it about?
   a) how to become a hypnotist
   b) making money out of hypnotism
   c) benefiting as a result of being hypnotised

2 a Read the text again carefully and think about the type of word which will fit in each gap. Try to predict what the answer will be.

 b Look at the options A–D and choose the option which you feel fits best in each gap. Use the Help clues if necessary.

TIP

Remember to answer all the questions, even if you have to guess. But if you have no idea about one item, leave it until the end. Once you've worked through and fully understood the whole text, it might be easier to guess the right answer.

3 Read through the text again when you've finished and check that the options you've chosen fit in with the overall meaning of the text.

HELP
➤ Question 1
 Which of these phrasal verbs means *found by chance*?
➤ Question 3
 Two of the verbs can be followed by *up*. Which one fits the context?
➤ Question 8
 Only one of these words makes sense after *but*. Which is it?
➤ Question 9
 Only one of these words is typically followed by a *to*-infinitive. Which is it?

For questions **1–15**, read the text below and then decide which answer **A**, **B**, **C** or **D** best fits each space. The exercise begins with an example **(0)**.

Can hypnosis make you prosperous?

I was **(0)** A some research into the use of hypnosis in business training when I **(1)**........ the website of a hypnotist who **(2)**........ courses in something called 'abundance training' or 'learning to accumulate wealth through hypnosis'. I was, to say the least, intrigued and so I **(3)**........ up for a workshop that was **(4)**........ to be held in a city-centre hotel.

The hypnotist began by explaining that people could be surprisingly slow to take advantage of money-making opportunities. To illustrate her **(5)**........ , she revealed the first page of her flipchart. Attached were a number of banknotes below the **(6)**........ : 'Free money'. The room fell silent. Then one participant **(7)**........ from his seat. I assumed he was going to leave the room, but **(8)**........ he stopped at the flipchart and pocketed a note. For a moment, nobody **(9)**........ to copy him; then there was a stampede.

Next came the actual hypnosis. I had always imagined it would be a vivid, dreamlike experience. In the **(10)**........ , it felt more like **(11)**........ breathing for relaxation, or listening attentively with your eyes shut. Once under hypnosis, I heard a voice telling me to **(12)**........ the obstacles that prevented me achieving abundance, and I climbed over the wall that appeared before me. It was a terrific feeling. Released from my trance, I left the hotel on a **(13)**........ of optimism. A stern letter from the bank awaited me at home, however, **(14)**........ me that once again I'd reached my credit-card **(15)**........ . I realised that 'achieving abundance' might take me a while.

0	**A** doing	**B** getting	**C** making	**D** seeking
1	**A** dropped into	**B** tripped over	**C** came across	**D** checked up
2	**A** sets	**B** deals	**C** guides	**D** runs
3	**A** enlisted	**B** signed	**C** enrolled	**D** joined
4	**A** shortly	**B** currently	**C** briskly	**D** eventually
5	**A** point	**B** issue	**C** matter	**D** topic
6	**A** term	**B** label	**C** heading	**D** mark
7	**A** stood	**B** rose	**C** spun	**D** left
8	**A** instead	**B** although	**C** however	**D** therefore
9	**A** risked	**B** chanced	**C** feared	**D** dared
10	**A** occasion	**B** fact	**C** truth	**D** event
11	**A** strong	**B** soft	**C** deep	**D** heavy
12	**A** triumph	**B** overcome	**C** outdo	**D** defeat
13	**A** wave	**B** stream	**C** flood	**D** drift
14	**A** reminiscing	**B** reminding	**C** recalling	**D** remembering
15	**A** deadline	**B** boundary	**C** limit	**D** extent

Language development

Relative clauses ▶ CB page 29, GR page 175

Relative pronouns

1 a Use each of the pronouns in the list once to complete the following sentences.

who   whose   whom   why   which
where   when   that

1 My friend got to meet Brad Pitt, ... was very exciting for her.

2 Is that the magician .... often appears on TV?

3 I'm interested in an area of the brain .... images are processed.

4 The dogs, ... trainer has supplied animals for a number of films, could do some incredible tricks.

5 These days, there are few occasions .... I need to wear a tie.

6 The director from .... we received the information shall remain anonymous.

7 My past is not something .... I'd like people to know much about.

8 I'd like to know the reason .... you didn't act sooner.

b In which sentence above can the pronoun be omitted?

2 Complete the text by putting one word in each gap.

Borley Rectory – 'The most haunted house in Britain'

Borley Rectory was built in 1863 on a site with a long history. All **(1)**.................... who lived there reported strange occurrences, as a result of **(2)**.................... it was named 'the most haunted house in Britain'. The house was first occupied by Henry Bull and his son Harry, **(3)**.................... of whom died in the 'Blue Room' there.

Later residents, several of **(4)**.................... wrote down their experiences, claim to have seen the figure of Henry Bull. The strange incidents, most of **(5)**.................... have never been explained, include objects being thrown, objects appearing and disappearing, sightings of people, writing appearing on walls. A nun, believed to have died there in the 15ᵗʰ century, is often seen walking along a path in the garden, which is **(6)**.................... it is known as 'The Nun's Walk'.

The house was destroyed by fire in 1939, **(7)**.................... which point the number of incidents in the area dropped sharply. The site, **(8)**.................... which a number of modern houses have now been built, is still a source of interest to many visitors.

3 Mark the option(s) that can fit in each space. There may be more than one.

1 Please show your ID card .... you visit the club.
   A every time   B all times   C whenever
   D each time that

2 You can use this phone .... you go.
   A where   B wherever   C anywhere
   D in which place

3 .... I do seems to go wrong.
   A All what   B Which   C Everything that
   D Whatever

4 I'd like to speak to .... is in charge.
   A whoever   B who   C the person who
   D whom

5 I explained .... I wanted him to do.
   A what   B whatever   C the things what
   D the things that

6 They both love sports; that's .... they get on so well.
   A why   B the reason that   C for why
   D because

7 I've been thinking about .... we did yesterday.
   A what   B the things that   C which   D it's what

8 I recommend all these books – you can borrow .... you want.
   A them   B any one   C whichever one   D one

Reduced relative clauses

4 In each text, make one sentence shorter by using a reduced relative clause: a present or past participle or *to*-infinitive.

1
Janine is very superstitious. She always wears a necklace with a locket that contains a lucky clover leaf. I don't know where she got it from or why she believes in it.

2
People who wish to learn more about the paranormal would be well advised to contact a local paranormal society. A number of such groups exist, especially in places where there are high numbers of incidents.

3
A number of people here can help you. However, Jeremy is the person who you should talk to if you want information about local customs. He has lived in the area all his life and is an expert.

4
There are many numbers that have huge significance. People who are asked to choose a lucky number most frequently pick three or seven. Thirteen is the least popular number.

English in Use
Gapped text (Paper 3 Part 6)

▶ CB page 28,
ER page 170

1 a Read the title of
       the text and look
       at the picture.
       What do you
       know or what can
       you guess about
       'The Indian Rope
       Trick'?

   b Read the whole
      text quickly to
      find out what it
      tells you about
      the trick, ignoring
      the gaps for the
      moment.
      1 Was the rope
         trick genuine
         or fake?
      2 Why were people in the West so fascinated by it?

2 Read the text again carefully and do the task. Use the
   Help clues if necessary. Remember that there are three
   phrases that do not fit into the text at all.

TIP

*In this example of the task, the options are all clauses which
come at the end of the sentence. So for each item, you need to
look at what comes before the gap to check if an option fits
grammatically – check the tense, singular and plural
references, etc. Then look at the text before and after the gap to
check that an option makes sense in the context of the whole
text.*

3 Read through the text again when you have finished
   and check that the options you have chosen fit in with
   the overall meaning of the text.

HELP
➤ Question 2
   The text before the gap mentions a *fake newspaper story*
   which was written in 1890. The correct option is in the
   past tense and mentions the effects of the story.
➤ Question 5
   The first part of the sentence says the story was in a
   relentlessly jokey style. Look at the words immediately after
   the gap to find out whether the writer liked this aspect of
   the book or not. This will help you choose the right
   option.

For questions **1–6**, read the following text and then
choose from the list **A–I** given below the best phrase to
fill each of the spaces. Each correct phrase may only be
used once. **Some of the suggested answers do not
fit at all**.

The Indian rope trick

The Indian rope trick of popular mythology can be
described relatively simply. The magician throws a
length of rope up into the air; it stiffens and stays
vertical, then a boy climbs up it and disappears. It's
one of those things that everyone appears to have
heard about, but **(1)**........ .

The Rise of the Indian Rope Trick by Peter Lamont is
the story of a 19th-century legend that began in 1890
when Chicago journalist John E. Wilkie wrote a fake
newspaper story **(2)**........ . Historian Peter Lamont
argues that the idea of the Indian rope trick, and its
fascination for 19th-century Western audiences, was
the product of a people so in love with rationality and
progress that it had to invent that sense of wonder
(3)........ . The rope trick matched the European idea of
a mystical East, of an imagined India **(4)**........ .

Peter Lamont tells the story in a relentlessly jokey
way, **(5)**........ . That aside, I found this a readable and
well-written book, with lots of marvellous comic detail
about the rivalries between magicians. He describes
Western magicians who stole tricks, faked Indian
identities and got up to all sorts of tricks in order not
to be outdone, **(6)**........ .

Did anyone ever see the trick? Well, lots of people
said they did – some clearly credulous, others a little
more reliable – and although various photographs
were taken, we may never know.

A which was bursting with fantastic feats

B which criticised the magicians of the time

C which gave a relatively easy answer

D which all makes for excellent reading

E which did become irritating after a while

F which they copied on their visits to India

G which its own culture lacked

H which nonetheless managed to catch the public
   imagination

I which relatively few claim to have actually witnessed

Language development

All the options A–I begin with a relative pronoun. Can
you find any more relative clauses in the main text?

Vocabulary
Film reviews
▶ CB page 30

1 a Think of a word that matches the following definitions. If you are stuck, choose from the nouns in this list.

adaptation   background   close-up   epic location   plot   scene   score   screenplay soundtrack

1 a film that tells a long story about brave actions and exciting events ....

2 a single piece of action that happens in one place ....

3 a place away from a film studio where scenes are filmed ....

4 the events that form the main story of a film ....

5 music written specially for the film ....

6 the recorded music from a film ....

7 the words that are written down for actors to say in a film, and the instructions that tell them what they should do ....

8 a film that is based on a book or play ....

9 the situation or events that explain why something happens in the way that it does ....

10 a shot in which the camera seems to be very near ....

b Complete the following extract from a film review with words from Exercise 1a.

2 Rewrite the following extract from a review in your notebook, replacing the parts in italics with expressions from the list, making any changes necessary. There are more expressions than you need.

box-office hit/smash   be a runaway success   sequel to remake   action packed   on the edge of one's seat a dramatic finale   lavish production   on a shoestring thrilling   blockbuster   cult classic

The Mexican film 'El Mariachi' is a great example of how good movies can be produced **(1)** *with a very small budget.* Made in 1992 by Robert Rodriguez for $7,000, it **(2)** *quickly became successful* at the box office and has become a **(3)** *very popular film with some enthusiasts.* The story, about an innocent musician who is mistaken for a killer who carries his gun in his guitar case, will keep you **(4)** *feeling excited* from start to finish. With some twists along the way, it leads to **(5)** *an exciting ending.* Rodriguez went on to make 'Desperado', starring Antonio Banderas, in a **(6)** *big, expensive film* that was meant to be a **(7)** *continuation of the story of* 'El Mariachi'. However, the film was not the **(8)** *popular and successful film* that everyone had expected and was criticised for being more of a **(9)** *different version of the same film*, as the stories were so similar.

3 Find and read some other film reviews in English, both positive and negative, and note down more useful expressions in your vocabulary notebook.

Doctor Zhivago, made in 1965, remains a classic of the period. This **(1)**...................... film, which spans many years in the lives of the central characters, is a simple love story. The basic **(2)**...................... of the poet doctor in love with two women is set against the **(3)**...................... of the Russian Revolution.

  The director, David Lean, makes good use of the **(4)**...................... , and the vast snow-covered fields are beautifully shot. The dialogue is superb, and the **(5)**...................... , which is an **(6)**...................... of the book by Boris Pasternak, won one of five Oscars for the film. Another was for the music, composed by Maurice Jarre, which has been described as 'the greatest **(7)**...................... in movie history'.

  Classic **(8)**...................... include one where Lean is able to show the horror of fighting just by using a **(9)**...................... of Yuri's face as he witnesses the destruction.

Listening

Multiple matching (Paper 4 Part 4)

▶ ER pages 170–171

1 a Read the instructions for the task.
   1 How many speakers will you hear?
   2 What will they all be talking about?
   3 How many tasks do you have to do?
   4 How many times will you hear the texts?

   b Read Task One carefully. Think about the vocabulary and expressions you would expect to hear connected with each sport and note them down.

   c Read Task Two carefully and highlight key words in the options A–H. This has been done for you in the first two options.

2 a 🎧 Listen to the recording once. The first time you listen, try to do Task One. Use the Help clues if necessary.

   b Listen again. This time try to do Task Two. Use the Help clues if necessary.

TIP

Don't worry if you don't understand every word in the recording – in Part 4, you are listening to identify the speakers and understand their main points, attitudes and opinions.

You will hear **five** short extracts in which various sportspeople are talking about superstitions that they have.

TASK ONE

For questions **1–5**, choose from the list **A–H** the sport which each speaker competes in.

TASK TWO

For questions **6–10**, choose from the list **A–H** the reason each person gives for carrying on with their superstition.

You will hear the recording twice. While you listen you must complete both tasks.

A skiing		
B motor racing		
C swimming	Speaker 1	1
D sailing	Speaker 2	2
E canoeing	Speaker 3	3
F wind-surfing	Speaker 4	4
G cycling	Speaker 5	5
H running		

A It takes my mind off the risks involved.		
B It helps me to prepare mentally.	Speaker 1	6
C It's just a joke really.	Speaker 2	7
D It helps me cope with nerves.	Speaker 3	8
E I don't know why I bother with it.	Speaker 4	9
F It reminds me of my objectives.	Speaker 5	10
G It is a family tradition.		
H It helps me when I'm feeling low.		

HELP
➤ Question 1
At the beginning, the speaker tells us that she doesn't use *valuable gear* in her sport. Which of the sports A–H doesn't require equipment? Listen to the rest of the text to hear confirmation of which is her sport.

➤ Question 2
At the beginning, the speaker tells us that he does his training *on the roads*. Which of the sports could this refer to? Listen to the rest of the text for confirmation of which is his sport.

HELP
➤ Question 6
Listen for why the speaker takes a coin to competitions. How does she feel before a race?

➤ Question 7
The speaker says *I can't think what makes me do it*. Which option does this match?

B It's only logical!

Language development
Speaking skills
▶ CB pages 32–33, ER pages 171–172

Giving full answers to questions

1 For each question, choose an appropriate response for Part 1 of the Speaking test.

1 Have you travelled far today?
   A Not really.
   B It depends, what do you call far?
   C No. I'm quite lucky in that I only live about 15 minutes from here.

2 Can you tell me a little about your family?
   A Let me see, I have a mother, a father, one sister, one brother, seven uncles and aunts and 14 cousins.
   B We have our own business. We run a hotel and restaurant that together employ about 14 people. It's hard work, particularly in the summer when the hotel is full. We have many tourists and that's why I need to study English.
   C I don't see that much of my family since I moved into my own flat a couple of years ago. I tend to spend more time with friends and just see my family a few times a year.

3 What do you like about your town?
   A My town is famous for its traditional industries. Tiles have been made here for over 200 years and are vital to the region's economy.
   B There are a lot of shops, cinemas, museums and art galleries and other places to visit.
   C The town itself is not so exciting, but it's where all my friends and family are. That's why I'm happy there.

Asking questions

2 Choose the most appropriate question to ask to find out the information required. Remember, you should avoid repeating the prompts word for word.

1 I'd like you to ask each other something about your leisure activities.
   A What are your leisure activities?
   B What kind of things do you like doing in your free time?
   C Do you like stamp collecting? I do.

2 I'd like you to ask each other about your attitude to sports.
   A I think sports are boring. Do you like music?
   B What is your attitude to sports?
   C How important is sport in your everyday life?

3 I'd like you to ask each other about your future plans.
   A What are you doing after the exam? Do you fancy going for a coffee?
   B What do you think you will be doing this time next year?
   C What are your future plans?

4 I'd like you to ask each other about changes you would like to make in your life.
   A If you could change anything about your life, what would it be?
   B What changes would you like to make in your life?
   C In the last few years what changes have you made in your life?

Reacting and asking for more information

3 a Complete the dialogue by putting one suitable word in each gap.

EXAMINER: I'd like you to ask each other about places of interest you have visited in this country.

CANDIDATE 1: Where have you most enjoyed visiting here?

CANDIDATE 2: Well, I (1)................... that one of my favourite places is the Museum of Modern Art. Have you been?

CANDIDATE 1: Not yet, but (2)................... it or not, I was planning to go next week. What do you like about it?

CANDIDATE 2: Well, you (3)..................., I didn't know much about art before I started going there, but I learn more each time I visit.

CANDIDATE 1: That's (4)................... . So what you're (5)................... is that it's worth visiting a few times?

CANDIDATE 2: Definitely. So, what's your favourite place?

CANDIDATE 1: Let me (6)................... . It's probably the old town with its ancient buildings. As a (7)................... of fact, I've been working in a shop there.

CANDIDATE 2: Oh, (8)................... you? What has that been like?

CANDIDATE 1: Hard work, but great for my English!

b ⌒ Now listen and compare your answers.

Language development

Articles

▶ CB page 35, GR page 176

Use of articles

1 Complete the sentences with *a/an, the* or ø (no article).

1 Graham is .... biologist and for .... last three years, he's been studying .... lifecycle of .... ant.

2 After .... accident, ... injured were quickly taken to .... hospital.

3 As .... MP (Member of Parliament), he does .... lot of work to help .... disabled people and .... elderly.

4 On .... Sunday we are going to .... coast for .... day. We'll probably have .... dinner in .... local restaurant.

5 Generally speaking, ... Spanish love .... fish and Madrid has .... second-largest fish market in .... world.

6 Before I go to .... sleep, I like to watch .... TV or listen to .... radio.

7 I'd like two coffees, please; .... large black one and .... one with .... cream.

Singular or plural verb?

2 **Correct the mistakes in these sentences.**

1 Some of the girl's clothing were torn.

2 He gave us some very useful advices.

3 None of the information he gave me were correct.

4 A number of students has complained about the poor quality of food in the canteen.

5 A lot of people enjoys watching sport.

6 The number of people interested in the job have surprised us.

Quantifiers

3 **Mark the correct quantifier in these sentences.**

1 I've got very *few / little* money left.

2 Please could you send me *some / any* information about your training courses?

3 We haven't had *much / many* success with our search so far.

4 Not *much / many* people would choose to live in such a remote place.

5 I'm afraid we haven't got *some / any* of these shoes in your size.

6 He's a child who needs *a lot of / enough* encouragement.

7 Could you try to make *little / less* noise, please?

8 We haven't got *enough / much* players for a team.

4 Complete each gap in this text with a word from the list. You will have to use some of the words more than once.

each
both
either
neither

Jane and Emily are twin sisters, separated at birth and reunited after 40 years. Since meeting again after such a long time, (1)................. Jane and Emily have been struck by the number of things they have in common. For example, they (2)................. work in the media, Jane as a television producer and Emily as a radio sound assistant. (3)................. of them is married, but (4)................. have steady partners. They (5)................. own their own house, but (6)................. has a car.

As I interviewed them, I noticed time and time again that, as I put a question to (7)................. sister in turn, the other seemed to know the answer before it had been given, as if they knew what the other was thinking. I asked if (8)................. of them felt threatened by meeting the other after all this time. 'Definitely not,' says Jane. 'It's great. (9)................. of us feels threatened at all.'

And why are they so similar? For once, they don't agree. Jane believes it's all in the genes, whereas Emily is convinced that the time they spent together in the womb accounts for their many similarities. Maybe they are (10)................. right!

Making uncountable nouns countable

5 **Fill each gap with a word from the list to complete the common phrase.**

bit   drop   heap   hint   piece   pinch
shred   slice

1 There isn't a .... of evidence against this man!

2 Before serving, add a .... of salt to taste.

3 Oh dear, I think I just felt a .... of rain.

4 I came across a very interesting .... of information.

5 I don't have much for breakfast; usually just a cup of tea and a .... of toast.

6 Maria's quite upset, and could do with a .... of support at the moment.

7 There was a .... of anger in his voice.

8 There was a .... of clothes in the middle of the floor.

English in Use
Open cloze (Paper 3 Part 2)

▶ ER page 169

1 a Read the title of the text and think about the topic.

b Read the whole text quickly for general understanding, ignoring the gaps for the moment.

   1 Why was the story of Frane Selak reported in the news?

   2 How many lucky escapes are mentioned in the text?

2 a Read through the text again and think about the type of word which will fit in each gap. For example, is it an article, a preposition, a pronoun, etc.?

b Look at the words before and after the gap and decide which word is missing. Use the Help clues if necessary.

TIP

If you aren't sure about an answer, try reading the sentence in the text using different words in the gap. If you're still not sure, leave this gap until the end.

3 Read the whole text again to check that the words you've chosen fit in with the overall meaning of the text.

HELP

➤ Question 1
   Look at the second part of the sentence after the comma.

➤ Question 3
   Which preposition goes here to give the idea of *entering water*?

➤ Question 5
   Which preposition do we use after the verb *to suffer*?

➤ Question 12
   Is it the definite or indefinite article that is needed in this phrase?

4 Look back at questions 1–15. How many of them tested:

   • use of articles?
   • use of pronouns?
   • a fixed phrase?
   • a phrasal verb?
   • prepositions which follow a particular noun or verb?

For questions **1–15**, complete the following article by writing each missing word in the space. Use only one word for each space. The exercise begins with an example **(0)**.

World's luckiest man wins the lottery

Frane Selak, a 74-year-old from Croatia, has been dubbed the world's luckiest man by his friends **(0)** ...after... hitting the jackpot with his first lottery ticket in 40 years. Frane's story was picked up by the world's media **(1)**.................... so much because of this particular stroke of luck, but because it comes after **(2)**.................... life characterised by lucky escapes.

The first came in 1962 when a train Frane was travelling on jumped the rails and plunged **(3)**.................... an icy river. Frane made **(4)**.................... to the riverbank suffering **(5)**.................... hypothermia, shock and a broken arm. A year later, he was thrown out of a DC-8 airliner when a door flew open. This time, Frane was lucky enough to land in a haystack and escaped **(6)**.................... cuts, bruises and shock. In 1970, he lost control of his car, **(7)**.................... plunged 300 feet down a precipice **(8)**.................... exploding. Frane, of course, managed to jump out just in **(9)**.................... , landing unhurt in a tree. It was after this accident that his friends gave him the nickname 'Lucky', but **(10)**.................... Frane says, 'There are two ways of looking at it – I am **(11)**.................... the world's unluckiest man or the luckiest. I prefer to believe **(12)**.................... latter.'

In all, Frane has survived seven major disasters, including accidents on most forms of transport. So is Frane **(13)**.................... forward to a quiet retirement on his £600,000 jackpot? It **(14)**.................... seem not. First, he'll be marrying his girlfriend, who is 20 years **(15)**.................... junior, then he'll be investing in a speedboat!

Language development

Look at all the uncountable nouns in the text. Can you find a phrase that is used to make an uncountable noun countable?

Writing
Information leaflet (Paper 2 Part 2)
▶ CB pages 36–37, WR page 190

Exam strategy

For any piece of writing, you should make a plan so that you don't include irrelevant information. Read the task carefully, then make your plan, using notes which you can expand when you write your answer. When writing an information leaflet, make sure that the information is clearly organised. You can use headings and bullet points to help you do this.

1 **Read the task below and answer these questions.**
   1 What is the purpose of the leaflet?
   2 What information do you have to include? Mark the relevant parts of the task.
   3 Should the style be formal or informal?

> You have been asked to write an information leaflet to promote a new leisure complex which is opening in your town. You should give a brief description of the complex, outlining why it is important to the town, describe its main facilities and plans for the future and mention any other points that you think are important.
>
> Write **the text for the leaflet** in approximately 250 words.

2 **Read part of a student's answer to the task on the right. Match four of the topics in the student's plan to each section (1–4) of the answer.**

   a   Describe facilities in the centre.   ....

   b   Inform readers about the opening.   ....

   c   Introduce the centre in an eye-catching way.   ....

   d   Outline future plans for the centre.   ....

   e   Explain the importance of the centre to the town.   ....

   f   Give further information about the centre or opening-day activities.   ....

3 **The student has not added any headings. Decide which of these headings would be suitable for each section of the leaflet.**
   A When will the New Metro Complex open?
   B What can you expect to find in the New Metro Complex?
   C THE NEW METRO COMPLEX
   D Why is the New Metro Complex important for this town?

① It's here at last! Are you bored? Are your evenings dull and uninteresting? Help is at hand!

Whether you are 14, 40 or 80, the New Metro Complex has something for you.

② Opening Day is September 15th, and for the first week there's a spectacular offer of BUY ONE GET ONE FREE on all available facilities. Don't miss out! Come to the old converted Cattle Market on September 15th!

③ The Complex offers a ONE-STOP SHOP for everyone in the town, a place where you can meet friends, relax and socialise, get fit or go shopping – all under one roof! As well as this, it will attract more people from the outlying towns and villages. This can only be good for local businesses!

④ In the welcoming atmosphere of the complex, you will find lots of different things. You will find three restaurants catering for a wide variety of tastes, and five cafés for a quick bite to eat. There is also an indoor sports arena which will host tournaments and provide facilities for local clubs. A five-screen cinema will show the latest films, and there will also be specialist boutiques. Finally, a multi-storey car park will ensure easy access to the complex.

4 In section 4, bullet points would help to make the information easier to read. Rewrite this paragraph, organising the information with bullet points.

5 Complete the sample answer, using the remaining topics from Exercise 2. Make some notes before you write.

Reading
Gapped text (Paper 1 Part 2)
▶ ER page 168

1 Read the title and subtitle of the text. What does *faking* mean?

2 Read the main text quickly, ignoring the gaps for the moment. Answer these questions to check your comprehension.

   1 What does Richard Wiseman want to find out?
   2 What research has his team already carried out?
   3 Why did the results surprise them?
   4 What does Richard Wiseman think really causes people's 'spooky' experiences?
   5 How is he planning to test this out?

3 a Look at question 1.
   • Read the text above the gap. It contains information about Wiseman's strange idea and what he plans to do.
   • Now read the text below the gap. It contains the phrase *evidence to support this explanation*.
   • Read extract E. It contains both a reference to a strange idea and an explanation.

   b Now look at questions 2–7 and repeat the procedure. In questions 2 and 3, words and phrases in the main text and extracts have been highlighted to help you.

TIP

Write in the letter of any answers you are sure about. If you're not sure which option fits a gap, then put a question mark (?) and return to it later.

4 When you have finished the task, read the whole text through to check it makes sense.

For questions **1–7**, you must choose which of the paragraphs **A–H** fit into the numbered gaps in the following magazine article. There is one extra paragraph which does not fit in any of the gaps.

FAKING A GHOSTLY FEELING

Scientists want to put people in a scary situation, just to test their reactions. Nathan Booth finds out about a strange experiment in a purpose-built 'haunted' house.

The image of a haunted house inhabited by the ghosts of its former occupants is a familiar one from literature and horror movies. But do such places really exist? A team of scientists aims to find out. Richard Wiseman, a
5 psychologist, is building his own 'haunted' house for the purposes of scientific research. He wants to be able to terrify visitors with spooky special effects that he's designed himself. By controlling where and when these effects appear, he hopes to find out much more about how and
10 why people have spooky experiences. 'We want to build our own haunted house, so that we're in total control,' says Wiseman. 'Then we might get significant scientific results.'

> **1**

Earlier this year, Wiseman and his team produced some well-documented scientific evidence to support this
15 explanation. They recorded the experiences of hundreds of volunteers, visiting some of the best-known haunted spots in the UK.

> **2**

Beforehand, Wiseman's team surveyed these sites, recording things such as air temperatures, magnetic fields
20 and lighting levels. Then they asked visitors to report exactly where they felt or saw anything strange. To their astonishment, they found that people's scariest experiences were often in the precise spots reputed to be haunted. And these same spots were often those where subtle variations
25 in temperature and magnetic fields had already been recorded.

> **3**

As a result, Wiseman thinks he can discover even more through experiments in which he dictates exactly when people are exposed to subtle environmental effects. 'The
30 only way you know if something is causal is if you control the signal,' he says. In addition, he wishes to prepare people psychologically before they visit a site.

4

He also intends to create the perfect environment for his research, where he would direct the lighting
35 effects and other features within the rooms. And as spook-master general, he could play with the effects; introducing minor changes in temperature and perhaps wisps of a draught here and there. 'It's the subtle things that count,' says Wiseman. 'Less is
40 more.' In earlier research, he discovered that people found the special effects less believable as they became more obvious.

5

What's more, such feelings become even stronger where they match instinctive reactions to natural
45 hazards that date back to the days of the first humans. Poisonous insects can lurk in cramped, shadowy corners, for example. That's why Wiseman considers control over lighting and room size to be crucial. 'I think many experiences are visually driven,'
50 he says. In a castle in Scotland, people often reported the strangest feelings when entering the darkest, tiniest rooms. Objects such as old furniture are also important for reinforcing expectations about where ghosts hide, and he expects his house to
55 have an 'Old World' feel.

6

So, at present, he is searching for disused buildings in the grounds of large aristocratic houses, which could be converted for the purpose, perhaps an old hunting lodge. Wiseman is contacting organisations
60 that manage historic properties open to the public to see if they're interested, reminding them that his previous experiments at Hampton Court attracted a record number of visitors.

7

However, surely there's a fatal flaw in the plan? If
65 they know it's all fake at the outset, won't people just laugh at any strange effects they experience? Wiseman is not discouraged. 'We would tell people they were part of an experiment,' he says. 'But with genuinely strange effects, it will only add to the
70 mystery.'

A Wiseman seems to have all the details worked out, but how likely is any of this to happen? He is optimistic because his house could pay for itself by becoming a tourist attraction in its own right, especially if it was associated with historic venues already full of ghostly folklore.

B An equally practical way of controlling the temperature in the house would be with air-conditioning units hidden behind the walls. 'People are very sensitive, so the temperature wouldn't have to drop much,' says Wiseman. 'You can feel a quarter of a degree change.'

C This provided Wiseman with a more earthly explanation for what some people feel. 'We showed that people had odd experiences in the same places, and now we know that these are based on environmental factors,' says Wiseman. He also found that it didn't matter whether volunteers knew beforehand where the most haunted spots were located. So, the idea that the experiences relied solely on prior knowledge was disproved.

D Indeed, his experimental haunted house could prove to be a bargain. Even if the team were to buy the house, the cost could be recouped by selling it after the experiments are completed. 'We could leave all the electrical equipment there so the owners could have the scariest house in the world,' he says.

E Yet surprisingly, for a man with such an unusual idea, Wiseman doesn't believe in ghosts. But he is sure that the sensations felt by people who have ghostly encounters, like fear and even nausea, result from a mixture of psychology and a spooky environment.

F It's the same in everyday life, we are sensitive to very slight alterations in our environment especially in situations where we feel nervous. As Wiseman explains, whenever we have preconceptions about ghostly goings-on, our sense of unease is heightened.

G One was Hampton Court, the former royal palace near London which is said to be haunted by the screaming ghost of Catherine Howard, fifth wife of Henry VIII, the notorious 16th-century English king. Another was the South Bridge Vaults, a series of underground rooms and corridors in Edinburgh, Scotland.

H Wiseman insists that he should be able to tell the volunteers beforehand whatever he wants: which spots may be haunted and so on. In other words, he's in total control. He is convinced this would make the results of the experiment more wide-reaching.

A The burden of fame

English in Use
Word formation (Paper 3 Part 4)
▶ CB page 42, ER page 170

Exam strategy

For this task, you need a good knowledge of prefixes, suffixes and spelling rules. When learning new vocabulary, make a note of other words that can be formed from the word you are learning, for example a noun formed from a verb or a negative form of an adjective. Also make a note of the spelling rules that apply when the form of a word changes.

1 a Read the title of the first text to identify the topic and think about what you are going to read.
   - Do famous people experience problems with friendships?
   - Are the friendships of famous people different from those of other people?

b Read the text through quickly for general understanding, ignoring the gaps for the moment. Who do famous people usually choose as their friends?

2 a Read the text again carefully and think about the type of word which will fit in each gap. Try to predict what the answer will be.

b Now fill in the gaps.

3 Read through the text again when you've finished and check that the words you've written fit in with the overall meaning of the text and are spelled correctly.

4 Repeat the procedure for the second text. Remember, each text stands alone and has a different topic.

For questions **1–15**, read the texts below. Use the words in the boxes to the right of the texts to form **one** word that fits in the same numbered space in the text. The exercise begins with an example **(0)**.

MAGAZINE ARTICLE

Famous friends

When it comes to picking friends, celebrities have a **(0)** tendency to pick other celebrities. This reflects the circles they move in, and one of the **(1)**................... of becoming a celebrity is **(2)**................... the chance to mix with the rich and famous. Very often, however, an air of **(3)**................... can hang around a high-profile friendship, where an **(4)**................... show of affection actually masks an underlying **(5)**................... . Friends clearly have to be chosen with **(6)**................... care, based on a degree of mutual **(7)**................... combined with equal standing in the eyes of the outside world. How else can we explain the intense friendships between stars who, in any other situation, would have very little in common?

(0)	TEND
(1)	ATTRACT
(2)	SUPPOSED
(3)	TENSE
(4)	OUT
(5)	RIVAL
(6)	TACTIC
(7)	ADMIRE

NEWSPAPER ARTICLE

Stella takes a stand

Well-known fashion designer Stella McCartney is someone who, despite the nature of her work, manages not to compromise on her **(8)**................... beliefs. Many of these have been inherited from her celebrity parents; her father, the internationally renowned pop musician Sir Paul McCartney, and her late mother, Linda, who established a **(9)**................... successful brand of vegetarian meals. The **(10)**................... of her views on certain issues is clear in her recent **(11)**................... of a most lucrative job offer for purely high-minded reasons. Stella turned down the chance of an **(12)**................... as **(13)**................... director of Gucci, the Italian fashion house, telling friends that she couldn't take the job because it would require her to assume direct **(14)**................... for the company's famous line of leather handbags. Stella is a vegan and so she finds the use of animal products, whether it be in food or as a fashion item, totally **(15)**................... .

(8)	PERSON
(9)	HIGH
(10)	STRONG
(11)	REJECT
(12)	APPOINT
(13)	CREATE
(14)	RESPONSIBLE
(15)	ACCEPT

Language development

Punctuation

▶ CB page 44, WR page 201

Capitals

1 Correct the following sentences by adding capitals where necessary.

1 the planet venus is warmer than mars because it is closer to the sun.

2 this winter, I'll be working every saturday in december in the run-up to christmas and new year.

3 my friend fabio's father has a house near lake como in the north of italy.

4 i'd like to study spanish in south america, in either argentina or chile.

5 she's the new doctor; she's taken over from doctor digby.

6 for more information, please contact barclays bank at 42 high street, biggleswade.

7 the sacred river ganges starts high in the himalayan mountains and eventually flows through bangladesh into the bay of bengal.

8 are you fascinated by fame? do you seek out celebrities? if so, read *stalkers weekly*, the new magazine for star spotters.

Apostrophes

2 Rewrite the following messages using contractions where appropriate and adding apostrophes as necessary.

① If you are going out for coffee, I would love a cappuccino!

② Please ask the maintenance man if he has fixed the tap in the kitchen. Apparently there has been a leak in there.

③ I need a laptop. Mine is broken so I am using yours. OK?

④ How is the report coming on? I will need it in the morning.

⑤ Who will be locking up tonight? I will not be here.

⑥ Janine says you cannot call her at home because she is not going to be there tonight.

⑦ Daniel called to say he will not be coming in today as he has got a headache.

⑧ Melanie says she has booked the Victoria Hotel. She says it is a great place and has its own pool.

⑨ Melissa says if she had known there was going to be a strike, she would have set off earlier.

⑩ Dave and Mike said they are not going to be more than ten minutes late.

Speech marks

3 Add speech marks and other punctuation where necessary to the following quotes.

1 It was the American journalist Henry Louis Mencken who said a celebrity is one who is known to many persons he is glad he does not know.

2 Fame and tranquility can never be bedfellows said Michel de Montaigne, the 16th-century French writer.

3 I may be a living legend said singer Roy Orbison but that doesn't help when I've got to change a flat tyre.

4 The actor Alan Alda once joked it isn't necessary to be rich and famous to be happy. It's only necessary to be rich.

5 It was the actor and film director Woody Allen who remarked I don't want to achieve immortality through my work. I want to achieve it through not dying.

4 Punctuate the text about Robert Garside.

robert garside is nothing if not dedicated for the last six years the 36-year-old briton has had just one goal to be the first person to run around the world since starting out in new delhi in october 1997 robert has dodged bullets in russia outrun thieves in mexico and found true love in venezuela garside who often feels homesick says i miss a really good pot of tea

in june 2004 he plans to set off on his next venture to become the first person to swim around the world covering a distance of approximately 25000 miles he says that as with the run the greatest problems will be isolation politics and the weather

English in Use
Error correction (spelling and punctuation) (Paper 3 Part 3)

▶ CB page 45, ER page 169

1 Read the title of the text below to identify the topic. Which of these adjectives would you use to describe the sort of people who usually read the news on television?

rich   friendly   fashionable   shy   formal
laid-back   fun   serious   confident

2 Read the whole text quickly for general understanding, ignoring the mistakes for the moment.
   1 What do most television viewers think about while they are watching the news?
   2 What impression do most people have about this newsreader?

3 Read the text again, sentence by sentence, and complete the task. Use the Help clues if necessary. Remember that:
   • the errors may be either spelling or punctuation
   • there is only one error per line, and some of the lines will be correct.

4 When you've finished, read the whole text again to check it makes complete sense.

HELP
➤ **Question 1**
Are all the punctuation marks on this line needed?
➤ **Question 3**
Check the spelling of the words on this line.
➤ **Question 4**
A punctuation mark is missing in this line.
➤ **Question 5**
This line contains a word that is often misspelled – check it carefully!
➤ **Questions 6–10**
Three of these lines are correct. Do you know which ones?

TIP

Punctuation errors could be either at word level, e.g. apostrophes for possessives, contractions, etc., or at sentence level, e.g. commas, full stops, capital letters, etc. To find some punctuation errors, you will need to read and understand several lines of text.

In **most** lines of the following text, there is **either** a spelling **or** a punctuation error. For each numbered line **1–16**, write the correctly spelt word or show the correct punctuation. **Some** lines are correct. Indicate these lines with a tick (✓) in the box. The exercise begins with three examples **(0)**, **(00)** and **(000)**.

The real person behind the TV newsreader

It's a strange job, reading the news on television. According to	0	✓
some recent reserch, 70% of all those watching the news are	00	research
thinking about the newsreaders appearance rather than listening	000	newsreader's
to what's being said. With thousands, of critical eyes on you every	1	
day, its not surprising that some people are quick to make	2	
judgemants and jump to the wrong conclusions. Do you know how	3	
other people see you It might not be something you've thought	4	
of very often, but I can guarentee you'd be surprised. In my case,	5	
I usually find that people think I'm rich because they assume that	6	
everyone who works in television is paid an enormous salary.	7	
When I meet people for the first time, they often coment that	8	
I'm smaller than I look on the screen, and just last weekend a	9	
friend said he'd been asked, if I was 'unfriendly' by someone who'd	10	
never met me. Luckilly he put the record straight! When I told	11	
friends about writing this column, one said, Be careful how much	12	
you reveal about yourself.' while I understand her concern, and	13	
won't be regaling you with endless tales of my Private life (you'd be	14	
bored senseless anyway), I would like everyone to know the real me,	15	
especialy if the alternative is that large, rich, unfriendly woman off the telly!	16	

Writing
Coherence

▶ CB page 46, WR page 200

1   Read the following paragraphs. For each paragraph:
   1   underline the topic sentence
   2   underline any linking devices used to organise the details
   3   cross out any sentences that are not relevant to the main idea.

① It is hard to say why the marriages of well-known actors seldom last. Some have said it is because of the pressure of being in the public eye. Others have suggested it is because actors spend a lot of time away from their partners as they are touring or filming. Many films take months to shoot, and there are often delays. Another possible reason is that the opportunities for being unfaithful are so much greater, especially if you are in constant contact with adoring fans. Some actors are gorgeous and have huge fan clubs. The final reason could be that actors are people who crave constant attention and need to be loved, and it is hard to maintain that level of devotion in a long-term relationship.

② I'm not that interested in fame. Some famous people have far more money than they need. For me, the most important thing in life is to know that I have used my time and energy well. So I'd rather have a lower-paid job where I was helping others than earn a fortune making money from those around me. Some people judge their success by how much they have gained for themselves, whereas I'd like to be judged on what I have given back, not on what I have taken from life. My mother has always gone out of her way to help people. The more people give, the more everyone has. When I'm old, I'd like to be able to look back on my life with a clear conscience.

2   Read the following paragraphs and choose the most appropriate topic sentence from the options A–C.

1 ....
Glossy magazines have always carried features on celebrities: *Hello* was the first successful magazine that was based solely on celebrity gossip and PR. It was quickly followed by a stream of similar publications. Initially, they tended to be very supportive of the celebrities and were happy to promote whatever image the people featured wanted to project. These were followed by others that were keener to get beneath the mask and find out what the individuals were really like. Finally, came the rise of Internet-based gossip sites that, less restricted by libel laws, find it easier to say what they like about people.

   A The last few years have seen the rise of celebrity magazines.
   B Interest in celebrities is constantly growing and changing.
   C There is a lot more to read than there used to be.

2 ....
Years ago, young people dreamt of such things as having their own successful business, being a top athlete or an accomplished musician. Fame was secondary, and came as a result of getting to the top of their profession. Nowadays, however, it seems as if the aim of many young people is simply to 'be famous'. How they achieve fame is not important. Fame itself is the goal. Hence the rise of 'reality' TV shows such as *Big Brother* and growing numbers of people wanting to work in the media. Being on TV is enough; what you do when you are on is less important. One direct result is that there is seldom anything worth watching.

   A People's attitude to fame is changing.
   B Young people have lost touch with reality.
   C TV is not as good as it was.

3   Look at the plan for a composition describing the job of a paparazzo.

   a Select a topic sentence for each paragraph.
      1 Other paparazzi are friends as well as rivals.
      2 To be successful, a paparazzo needs as many contacts as possible.
      3 A paparazzo's days are long and often boring.
      4 A paparazzo is nothing without his camera.

   b Write the notes into a coherent composition. Link the ideas in each paragraph using linking devices.

The job of a paparazzo

Paragraph 1: ....
   • *typical day, start early in the morning, finish late at night*
   • *spend a lot of time standing around and waiting*
   • *depressing at times, no picture, no pay*
   • *always hoping for the one special piece of good luck*

Paragraph 2: ....
   • *other paparazzi are in the same situation*
   • *chat, compare work, share ideas, experiences*
   • *makes the job more enjoyable, less lonely*

Paragraph 3: ....
   • *take your camera everywhere – something important could happen at any time*
   • *have to practise – must be able to use it quickly and accurately*
   • *keep it in good working order, update for new technology – can't afford to be let down by it*

Paragraph 4: ....
   • *rely on contacts to give information and tip-offs*
   • *must get on well with people, hotel porters, barmen, taxi drivers, hairdressers*
   • *they are in contact with rich and famous – might phone one day with the big story*

Listening
Sentence completion (Paper 4 Part 1)

▶ ER pages 170–171

1 a Read the instructions for the task below.
   1 Who are you going to hear?
   2 What will she be talking about?

   b Read the sentences. Think about the topic and what you expect to hear.
   • How much do you find out about the television programme from the sentences?
   • What do you find out about the order of information in the talk?

   c Try to predict the type of information you will be listening for. For example:
   1 In which question are you looking for someone's occupation?
   2 Which answer is likely to be an adjective?
   3 Which answers are likely to be abstract nouns?

2 ◯ Listen to the recording once and complete the sentences. Use the Help clues if necessary. Remember that:
   • although you won't hear exactly the same sentences, the information comes in the same order as the sentences on the page
   • your answers need to fit into the sentence grammatically.

HELP
➤ Question 1
You are listening for the actual words the speaker uses. Listen for the phrase *what I call …* The answer comes directly afterwards.
➤ Question 4
What were the bags full of? Be careful, because two possible things are mentioned, but only one is correct.
➤ Question 5
The word *and* is already in the box. This is there to help you. Add two more words which, together with *and*, will give you the answer.
➤ Question 6
Do you know any other words or expressions for *old-age pensioner*? Three are mentioned in the recording. Listen for the other one that Anita thinks is patronising.

3 Listen again to check and complete your answers.

4 Look at these wrong answers that students gave to some of the questions. Listen again and decide why these answers are not correct.
   2 costume designer   6 such as senior
   5 anger   8 emplymant

You will hear the well-known businesswoman Anita Roddick talking about a TV programme in which she pretended to be an old person. For questions **1–8**, complete the sentences. **You will hear the recording twice.**

HOW DOES IT FEEL TO BE OLD?

Anita uses the words [1] to describe what she did to find out about old age for the programme.

Anita feels that the programme's [2] made her look older than necessary.

Anita says that she felt as if she was [3] when disguised as an old person.

Anita carried shopping bags full of [4] to see if anyone would offer to help her.

Anita's impression was that people had feelings of and [5] when she crossed the road slowly.

Anita feels that it is no longer appropriate to use terms like ' [6] ' and 'old-age pensioner'.

Anita prefers the term 'elder' because it suggests both [7] and respect.

Anita gives the example of Sweden as a country where older people stay in [8] longer.

B What I believe in

Language development
Modal verbs
▶ CB page 50, GR page 177

Expressing necessity

1 **Complete the sentences using a suitable form of** *must, have (got) to* **or** *need to.*
1 All students .... register with the faculty before 15 September.
2 When he gets home from work, he .... just sit and chill out for half an hour.
3 Food .... be consumed in the library.
4 I should be free that day, but I .... check in my diary to make sure.
5 The report isn't urgent and .... be completed until next week.
6 I can't find my key. I .... left it at home.
7 I won't be ready for another half hour, but you .... wait for me. I can catch you up later.
8 It was very kind of you to clean the flat for me, but you .... done it because we have a cleaning lady.

Expressing advice

2 **Complete the sentences using a suitable form of** *should, ought to* **or** *must.*
1 It's a lovely little town. You really .... go there!
2 .... I tell the police what I saw?
3 You really .... drink so much. It's bad for you.
4 You were very silly to leave the car unlocked. You .... locked it.
5 You .... tell your tutor if you're falling behind with your work.
6 Do you think we .... take some drinks with us?

Expressing ability

3 **Complete these sentences using a suitable form of** *can, could* **or** *be able to.*
1 I looked for your book, but I .... find it.
2 After a lot of effort, we .... hook the bag out of the water.
3 If I had known that you needed some extra bags, I .... lent you one.

4 Next week, I'll have more time, so I .... get started on this work.
5 I've been trying to phone Jim all morning, but I .... get hold of him.
6 I'm afraid I .... come to the party this evening.
7 When I was younger, I .... run around for hours without getting tired.
8 I've been practising like mad, and I .... juggle now!

Expressing possibility/probability

4 **Complete the sentences by choosing the correct modal.**
1 The temperature *can / could* reach 40 degrees tomorrow.
2 We *might / should* go to Italy this summer, but it's not definite yet.
3 He's not answering his phone. I suppose he *might have / can have* popped out of the office.
4 These animals *must / can* grow to over two metres long.
5 We're leaving at ten o'clock, so as long as the traffic isn't too bad, we *should / would* be there by 12.
6 It looks fairly straightforward, so there *can't / shouldn't* be any problems.

Expressing deduction

5 **Rewrite the two sentences as one sentence, using a modal to express the meaning in the second sentence.**
0 Although it seems unlikely, he is telling the truth. There is no other explanation.
   Although it seems unlikely, he must be telling the truth.
1 This is not the building we're looking for. It's not possible.
   ....
2 I suppose that maybe he phoned while I was out. It's possible.
   ....
3 Someone broke into the house while we were out. That is the only explanation.
   ....
4 Michael was in New York all last week, so it wasn't him that you saw. It's not possible.
   ....
5 He didn't crash the car. It's impossible.
   ....

Same verb, different meanings

6 For each set of sentences, decide which modal verb fits all five sentences.

1 a 'No one is answering.' 'There .... be a problem with the phone.'

b I'm so full, I .... n't eat another thing!

c In my last job, I .... start work any time I wanted.

d .... you do me a favour? .... you feed my cat while I'm away?

e 'I really need to lose some weight.' 'You .... join a gym.'

2 a .... you let me know when Mr Burns arrives?

b I think it .... be better to keep that opinion to yourself.

c I can't remember what time I got home, but it .... have been around ten.

d I .... love to go to Peru.

e Ruth was very reliable. She .... always be the first to arrive in the morning.

3 a We are hoping our petition .... make the councillors change their minds.

b Mr Jenkins .... see you now, if you .... come this way.

c .... you please be quiet. This is a library!

d 'What's that noise?' 'That .... be Peter practising the violin.'

e How much water .... the swimming pool hold?

4 a The jury .... rise.

b I .... attempt to explain the differences between the two systems.

c What .... I wear for the party?

d .... I keep an eye on your house while you're away?

e Let's agree to differ on that topic, ... we?

7 Read the letter and then decide which word or phrase (**A**, **B** or **C**) fits each gap. Only one answer is possible.

Dear fellow traveller

Welcome to everyone who has signed up for our Jungle Safari Adventure Tour. Please read the following carefully as it contains important information about your holiday.

Passports / visas

I **(1)**....... like to remind you that **(2)**....... to make sure that your travel documents are in order. Your passport **(3)**....... valid for at least six months beyond your return date or you will not be **(4)**....... entry to the country. In addition, you will require a visa. Please note that, in light of recent events, the visa regulations have changed and many people who previously **(5)**....... a visa now do so.

  You are **(6)**....... obtain the visa in person at the embassy. It **(7)**....... be done by post. If applying by post, you must allow two weeks, and it is **(8)**....... use registered post. If applying in person, you **(9)**....... submit your details before 11 a.m. All applications **(10)**....... two recent photos.

Health

If you received a note about yellow fever, please ignore it. Our representatives **(11)**....... given it to you, as it does not apply to this trip. If you have not had a hepatitis vaccination because you thought that you **(12)**....... one, then please think again. We recommend that all travellers have it.

  There **(13)**....... be a lot of mosquitoes around, so we recommend that you take malaria tablets. For them to be fully effective, you **(14)**....... start taking them a week before departure.

  If you are taking any prescription medicines, you must inform the guide. Please ensure that you have enough for the whole trip. Also, it's **(15)**....... to take a spare pair of glasses.

Wildlife

You can, of course, take as many photos as you wish of all the amazing plants and animals that you will see. However, you **(16)**....... take enough film for your entire trip, as it is unavailable once we arrive. You are, however, **(17)**....... bring any plant samples back with you. Be warned that some plants are very poisonous, and children in particular **(18)**....... be allowed to touch them. The guides will explain which they are.

If you have any further questions, please contact me at the address above.

---

1 **A** would	**B** will	**C** could
2 **A** you require	**B** you must	**C** it's up to you
3 **A** could be	**B** must be	**C** needs be
4 **A** obliged	**B** required	**C** allowed
5 **A** did not need	**B** need not	**C** must not have
6 **A** not supposed to	**B** not obliged to	**C** need not
7 **A** can	**B** ought to	**C** is allowed to
8 **A** required to	**B** advisable to	**C** forbidden to
9 **A** are obliged to	**B** had better	**C** require
10 **A** are allowed	**B** require	**C** are obliged
11 **A** must not have	**B** need not have	**C** should not have
12 **A** didn't need	**B** needn't have had	**C** must have
13 **A** should	**B** will	**C** are to
14 **A** are allowed to	**B** can	**C** must
15 **A** required	**B** forbidden	**C** advisable
16 **A** will need to	**B** must not	**C** are allowed to
17 **A** mustn't	**B** not allowed to	**C** can't
18 **A** needn't	**B** should not	**C** may not

English in Use
Gapped text (Paper 3 Part 6)
▶ ER page 170

1 a Read the title of the text to identify the topic. What type of tools (equipment) do you think that schools need to buy and update regularly?

 b Read the whole text quickly to find out what it is about, ignoring the gaps for the moment.

 1 Why is providing computers a problem for schools in poorer areas?

 2 How can the 'Tools for Schools' scheme help?

2 Read the text again and do the task. Use the Help clues if necessary.

3 Read through the text again when you have finished and check that the answers you have chosen fit in with the overall meaning of the text.

HELP
▶ Question 2
Think carefully about what *it* refers to in this sentence – it will help you rule out some of the options.
▶ Question 4
What is the subject of the modal verb in this sentence? Think about which of the phrases follows on logically from this subject.
▶ Question 6
Which options follow on grammatically and logically from *the charity*?

Language development

Look at all the verbs in the text. How many modals can you find? Underline them.

For questions **1–6**, read the following text and then choose from the list **A–I** given below the best phrase to fill each of the spaces. Each correct phrase may only be used once. **Some of the suggested answers do not fit at all**.

Tools for schools

It's hard for schools and adult education groups working in poorer areas to keep their computer technology up to date. Yet courses in word-processing and IT skills are a high priority for their students. A large school, keen to teach with the latest digital technology, might feel justified in investing in brand-new equipment regularly. But many small educational institutions just want something on which they **(1)**........ . That's where the charity known as 'Tools for Schools' can step in and help. By going through the charity, it **(2)**........ . For example, a mere £175 will buy a one-year-old Internet-ready computer. And if even that is beyond a group's means, a machine with a slightly less up-to-date processor starts at £55 for those who **(3)**........ . The charity persuades large companies which are upgrading their IT systems that giving their old computers to a needy cause **(4)**........ . The charity then spruces the machines up, giving them a thorough clean and health check inside, so that they look, and work, just like new computers when they arrive at the schools.

When the scheme was first introduced, it was so popular that demand soon exceeded supply, and the charity had to work hard to find more companies who **(5)**........ . Happily, this didn't prove too difficult, so that now within two weeks of receiving and processing an order from a school, the charity **(6)**........ .

A would be willing to participate when they updated their equipment
B can give practice in the basics of keyboard skills and Internet access
C will be possible to access the information
D could live without the Internet access
E can take up to two weeks to do so
F should be able to get donated equipment up and running in the classroom
G ought to be able to benefit from the scheme
H may be possible for schools to obtain computers without spending a lot
I must be better than just ditching them

Reading

Multiple-choice questions (Paper 1 Part 3)

▶ ER page 168

1   Read the title of the text and the subheading.
  1   What do you think is meant by the phrase *ethical employer*?
  2   Who do you think the article is aimed at?

2   Read the text quickly to check whether your predictions about the text and topic were correct. A number of organisations and people are mentioned in the text. As you read, make a note of why each of these is mentioned.

London University	Axiom Software
Rachel Hare	Tom Chance
Ethical Consumer Magazine	*People and Planet*
Lauren Steadman	Reading University
the Industrial Society	Helen Wallis

3   Read all the questions and highlight the key words in each one. The first two have been done for you. The questions follow the same order as the text, and there is one piece of text for each question.

4   a   Read question 1. This relates to the first paragraph of the text.

  b   Read this piece of text carefully, then look back at the question. It asks what the research has shown us about companies which claim to be socially responsible. The paragraph tells us that:
    1   we should not necessarily believe their claims
    2   employees expect companies to live up to their claims
    3   good graduates want to work for ethical companies.

  c   Now look at the options. Which one is closest to one of these three things?

  d   Now look at the other three options – look carefully at the text to see why they are wrong.

5   Follow the same procedure for question 2, which relates to the second paragraph of the text. Again, the key information has been highlighted for you.

6   Now continue to answer the rest of the questions. Always read the section of text carefully, to find your own answer to the question, then find the option which is closest in meaning to your own answer.

Read the following magazine article and answer questions **1–6**. Mark the letter **A**, **B**, **C** or **D**. Give only one answer to each question.

How to choose an ethical employer

Students and graduates shouldn't underestimate their power to bring about change by choosing an ethical employer.

According to some research findings published this week, we should be slightly sceptical when large companies say that they are committed to 'socially responsible behaviour'. Such companies could actually be chiefly interested in their public-relations image. They make these claims as a way of attracting customers and shareholders who want to be involved in a business that is 'ethical'. The research does highlight one positive trend, however. It seems that companies which claim to be socially responsible are facing increasing pressure from their employees to put these principles into practice. What's more, the researchers say there is even evidence to suggest that those companies which continue to have a negative impact on the environment and on the communities in which they work may fail to attract the most able candidates in the job market. Could this be an incentive for them to change their ways, and an opportunity for young people to have some influence?

'I think most people who are concerned about society or development as a whole want to work for a company whose policies are not hurting parts of society or stopping their development,' says Rachel Hare, a student at London University. Another survey, this time by graduate careers publisher Axiom Software, bears out these sentiments. It found that 79% of UK graduates would prefer not to work for a company with a poor ethical record. What's more, over half of UK graduates said they would choose a job which fitted their ethical principles rather than one with a more lucrative salary or prospects – despite having student debts to pay off. But establishing which companies are truly socially responsible, as opposed to those simply hiding behind their public-relations image, is no easy task.

Some companies involved in oil, tobacco and timber have been publicly criticised for their behaviour, but many apparently harmless companies maybe equally irresponsible. It depends where they invest, where their raw materials come from and to whom they sub-contract work. Some companies have what's known as a Company Social Responsibility (CSR) policy; others go as far as to engage the services of highly qualified consultants to advise them on human rights and environmental policies. 'It's a potential minefield for students,' says Lauren Steadman, co-editor of *Ethical Consumer Magazine*. 'We get lots of calls asking for help in assessing whether or not a company is ethical. There's a lot of 'greenwash' where companies have sophisticated PR and produce reports without much substance to try to look good. Students need to be sceptical.'

But to be sceptical, students need to be informed. It was in response to a growing demand for advice on such issues that the first ethical careers service in the UK, *People and Planet*, was set up. Manager Helen Wallis tours universities giving workshops for students on how they can find a job that fits with their beliefs. Everyone has their own idea of what is ethical, and what one person will question, another will accept. For example, Tom Chance from Reading University has his own boundaries: 'I wouldn't work for an oil company full stop. I don't think I'd ever be that desperate for a job. I wouldn't work with anything to do with logging, genetically modified food or child labour.' Other students appreciate the chance to talk through the issues in order to arrive at their own particular priorities.

Once an individual has sorted out in their own mind what they consider to be acceptable working practices, Helen helps them investigate whether the company they are interested in is living up to those standards. 'You can find out what social and environmental policies the organisation has by looking at its reports and mission statements,' she says. 'Then look at its website or annual review for proof that those things have been achieved. You can also look for facts it's not going to be publicising by doing your own web search. Has there been anything in the media criticising their practices, or are there independent reports from campaigning groups and charities?' says Helen. 'Finally, when candidates are asked at interview if they have any questions, they should take advantage of the opportunity, and not be fobbed off. Companies should be able to justify what they say they are doing.'

So, students and graduates shouldn't underestimate their power to bring about change; after all, most of them will spend more than 70,000 hours of their lives in the workplace. Research by the Industrial Society a couple of years ago claimed 65% of businesses would change their policies if pushed by employees. To quote Helen Wallis: 'Choosing a socially and environmentally responsible career and persuading your employer to respect your values has enormous potential to benefit both the community and environment.'

1 What does recent research say about companies which claim to be socially responsible?
   A Their claims may not always be very sincere.
   B Their shareholders may not support their principles.
   C Their customers may not really believe their claims.
   D Their employees may not always be aware of their policies.

2 What did Axiom Software discover about graduates in the job market?
   A Most have unrealistic expectations of ethical employers.
   B Most see financial necessity dictating their choice of employer.
   C Most would avoid working for companies believed to be unethical.
   D Most do not know which companies claim to have ethical principles.

3 In the third paragraph, the writer is suggesting that some companies
   A may be less ethical than they appear.
   B have tended to be rather unfairly criticised.
   C have misused the services of experts in the field.
   D may not respond well to enquiries about their policies.

4 Through its workshops, the careers service *People and Planet* aims to
   A promote a general awareness of the idea of ethical employment.
   B help students to establish their own criteria for judging employers.
   C reach a standard definition of what represents an ethical employer.
   D discourage students from working in certain sectors of the economy.

5 Helen Wallis encourages individual students to
   A share any information they uncover about a company's activities.
   B find independent confirmation of information obtained from the media.
   C look for evidence that a company's ethical policies are actually effective.
   D make their views known to companies in advance of attending an interview.

6 In the article as a whole, the writer is
   A critical of employers who have no ethical policy.
   B sceptical about the findings of various research projects.
   C sympathetic towards companies failing to meet ethical targets.
   D supportive of students who wish to work for ethical employers.

Writing

Report (Paper 2 Part 1)

▶ CB pages 52–53, WR page 191

Exam strategy

Read all parts of the Part 1 task carefully. When writing a report, remember to include topic sentences, as these will help you to present your information clearly. Make sure you use linking words so that your points are clearly connected. Remember to use an impersonal style.

1 Look at the task on page 52 of the Coursebook again. Read the first part of a student's answer below.

2 The student has not used topic sentences. Choose the best topic sentence to begin each paragraph from this list.
   a) On the whole, the day was a great success.
   b) Some events were more successful than others.
   c) The purpose of this report is to describe the fundraising day held on June 16th.

3 Choose and add appropriate linking words and phrases from the list below where indicated by numbers 1–5 in the text.
   Apparently   On the other hand   Finally
   This was in spite of the fact that   In addition

4 Change the underlined sentences into the passive to make them less personal.

5 Write the 'Recommendations' and 'Conclusions' paragraphs, using the information given. Remember to include a topic sentence. Use linking words and the passive where appropriate.

Report

Introduction
It was an extremely enjoyable day. I will evaluate its success and make recommendations for future events.

Overview
Events organised included house-to-house collection and street collection, a jumble sale, an appeal for money in the local paper. <u>They raised more money than on the same day last year</u>, and more people attended. <u>About 50 people organised the event</u>, mostly students from the university.

Evaluation of events
It was clear that one event raised a lot more money than the others, and this was the house-to-house collection. This raised 40% of the overall total. This may be because <u>people felt obliged to give money when collectors approached them directly</u>. **(1)** The street collection was very successful financially, probably for the same reason (it accounted for 30% of the total). **(2)** <u>Everyone attending the jumble sale enjoyed it</u>, but it only raised 20% of the money. **(3)** The sale was very popular, being the only interactive event of the day. **(4)** The last 10% came from various activities including an appeal in the local newspaper. **(5)** These were less successful because they lacked the personal touch of the house-to-house and street collections.

Recommendations
Events with a personal touch were very successful, so suggest:
• provide greater range of interactive activities, e.g. ...
• give all officials a badge so that ...
• advertise the event well in advance so that ...

Conclusions
• very successful day
• with some careful thought and planning – could raise even more money next year

A Making choices

English in Use
Lexical cloze (Paper 3 Part 1)

▶ CB page 58, ER page 169

1 Read the title of the text, then read the whole text quickly for general understanding, ignoring the gaps for the moment.
   1 What is David Adjaye's profession?
   2 Which building has made him well known internationally?
   3 What job does Karen Wong do?

2 Read the text again carefully and try to predict what each answer will be. Then look at the options **A–D** and complete the task. Use the Help clues if necessary.

TIP

Remember that each of the items will be testing a slightly different area of language knowledge. So sometimes you are looking for collocations, sometimes for fixed phrases and sometimes for other grammatical relationships between words. Some items, however, simply test whether you know the correct word in the given context – so always think about the meaning of the text as a whole.

3 Read through the text again when you've finished and check that the options you've chosen fit in with the overall meaning of the text.

HELP
➤ Question 2
Which of these words can be followed by the preposition *for*?
➤ Question 6
All of these words are used to describe something extra. Only one completes this fixed phrase, however. Which is it?
➤ Question 9
Only one of these words collocates with *great*. Which is it?

David Adjaye

For questions **1–15**, read the article below and then decide which answer **A**, **B**, **C** or **D** best fits each space. The exercise begins with an example (**0**).

A successful working relationship

For centuries, the typical architectural practice has had at its (**0**) ..A.. the skill and reputation of one extremely gifted individual. This creative genius has generally been supported by a (**1**)........ of talented juniors, (**2**)........ for bringing the master's designs to life. Normally it is impossible to (**3**)........ out one especially important underling, but in the office of one of London's fastest-rising architectural stars, David Adjaye, identifying that pivotal (**4**)........ is simple. It is Karen Wong, managing director of his ever-expanding business.

In his (**5**)........ thirties, David Adjaye, is one of the city's most fashionable architects, designing, amongst other things, the private homes of celebrities such as the actor Ewan McGregor. In (**6**)........ to this, Adjaye's impressive design for the building that will (**7**)........ the Nobel Peace Centre in Oslo is also (**8**)........ him a lot of international recognition.

Karen Wong is an arts graduate from Boston, Massachusetts, who possesses one of the sharpest minds and most efficient personalities working in architecture today. David is in great (**9**)........ , not only for his architectural skills, but also for public (**10**)........ and media interviews. Meanwhile, Karen is the backbone of the office, taking the (**11**)........ off David's shoulders by (**12**)........ with clients, contractors and others. Every creative genius needs a firm (**13**)........ to work from, and David is lucky to have Karen. She not only understands creativity, but is also (**14**)........ of realising a project. It's a combination that is quite (**15**)........ in the artistic world these days.

0	**A** heart	**B** middle	**C** essence	**D** focus
1	**A** cast	**B** side	**C** team	**D** crew
2	**A** responsible	**B** agreeable	**C** liable	**D** dependable
3	**A** separate	**B** select	**C** stand	**D** single
4	**A** issue	**B** figure	**C** factor	**D** aspect
5	**A** last	**B** end	**C** late	**D** final
6	**A** addition	**B** supplement	**C** attachment	**D** extension
7	**A** home	**B** reside	**C** lodge	**D** house
8	**A** lending	**B** gaining	**C** bearing	**D** drawing
9	**A** demand	**B** claim	**C** request	**D** call
10	**A** invitations	**B** encounters	**C** audiences	**D** appearances
11	**A** bother	**B** load	**C** matter	**D** bulk
12	**A** handling	**B** treating	**C** dealing	**D** managing
13	**A** ground	**B** base	**C** root	**D** core
14	**A** capable	**B** practised	**C** skilful	**D** experienced
15	**A** infrequent	**B** scarce	**C** rare	**D** unfamiliar

Language development
Word formation
▶ CB page 60

Spelling

1 Add *a* or *e* to complete these nouns. Use your dictionary to check your answers if necessary.
   1 differ__nce
   2 persist__nce
   3 confid__nce
   4 appear__nce
   5 perform__nce
   6 correspond__nce
   7 depend__nce
   8 assist__nce
   9 exist__nce
   10 prefer__nce

2 Add *a* or *i* to complete these adjectives.
   1 respons__ble
   2 believ__ble
   3 collaps__ble
   4 defens__ble
   5 adapt__ble
   6 suit__ble
   7 revers__ble
   8 break__ble
   9 flex__ble
   10 adjust__ble

Negative prefixes

3 Make these words negative and underline the odd word out in each case in terms of its negative prefix.
   1 safe   secure   predictable   well
   2 able   capable   formal   adequate
   3 responsible   relevant   realistic   rational
   4 patient   pleasant   probable   mature
   5 legal   logical   literate   lucky

Word families

4 Complete each sentence with the correct form of the word in capitals. Decide if you need to make the word negative or plural.

1 GENERAL
   a It's dangerous to .... from a limited number of examples.
   b It's impossible to make .... about what men and women are like.
   c I find my colleagues are .... very pleasant and helpful.
   d The discussion got no further than .... ; another meeting will be needed to decide on action.

2 INTEND
   a The plane had to divert from its .... destination due to bad weather.
   b He's full of good .... , but he never actually does anything.
   c He said his rudeness was .... and that he regretted it.
   d His speech was .... vague and lacking in concrete promises.

3 DEPEND
   a His friends knew that he was utterly reliable and ....
   b The company plans to split into two separate .... companies.
   c Western countries need to reduce their .... on oil.
   d This small state has been fighting for .... for nearly 20 years.

4 POWER
   a The new Mercedes has an even more .... engine.
   b He was .... to stop the children from drowning.
   c The course aims to .... young people by giving them confidence.
   d Her uncle was a tall man, and .... built.

5 ORIGIN
   a The old house still has a lot of its .... features.
   b No one knows the .... of this custom.
   c She is a young artist with a lot of talent and ....
   d I'm .... from Canada, but I've lived in London for 20 years now.
   e A lot of their ideas are rather dull and ....

6 PLEASE
   a It was a .... to meet you.
   b What a .... surprise! It's lovely to see you.
   c Shareholders who are .... with this decision should write to the chairman to complain.
   d His landscape paintings are .... to the eye, if not very exciting.
   e One way to make reading .... is to find books that your children will love to read.

7 VARY
   a The music is played on .... kinds of instruments.
   b The students on the course come from very .... backgrounds.
   c The quality of her work is rather ....
   d Several government ministers hold opinions which are at .... with the official government view.
   e We tried several different methods, with .... degrees of success.
   f They sell a very wide .... of cheeses.
   g He has been .... described as courageous and foolhardy.

English in Use

Word formation (Paper 3 Part 4)

▶ CB page 61, ER page 170

1 Read the title of the first text to identify the topic. Then read the whole text quickly for general understanding, ignoring the gaps for the moment.
  1 What is job-sharing?
  2 According to the text, do job-sharers do their job better than full-time colleagues?

2 Read the text again carefully and think about the type of word that could fit in each gap. Then complete the task by filling in the gaps. Remember to check if the word:
  • is singular or plural
  • has a positive or negative meaning.

3 Read through the text again when you've finished and check your answers.

4 Repeat the procedure for the second text.

For questions **1–15**, read the texts below. Use the words to the right of the texts to form **one** word that fits in the same numbered space in the text. The exercise begins with an example (**0**).

INFORMATION LEAFLET

Find your ideal job-share partner

If you want to work part time and achieve greater job (**0**)satisfaction , then job-sharing, where the hours, duties and salary of one job are literally divided between two people, may be just the thing for you. Whether you're looking for a new job, or wish to share your (**1**)................... one with someone else, a new employment agency with a website (**2**)................... Share a Job could help. It (**3**)................... in bringing together people with complementary skills and experience, then helps them to make job-share (**4**)................... to employers. For a job-share to work, both partners have to be extremely (**5**)................... and must be equally willing to share the overall (**6**)................... for the job. What's more, employers are now viewing job-shares more (**7**)................... , as recent research has shown that job-sharers tend to out-perform their full-time colleagues.

(**0**) **SATISFY**
(**1**) **EXIST**
(**2**) **TITLE**
(**3**) **SPECIAL**
(**4**) **PROPOSE**
(**5**) **ADAPT**
(**6**) **RESPONSIBLE**
(**7**) **FAVOUR**

MAGAZINE ARTICLE

Working as a team

Developing a good working (**8**)................... with colleagues is not always a bed of roses, and most employers nowadays are aware that disputes between staff can have a negative effect on a company's performance. For this reason, team-building courses have become very (**9**)................... in recent years. Employees are sent on (**10**)................... courses in the hope that they will gain a better understanding of each other's (**11**)................... and weaknesses. Some courses appeal to the more (**12**)................... side of people's character and include activities such as skydiving, whilst others are more (**13**)................... , like art and musical workshops. These may allow people to demonstrate (**14**)................... talents, not always obvious from their normal duties. However, the organisers are keen to stress that such courses are only (**15**)................... to the employees if they are followed up by meaningful discussions afterwards.

(**8**) **RELATION**
(**9**) **FASHION**
(**10**) **RESIDE**
(**11**) **STRONG**
(**12**) **ADVENTURE**
(**13**) **CREATE**
(**14**) **HIDE**
(**15**) **BENEFIT**

Language development

When you have checked your answers to the task, add any new words to your vocabulary notebook and use your dictionary to help you complete a word family for each item. Remember to review these words regularly and try to use them in your writing and speaking.

Listening
Multiple-choice questions (Paper 4 Part 4)

▶ ER pages 170–171

1 a Read the instructions for the exam task.
1 How many speakers will you hear?
2 What will they all be talking about?
3 How many questions are there for each speaker?

b Read the questions carefully and highlight key words. This has been done for you in the first two questions. Think about the type of decision that each speaker is talking about.

c Check you understand all the words in the options.
1 What does the phrasal verb *to fall back on* in question 2 mean?
    a) to do something again
    b) to depend on something
    c) to discover something
2 What does the adjective *laid-back* in question 6 mean?
    a) tired   b) secretive   c) relaxed

2 ⌒ Listen to the recording once and try to answer the questions on each speaker. Use the Help clues if necessary.

TIP

Don't worry if you don't understand every word in the recording – in Part 4, you are listening for the speakers' main points, attitudes and opinions.

HELP
➤ Question 1
The speaker tells us her reasons at the beginning of the text before she mentions the shop. Which option matches the gist of what she is saying?
➤ Question 2
Listen for the phrase *looking back* – the speaker uses it when she tells us how she feels now about her decision.
➤ Question 3
The speaker says he was frustrated in his job in architecture – listen for what it was that frustrated him.

3 Listen again to check and complete your answers.

You will hear **five** short extracts in which different people are talking about difficult decisions they have made. Each extract has two questions. For questions **1–10**, choose the correct answer **A**, **B** or **C**. You will hear the recording twice.

Speaker 1
1 Why did the **first speaker** buy a health-food shop?
    A She was looking for a new source of income.
    B She had some money that she wanted to invest.
    C She wanted to develop her interest in business.
2 How does she feel now?
    A glad that she had her savings to fall back on
    B grateful for the support of her friends
    C amazed at her own personal courage

Speaker 2
3 The **second speaker** left his job as an architect because
    A it was less creative than he expected.
    B it involved too much responsibility.
    C it lacked the career opportunities he had hoped for.
4 What does he say is the main disadvantage of his present job?
    A the low salary
    B the unpredictable hours
    C the length of the training period

Speaker 3
5 The **third speaker** says her decision to travel to India allowed her to
    A fulfil a long-held ambition.
    B avoid her family problems.
    C enjoy a new independence.
6 How has the experience affected her?
    A She is more honest with people.
    B She has become more patient.
    C She has a more laid-back attitude.

Speaker 4
7 How does the **fourth speaker** feel about being at home with his children?
    A embarrassed that his wife has such a well-paid job
    B concerned that he is often disorganised
    C surprised about how tiring his role is
8 How does he say his friends react to his role?
    A They are sympathetic to his problems.
    B They would like to be in his position.
    C They tend to regard him as lazy.

Speaker 5
9 The **fifth speaker** says that the main benefit of her new life in Africa is
    A learning new skills.
    B living in an unrestricted environment.
    C enjoying a different climate.
10 What aspect of her new lifestyle does she find difficult to cope with?
    A a limited social life
    B her isolated location
    C the relationship with her neighbours

B Human nature

Vocabulary
Relationships
▶ CB page 64–65

1 Match the sentence halves and underline the correct particle in each phrasal verb.

1 I'm very lucky because I get *on / off* with
2 She fell *for / to*
3 In most respects, Danny takes *over / after*
4 My brother and I fell *off / out* over
5 We should all look up *on / to*
6 Laura relies *on / with*
7 In the past, he's been badly let *down / off*,

a Peter for his courage and determination.
b a girl we both liked.
c my in-laws very well.
d her mother to look after the two children.
e so he finds it hard to trust people.
f Harry the moment she saw him.
g his paternal grandfather.

2 Complete the sentences using an appropriate idiomatic expression from the list in the correct form.

get your own way   hit it off   lose touch
run in the family   see eye to eye
the black sheep (of the family)

1 Patrick is treated as the odd man out, the misfit,
....
2 A: Do you and your mother-in-law get on?
   B: Not really. We've never ....
   about anything.
3 It's not good parenting to spoil children and let
   them .... all the time.
4 A: So they're going out together?
   B: Yes, they met at my party and obviously
   .... immediately.
5 A: She's very attractive, just like her mother.
   B: Yes, good looks must ....
6 A: Do you see much of Ian these days?
   B: No, I'm afraid I .... with him.

3 Complete the text below with words and phrases from the list.

acquaintances   associate   circle of friends
close family   colleagues   companion   confidant
ex   extended family   flatmate   friend of a friend
mate   partners   siblings

For many couples, deciding when and where to get married is the easy part. The trouble starts when they have to decide who to invite to the wedding. Some like to keep it small and stick to just their
(1)... such as parents and
(2)... . However, for a bigger wedding how much further do you go into the
(3)... ? Uncles, aunts, first or second cousins?
   Most people will invite friends, and there is often a special role for their best friend or a special
(4)... that they have turned to over the years – but how widely into your
(5)... do you go? However large your wedding, you have to distinguish between those who are friends and those who are just (6)... . And do you have to invite the
(7)... who you've never met but was the one that made the cake?
   Many people have friends at work, but if you invite one or two, you could upset other
(8)... who are not invited. And the numbers double if you include their
(9)... – that's before you even start with the children.
   The list goes on. What about the travelling (10)... you spent months with a few years ago or the (11)... you used to live with? You may have a close business
(12)... who is important to you and who you see a lot of – but do you really want to mix business and pleasure?
   Something that is generally agreed is that the one person you don't usually invite is your
(13)... !

Language development
Noun clauses
▶ CB page 67, GR page 179

that-clauses

1 Rewrite each sentence using a *that*-clause, starting
   with the words given.
   1 My brother passed his exam with flying colours,
     which came as no surprise to me.
     It ....
   2 How could you accuse me of such a thing? It
     horrifies me.
     I'm ....
   3 The deal is likely to be finalised tomorrow.
     It ....
   4 I'm delighted to be able to bring you this good
     news.
     I'm ....
   5 Funding for the project has been cut, which is
     ridiculous.
     It ....
   6 There is no proof of his involvement in the fraud.
     There ....
   7 I really regret not going to university when I was
     young.
     I ....
   8 Her guilt was obvious to the jury.
     It ....

2 Read the following text then choose the best phrase
   from the list A–I to fill each of the spaces. The first is
   given as an example (0).

Clauses beginning with a question word

3 Complete the sentences with a suitable word from the
   list.
   who   what   where   when   which   why   how

   1 I can't decide .... to use the money I won.
   2 I know he's off work at the moment, and I'm not
     sure .... he'll be back.
   3 Scientists don't understand .... some people
     are more likely to suffer from the disease than
     others.
   4 Can you remember .... you left your bag?
   5 We haven't decided yet .... film we're going
     to see.
   6 I think you should tell the police .... you
     know.
   7 I know I've got to phone someone, but I've
     forgotten .... it is.

The genius in every child.

The idea **(0)** ..D.. is not new. It doesn't mean **(1)**........ or write music like
Beethoven but that every child has the capacity for greatness. Babies are
born with wonder, curiosity and a vast capacity for learning. Young children
have vivid imaginations, creative minds and sensitive personalities. It is
important **(2)**........ as the children grow and mature.

It is sad **(3)**........ by following a curriculum that is too rigid and restricted.
Added to this is the problem **(4)**........ with its violence, mediocrity and poor
role models.

The good news is **(5)**........ to help children develop their natural genius. To
do this, adults have to set an example, so it is essential **(6)**........ . When
children are surrounded by creative adults, they too will become more
creative.

Secondly, adults need to provide simple toys and activities to stimulate a
child. Einstein said **(7)**........ to awaken his love of learning. Then create an
atmosphere that is free from criticism, comparison and pressure. Finally,
understand **(8)**........ . Forget IQ tests and let kids succeed in their own ways.

A that schools restrict genius
B (that) a simple compass
  was all it took
C that educators (parents
  and teachers) help
  preserve these
  characteristics
D that every child is a genius
E that they find within
  themselves their own
  creativity and sense of
  wonder
F that the mass media
  suppresses creativity
G that every child can think
  like Einstein
H that each child will be a
  genius in a different way
I that there is much a
  teacher or parent can do

4 Complete the sentences with a suitable question word.

1 .... she said was very interesting.

2 .... these animals behave in the way they do is still a mystery.

3 .... I choose to spend my evenings with is my own business!

4 .... you treat your children when they are young will affect the way they develop into adults.

5 .... you know is more important than .... you know.

5 Underline one or both of the options in these sentences.

1 *If / Whether* I go to the party or not depends on what time I get back from work.

2 I'm in such a rush I don't know *if / whether* I'm coming or going.

3 The question is not *if / whether* he did it but **when** he did it.

4 We can't agree on *if / whether* to move house or not.

5 I'm not sure *if / whether* I want to go to France on holiday.

6 I've seen a great car. I have to decide today *if / whether* to buy it.

7 I can't make out *if / whether* she is trustworthy or not.

8 I'm going out *if / whether* you like it or not.

to-infinitive and *-ing* clauses

6 Complete the text by putting the verbs into the correct form.

(1)......................... (*grow up*) in a big family can be tough. The most difficult thing is **(2)**.......................... (*keep*) your independence. Sometimes it's impossible **(3)**......................... (*assert*) yourself when you have so many brothers and sisters. But for me, **(4)**......................... (*criticise*) my family would be unfair. I am pleased **(5)**......................... (*say*) they have always been great. **(6)**......................... (*go*) away to university was a big thing for me. I was proud **(7)**......................... (*be*) independent, but also proud of **(8)**......................... (*have*) my supportive family behind me.

7 Rewrite these sentences using a *to*-infinitive clause, starting with the words given.

1 Discussing problems with a friend can be helpful.
It ....

2 He aims to become a top chef by the age of 30.
His aim ....

3 Tom wants us to meet Mary. He's really keen.
Tom's really keen ....

4 We have to cut costs. It's the only way the company can survive.
The only way ....

5 Human beings can solve problems. This is one of the definitions of intelligence.
The ability ....

6 The oldest child in a family tends to be the most ambitious.
The tendency is ....

7 Younger siblings want to establish their own identity. That is their main priority.
The main priority of ....
....

8 Therapists can help people recognise patterns of behaviour they need to change. That is the most valuable contribution they can make.
The most valuable contribution ....
....

8 Starting a sentence with a *to*-infinitive clause is more common in formal, written English. In everyday language, starting with introductory *It* or an *-ing* clause is preferred. Rewrite these sentences in two ways.

1 To meet the Dalai Lama would be a great honour.
a It..
....
b Meeting..
....

2 To spend time on your own is very important.
a It..
....
b Spending ....
....

3 To find out his true identity would be very hard.
a It..
....
b Finding ....
....

4 To say that the company is not interested in making money is ridiculous.
a It..
....
b Saying ....
....

English in Use

Open cloze (Paper 3 Part 2)

▶ ER page 169

1   Read the title of the text, then read the whole text quickly for general understanding, ignoring the gaps for the moment.

   1   Why do the children in this school do special physical exercises?

   2   What effect have teachers noticed on the children's behaviour?

2   Read through the text again and think about the type of word which will fit in each gap. Look at the words before and after the gap and decide which word is missing. Use the Help clues if necessary.

3   Read through the whole text again when you've finished and check that the words you've chosen fit in with the overall meaning of the text.

HELP

➤ **Question 1**
   An auxiliary verb is needed here, but it's not a modal verb.

➤ **Question 3**
   In this question, a word is missing from a fixed phrase.

➤ **Question 6**
   Read the whole sentence carefully. Is a relative pronoun or a conjunction needed here?

➤ **Question 12**
   Which preposition completes the idea of *incorporate*?

Language development

Read the text again. Can you find one sentence that begins with an -*ing* clause, and one that begins with *It* and contains a *to*-infinitive clause?

For questions **1–15**, complete the following article by writing each missing word in the space. **Use only one word for each space.** The exercise begins with an example (**0**).

Give the brain a breather

If you didn't know what was going (**0**)........*on*........ , you might think the children at Westfields Primary School were demonstrating a bizarre dance routine. They are swinging their arms above their heads – to the right and the left – and as they (**1**).................... so, they are also reciting the alphabet.

What they are actually doing (**2**).................... having what the school calls a 'brain break' – in (**3**).................... words, using a specially designed physical exercise to help them concentrate and learn. The exercises (**4**).................... supposed to help different parts of the brain to work in harmony, and many of them involve (**5**).................... are called 'cross-lateral' movements, (**6**).................... , it is thought, help the left and right sides of the brain to work together. An example of this is marching on the spot whilst at the (**7**).................... time touching your left knee with your right hand, (**8**).................... vice versa. Another exercise, known (**9**).................... 'Nose and Ears', involves putting your right forefinger on your nose, crossing over your left hand to touch your right earlobe, then swapping. It is actually quite difficult to make (**10**).................... that your arms always end up crossed over.

Westfields is (**11**).................... of a growing number of schools to incorporate such exercises (**12**).................... the school day. Doing the exercises helps the children settle down quickly after break time, and can help when concentration begins to flag, halfway (**13**).................... a lesson. In (**14**).................... to their beneficial effects, the exercises are also fun – so they (**15**).................... down extremely well with the children.

Writing

Competition entry (Paper 2 Part 2)

▶ CB pages 68–69, WR page 192

Exam strategy

A competition entry should engage its readers, so it is very important to keep their attention. Make your writing interesting by using colourful vocabulary and varying the type of sentence you use. Think of a good title if the entry is an article.

1 Read the task below and answer these questions.

  1 What type of text is the competition entry?

  2 What must you write about? Underline the part that tells you.

  3 What style will be appropriate?

    a) formal   b) informal   c) neutral

Want to become a writer? Enter the competition below!

An international magazine wants to run a series of articles on the importance of family, and has invited readers to submit articles about why they think the family is still the most influential part of a young person's life. The best entries will be published as part of the series.

This is your chance to see your name in print!

Write your **competition entry** in approximately 250 words.

---

2 Read a student's answer on the right. Which plan, A or B, has the student followed?

A	B
• introduction establishing topic	• introduction establishing topic
• advantages and disadvantages of friends	• what young people need
• advantages and disadvantages of family	• reasons why only family can give support
• conclusion	• conclusion

3 Substitute the words and phrases from the list below for the underlined parts of the answer to make it more interesting.

a vast array   incredible demands   blood is thicker than water
through thick and thin   bombarded on all sides
the going gets tough   play a part   bedrock

4 a Look at the highlighted sentences at the end of the second paragraph. Look at the different ways of writing these sentences below, and match them to the sentence types a–d.

1 I don't think this is what friends do.	a rhetorical question and exclamation
2 This is not what friends do!	b rhetorical question
3 Is this what friends do?	c statement
4 Is this what friends do? I don't think so!	d exclamation

It is often said that the role of the family is less important nowadays than in the past. I'm not convinced that this is actually the case. **(1)** Relatives are closer than friends.

It's perfectly true that young people today have **(2)** a lot of pressures put on them – they are expected to do well at school, to get good jobs, to look good, to keep up with the latest fashion – they are **(3)** hit everywhere by **(4)** lots of stresses. What they need is someone to talk things through with – someone they can trust to give independent yet caring advice, who won't make them feel small or imply that they are getting it wrong. Is this what friends do? I don't think so! It's the family.

It is the family, too, who rally round when **(5)** things become difficult, not friends – friends have their own problems. No one understands a young person better than the family who brought them up. Where do young people get their role models from? Is it the exotic media stars admired by so many? Of course, these stars do **(6)** contribute something, but ultimately they are removed from real life and probably have problems of their own! No, it's the family, the people who can be relied on to be there **(7)** always.

In the past, the family was the **(8)** basis of society, and in spite of rising divorce rates, this remains the case today. There certainly is 'no place like home', and no one is a better friend than a parent!

---

  b Which of the sentence types in Exercise 4a

    1 states an opinion?

    2 states an opinion strongly?

    3 involves the reader?

    4 involves the reader and states an opinion strongly?

  c Find two more exclamations and two more rhetorical questions in the student's answer.

5 Choose the best title for the article.

  a) Blood is thicker than water

  b) A family united

  c) The pressures of being young today

6 Plan and write your own answer to the task.

Reading

Multiple matching (Paper 1 Part 4)

▶ ER pages 168

1 Read the title and the subtitle of the text. Answer these questions before you read on.
1 What do the people in the text have in common?
2 What does *high-flying* mean?
3 What is *sibling rivalry*?

2 Read the text quickly to find out:
1 in which field each pair of twins is a high-flier
2 how the twins feel about each other.

3 a Read the instructions for the exam task, then read all the questions and highlight the key words. The first four have been done for you.

b Read section A (about Bryony and Kathryn Frost) carefully and mark any sections of text that contain similar ideas or information to the questions 1–16. For example:
1 Look at question 2. Find the sentence in section A of the text that seems to have the same meaning. Mark the parts that match *a family member has suffered as a result of their relationship*. Find the phrasal verb that means *someone felt excluded*.

2 Look at question 3. Find the phrases in section A of the text that are similar to *fall out over unimportant matters*.

You have now found two questions which match option A. There are two more. Can you find them?

c Now read section B (about Neil and Adrian Rayment) carefully. Look at question 11 and find the phrases in the text that match *people assume them to be identical in every respect* and *resents the fact that*. When you scan the whole text, there are several places where the attitude of people to identical twins is mentioned, but only one pair of twins resents the attitude.

4 Now continue to find the rest of the questions in the text.

Answer questions **1–16** by referring to the magazine article opposite about twins. Choose your answers from the people listed **A–D**. Some of the choices may be required more than once.

A Bryony and Kathryn Frost   **B** Neil and Adrian Rayment
C Louise and Jane Wilson   **D** Anita and Carole Pitman

Which pair of twins

recognises that their natural similarities are a bonus professionally?	1 ....
feels that a family member has suffered as a result of their relationship?	2 ....
only tends to fall out over unimportant matters?	3 ....
recognises that they might each be more cautious on their own?	4 ....
feels that some people have taken unfair advantage of their relationship?	5 ....
has recently realised a long-held career ambition?	6 ....
experienced contrasting reactions to being parted from each other?	7 ....
is convinced that their working partnership will be temporary?	8 ....
recognises that their professional talent is inherited?	9 ....
has a laid-back attitude to their professional rivalry?	10 ....
resents the fact that people assume them to be identical in every respect?	11 ....
enjoys a stronger bond than may at first be apparent to others?	12 ....
realises they may be influenced by false impressions of their personalities?	13 ....
feels their relationship enables them to avoid serious professional disagreements?	14 ....
admits to being apprehensive at the prospect of a life apart?	15 ....
accepts that having different interests has been of benefit to them?	16 ....

MIRROR IMAGESMIRROR IMAGES

What is it about the relationship between twins that can produce such a creative bond? We asked four pairs of high-flying twins to tell us about how they cope with a situation that must be the ultimate in sibling rivalry.

A Bryony and Kathryn Frost: Athletes

The Frost twins are professional athletes – middle-distance runners, who have been racing for as long as they can remember. The 18-year-olds have eyes the colour of swimming pools and long, white-blonde hair. Kathryn wears
5 hers up, otherwise it would be impossible to tell them apart. They train, compete and live together in a house with their parents and brother, Richard (21) who's in computers. The longest they have spent apart was when Kathryn went to Italy for a week. Although they compete in the same races,
10 they don't seem to be competitive. 'We have a love-hate relationship,' says Kathryn. 'Bryony and I spend a lot of time together. She's not really my friend, more a part of me. Sometimes she's faster than me, then suddenly, I'm better than her. It's not something we get worked up about.' Bryony
15 agrees: 'At the moment, she'd beat me, but so what?'

Bryony tells me they have quite a close relationship with their brother. 'He did feel left out because there was Mum and Dad, me and Kathryn. I feel sorry for him.'

'I love him, but I'll never know him like I know Kathryn,'
20 adds Bryony. Asked what they do row about, Kathryn says it's invariably over petty things, such as who gets in the shower first. 'We haven't developed separately, so we've got the same strengths and weaknesses, but our mood swings can be identical, too! We have to learn to give each other some
25 space.' The Frost twins will inevitably have to face up to building separate lives, but neither relishes the prospect. 'I'd be more likely to make an effort on my own,' admits Kathryn, 'but it's scary.'

B Neil and Adrian Rayment: Actors

When the Rayment twins are asked who's the better actor of
30 the two, Neil laughs. 'Don't wind us up! We don't even like to think about it.' But it's a reasonable question, considering they appear as identical bad guys in their latest sci-fi film. What's more, they are soon to be seen as the leads in *Team One*, an all-action martial-arts feature. These two films
35 represent the Rayment twins' big break. Although the pair previously ran their own separate businesses, they have been avid film fanatics for years; ready to grab any acting part that turned up since the age of 19.

As their twin careers seem to be taking off big time, how
40 will they develop – together or apart? Adrian says that he doesn't see them following the same path. 'We're both trying to tie down this new craft, acting. I'm sure we'll head in different directions because we have different styles, but maybe not for a while.' As Neil explains: 'Our lifestyles and
45 goals are the same, but we have different outlooks. Adrian's a bit more calculated, he thinks before he steps in, whereas I'm impulsive.'

Indeed they don't always see eye to eye, but despite the occasional heated discussion (usually about acting
50 techniques), they enjoy working together. 'It's being with someone you know inside out,' says Neil. 'There's this unexplained synchronicity on screen which looks really cool and the producers appreciate it. When we move together, the timing's already there, both physically and mentally.'
55 'We've been pushed together since we were born, forced

to accept people's indifference to our distinct personalities,' says Adrian. 'We tolerate it. But after 24 hours with us, someone we've just met is able to tell us apart.'

C Louise and Jane Wilson: Artists

The first time Louise and Jane were apart for any length of
60 time was when they were studying at different universities. The former found the separation 'a bit traumatic'; the latter viewed it as 'a terrific challenge'. Although in different cities, they found themselves working on similar ideas and experimenting with photography. They ended up producing
65 all but identical photographic displays on completion of their courses. 'We produced two of everything,' says Jane, who has dark hair and wears black, unlike her sister who favours lighter colours. They are not identical; in fact, you might not even think they were sisters. 'The colleges had to
70 confer to make sure we got the same marks,' says Louise. They haven't stopped working together since. 'We did paintings together in our first year in business,' says Jane. 'They were fakes, poor copies. Then in the second year, we returned to photography.'
75 So it was that they began to photograph 'different environments and spaces'. They now live in separate areas of London, but come together most days in their studio. Asked if they argue like all good business partners, they say they do, but have never had any irreconcilable differences.
80 'Obviously, working with Jane there's an enormous element of trust within a familial bond, so there's no need to define who's responsible for what,' says Louise. Jane agrees: 'A lot of producing art is collaborative, but it's only now becoming more acceptable to art galleries.
85 Until recently, they wanted to give us just one fee for our exhibitions!'

'That's taking sisterly love a bit far!' laughs Louise.

D Anita and Carole Pitman: Musicians

The Pitman twins – Anita on piano, Carole on violin – are a renowned classical musical duo. They have a brother, 16
90 months their senior, a mechanical engineer. 'We miss him because he's living in France,' says Carole. 'But we still feel close. As kids, being similar in age and all looking alike, people used to take us for triplets. But he's quite different to us now – we take after our mother, who's very musical.
95 Although we always had a three-way dynamic – it wasn't always us against him.'

The twins had a five-year period when Anita was at university and Carole worked in a bank, which they now feel was advantageous to them both intellectually and socially.
100 When it was over, they were ready to come back together. They made music together as a hobby, until their talent was discovered and they were unexpectedly offered a recording contract. Now they have the best of both worlds, recognising they need each other, but quite able to stand on their own
105 two feet.

'I'm not worried that we can only ever work as twins,' Carole says. 'But at the moment it's something we can capitalise on, and that's great. We're not yet in a situation to be choosy!'
110 'We feel we take more risks precisely because there's two of us. We spur each other on,' Anita says candidly. 'Deep down, we're very similar, but people often label Carole as more confident, and me as less so, and there's a danger of living up to that label after a while.'

A | In the slow lane

English in Use
Word formation
(Paper 3 Part 4)
▶ CB page 74, ER page 170

1 Read the title of the first text to identify the topic. Then read it through quickly for general understanding, ignoring the gaps for the moment.

2 Read the text again carefully and try to decide what type of word will fit in each gap. Then fill in the gaps, using the Help clues if necessary. Remember to check if the word:
   - is singular or plural
   - requires a suffix or prefix
   - has a positive or negative meaning.

3 Read through the text again when you've finished and check that the words you've written fit in with the overall meaning of the text and are spelled correctly.

4 Repeat the procedure for the second text.

HELP
▶ Question 1
   Which suffix is added to this verb to create the noun? Are there any spelling changes?
▶ Question 7
   You are looking for a noun that means *a collection of various things*. You need to add both a prefix and a suffix to the base word.
▶ Question 9
   You need to make a negative adjective from this verb.
▶ Questions 10–15
   Three of these items require plural nouns. Do you know which?

For questions **1–15**, read the two texts below. Use the words in the boxes to the right of the texts to form **one** word that fits in the same numbered space in the text. The exercise begins with an example **(0)**.

BOOK REVIEW

The pleasures of slow food

In a world **(0)** increasingly dominated by fast food, *The Pleasures of Slow Food* is a **(1)**................. of heritage recipes, artisan traditions and the rapid **(2)**................. of a philosophy which aims to make good food a part of everyday life. 'Slow Food' is the name of a 65,000-strong international **(3)**................. , which numbers amongst its members some of the most distinguished names in the food world. The book showcases over 60 recipes from the world's most **(4)**................. chefs for dishes in which local handmade ingredients feature **(5)**................. alongside traditional cooking methods. There are also profiles of some of Slow Food's leading **(6)**................. , such as Italian cheesemaker Roberto Rubino. This engaging **(7)**................. of fantastic recipes and personal stories makes for an enjoyable way to bring the best of the world's food to your table.

(0)	**INCREASE**
(1)	CELEBRATE
(2)	GROW
(3)	MOVE
(4)	INNOVATE
(5)	PROMINENT
(6)	SUPPORT
(7)	SORT

ARTICLE IN A MARKETING JOURNAL

Fast food slows to a stop

Things are changing in the fast-food business. In **(8)**................. to tougher legislation and **(9)**................. shifts in consumer taste, fast-food chains have sought to introduce healthier meal **(10)**................. onto their menus, whilst revamping their outlets to create a new image. But as burgers are bumped off the menu in favour of salads, market **(11)**................. are beginning to question the **(12)**................. of such a radical change of direction. Better, they argue, to promote reduced-fat or low-salt versions of traditional **(13)**................. rather than allow the **(14)**................. to grow that these are inherently unhealthy.

Meanwhile, the traditional burger and fries should, they suggest, be marketed as an **(15)**................. , as a special treat for the 'what-the-hell' times. After all, we all eat ice cream and feel good about it, but nobody pretends that it's particularly healthy.

(8)	RESPOND
(9)	DENY
(10)	OPT
(11)	ANALYSE
(12)	WISE
(13)	PRODUCE
(14)	PERCEIVE
(15)	INDULGE

Language development
When you have checked your answers to the task, add any new words to your vocabulary notebook and use your dictionary to help you complete a word family for each item. Remember to review these words regularly and try to use them in your writing and speaking.

Language development 1
Modifying gradable and ungradable adjectives

▶ CB page 77, GR page 180

Gradable and ungradable adjectives

1 a Complete the table below with pairs of adjectives from the list which are related in meaning.

amazed angry bad delighted disastrous fascinating huge hungry identical interesting irate large minute pleased priceless rare ravenous similar small surprised unique valuable

	Gradable (+ *very*)	Ungradable (+ *absolutely*)
0	surprised	amazed
1		
2		
3		
4		
5		
6		
7		
8		
9		
10		

b Complete these sentences with an appropriate adverb from the list. Then write '+' if it makes the adjective stronger, and '–' if it makes it weaker. Use each word once only. In some sentences, more than one adverb is possible.

slightly quite fairly utterly completely absolutely a bit rather

1 I was .... surprised to see my name on the shortlist of candidates.
2 A .... large crowd had turned out to welcome the team home.
3 The wildlife of this region is .... unique – these creatures are found nowhere else.
4 If the project lost its funding now, it would be .... disastrous for all the people involved.
5 The two pictures are .... identical.
6 She looked puzzled and .... angry.
7 I was .... amazed to discover that he had served in the army.
8 Shall we have some lunch? I'm starting to feel .... hungry.

2 Use the following adverbs to change the register of the sentences below as indicated in brackets.

a bit dead somewhat incredibly rather most

1 The article on climate change was ~~very~~ .... informative. (*formal*)
2 I thought the lecture on greenhouse gases would be ~~very~~ .... boring, but it turned out to be quite interesting. (*informal*)
3 The results of the initial tests were ~~slightly~~ .... surprising. (*formal*)
4 I'm ~~slightly~~ .... worried about what's in this food. (*informal*)
5 I found the first exam ~~very~~ .... difficult. (*informal*)
6 You look ~~slightly~~ .... confused. Can I help you? (*polite*)

3 a One of the adjectives on the right does not collocate with the adverb on the left. Cross it out.
1 **bitterly** cold / disappointed / opposed / sensitive
2 **deeply** ashamed / critical / hurt (emotionally) / moving
3 **heavily** dependent / armed / criticised / useless
4 **highly** controversial / respected / unacceptable / valued
5 **painfully** slow / aware / useless / shy
6 **perfectly** educated / satisfactory / genuine / understandable
7 **totally** disturbed / harmless / incompetent / unacceptable
8 **utterly** alone / appalled / healthy / miserable

b Write down which of the adverbs in Exercise 3a could be used with the words you crossed out.
1 *highly sensitive*
2 ....
3 ....
4 ....
5 ....
6 ....
7 ....
8 ....

c Complete the sentences with an appropriate adverb/adjective collocation from Exercise 3a or b. Use each collocation once only.
1 The convoy was attacked by a small group of .... soldiers.
2 Your concerns are .... However, there is little that the company can do.
3 The independent report was .... of the government's policy towards road building.
4 All Western economies are .... on oil.

5 I should take a warm coat with you as there's a .... wind blowing today.

6 The deliberate polluting of the sea is .... and ship owners will be prosecuted in all cases.

7 The government is .... of the need to change policies, but is concerned about the cost.

8 It is a beautiful and .... film.

9 The author of the report is a .... university lecturer and leader in his field.

10 People were confident that the minister would make great changes, but he turned out to be ....

Confusing adjectives/adverbs

- Some adverbs have the same form as adjectives e.g. He works **hard** (adv.). He's a **hard** (adj.) worker.
- Some adverbs have two forms, with different meanings, e.g.
  I had to stay **late** at the office. (after the usual time)
  What have you been doing **lately**? (recently)

4 Underline the correct word in the contexts below. In some cases, both are possible.

1 Remember to hold on *tight / tightly* when we go round the corners.

2 You shouldn't have been driving so fast; it serves you *right / rightly*.

3 The group's supporters are *most / mostly* students.

4 He is so unreliable you can guarantee he'll arrive *late / lately*.

5 When he heard the news, he didn't say much but I could tell he took it *hard / hardly*.

6 They worked for three days, *hard / hardly* stopping to eat or rest.

7 As I left the house, it was raining *hard / hardly*.

8 Do you like these shoes? I got them *cheap / cheaply* in the market.

9 Be careful; there are lots of snakes in the forest, some of them are *dead / deadly*.

10 He was *dead / deadly* tired that night and that's probably what led to the crash.

11 Open the window as *wide / widely* as you can so we can get rid of the smell in here.

12 Organic food is now much more *wide / widely* produced than it was a few years ago.

13 The cost of public transport puts people off. They should be able to travel *free / freely* within the city.

14 The information is *free / freely* available in the public library.

English in Use

Register transfer (Paper 3 Part 5)

▶ ER page 170

1 a Read the instructions to the task on page 53. Then read the email quickly for general understanding. Answer these questions.

   1 Who has written the email?

   2 Where should Kate include all this information?

   3 Is the email relatively formal or informal in style?

  b Now read the hotel leaflet, ignoring the gaps for the moment.

   1 Who is the leaflet intended for?

   2 Is the leaflet relatively formal or informal in style?

2 a Look at the words and phrases in bold in the email. Find and mark the same information in the leaflet. Notice how the style of the two texts is different.

  b Now look at the gaps in the leaflet. Answer these questions to help you complete gaps 1, 2, 4 and 6.

   1 Look at question 1. The correct answer completes a formal phrase with the same meaning as *if you ask him*. Which word does this best?
      a) order   b) demand   c) request

   2 Look at question 2. The correct answer completes a formal phrase which communicates the same ideas as *he needs to know the day before*. Which is it?
      a) notice   b) advice   c) caution

   3 Look at question 4. Underline the adverb in the email leaflet which relates to this gap. The answer to question 4 is an adverb with a similar meaning that collocates with *recommended*.

   4 Look at question 6. The correct answer has the same meaning as *to try out*. Which is it?
      a) to test   b) to sample   c) to experiment

3 Now complete the task using the same techniques. Remember that:

- the correct words must fit in with the style of the text.
- the answer must fit grammatically.
- the words you need do not occur in the first text.
- you must use no more than two words in each gap.
- you should read the text through when you have finished to make sure the text makes complete sense.

For questions **1–13**, read the following email from the manager of a hotel to her assistant. Use the information in it to complete the numbered gaps in the leaflet for guests. The words you need **do not occur** in the email. **Use no more than two words for each gap**. The exercise begins with an example **(0)**.

EMAIL

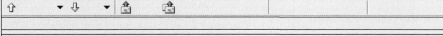

> Kate,
> Points to include in the guests' leaflet:
> ● The restaurant – Tell them there's a buffet menu (lots of choice) and that the chef **will cook** special dishes if they ask him (but he needs to know the day before). Stress that, if we can, we use fruit and vegetables **grown on local farms**, and that the fish is especially good because most of it comes off local fishing boats. Don't forget to say that if they want to try out the local specialities, then they should look out for the Chef's Special **every day**. Tell them he uses age-old family recipes as his starting point for these.
> ● Swimming pool – Make it clear that, for safety reasons, no swimming is allowed after midnight, and children must always have an adult with them when they're round the pool.
> ● Rooms – Tell them always to lock doors and ask them to leave their used towels in the bath.

HOTEL LEAFLET

Welcome to the
GOLDEN PALMS HOTEL
Mirador Restaurant
A buffet menu is available with an **(0)** ...*extensive*... selection of dishes on offer. Our chef is willing to prepare special dishes on **(1)**............................ , as long as he is given 24 hours' **(2)**............................ . As far **(3)**............................ , only locally produced fruit and vegetables are served, and the fish dishes are **(4)**............................ recommended, as the **(5)**............................ of the fish used is locally caught. Guests are invited **(6)**............................ the local cuisine by choosing the daily 'Chef's Specials', which he **(7)**............................ age-old family recipes.

Swimming pool
A heated swimming pool is available for guests, but in **(8)**............................ of safety, swimming after midnight is **(9)**............................ . Children should **(10)**............................ by an adult **(11)**............................ times in the pool area.

Rooms
Please **(12)**............................ that all room doors are kept locked. Used towels should be **(13)**............................ in the bath.

Language development

The texts on this page contain examples of words from two word families, *special* and *local*. Can you find these words?

Listening
Multiple-choice questions (Paper 4 Part 3)

▶ ER pages 170–171

1 Read the instructions for the exam task. Then read the multiple-choice questions and highlight the most important ideas in the questions and options. This has been done for you in questions 1 and 2.

2 🎧 Listen to the whole recording once, and try to answer the questions. Use the Help clues if necessary.

3 Listen again to check and complete your answers.

TIP

Listen to the interviewer's questions – they'll help you to keep your place – but the answers will come from the main speaker.

HELP
➤ Question 1
Christopher's answer comes after he mentions the 'business potential' of walking tours. There is a gap in the market, but who will go on the tours?
➤ Question 2
There are two parts to each of the options – how Christopher feels, and what he has those feelings about. Listen to his whole answer to this question before choosing the correct option.
➤ Question 3
Listen to the whole of Christopher's answer to the interviewer's question. What point is he making about the people both at the beginning and the end of his answer?

You will hear an interview with a man called Christopher Winney, whose holiday company organises environmentally friendly walking tours. For questions **1–6**, choose the best answer **A**, **B**, **C**, or **D**. You will hear the recording twice.

1 Christopher explains that he started the ATG Oxford holiday company because
   A he had little hope of getting further work as a writer.
   B he saw a gap in the market for holidays aimed at older people.
   C he believed organised walking holidays would have a wide appeal.
   D he had always wanted to set up an environmentally friendly company.

2 When discussing the company's finances, Christopher says he is
   A worried that his holidays may be overpriced.
   B determined to spend the company's profits wisely.
   C fortunate in being free of personal money worries.
   D restricted by his agreement with charity organisations.

3 What does Christopher say about the sort of people who go on ATG holidays?
   A They tend to expect a high standard of service.
   B They need to build up their level of fitness.
   C They have to have a good sense of humour.
   D They often have similar views about things.

4 When asked about the decision to stop advertising the company's holidays, Christopher says he is
   A worried that the level of business may still decrease as a result.
   B convinced that the previous style of advertising was ineffective.
   C pleased that clients have generally responded well to his motives.
   D concerned that the environmental message may have been weakened.

5 In Christopher's opinion, responsible tourism is best achieved through
   A the support given to carefully selected staff.
   B the monitoring of activities offered to clients.
   C the insistence on using only organic produce.
   D the simple nature of the accommodation provided.

6 How does Christopher feel about the current state of environmentally friendly tourism?
   A concerned at the attitude of some sections of the media
   B alarmed at the prospect of larger companies moving in
   C unsure what can be done to win more tourists over
   D satisfied to see the growing acceptance of the idea

Vocabulary

The environment

▶ CB pages 80–81

1   **Match these words to their definitions.**

1 sustainable
2 biodiversity
3 renewable energy
4 hydroelectric
5 environmentally friendly
6 tidal
7 biosphere
8 solar

a   a form of energy that replaces itself naturally, or is easily replaced because there is a large supply of it
b   the part of the world in which animals, plants, etc. can live
c   the variety of plants and animals in a particular place
d   able to continue without causing damage to the environment
e   relating to the sun
f   using water power to produce energy
g   relating to the regular rising and falling of the sea level on the shore
h   used about products and methods that do not damage the environment

2   **Complete the text with expressions from Exercise 1.**

A **(1)**.. is any naturally occurring energy source that we can tap into without depleting the world's finite resources, without contributing to the greenhouse effect, and often without causing any pollution. Renewable energies are therefore **(2)**.. , and the effect they have on the **(3)**.. is considerably less than with fossil fuels.

     Some forms of renewable energy, such as **(4)**.. power in countries with high rainfall, are already well established. **(5)**.. power is cost efficient in dry, sunny countries, as is wind power in exposed places. **(6)**.. energy has not yet been effectively harnessed, as it requires huge off-shore construction. All these energy forms are **(7)**.. , as they have low emissions and result in very little damage to a region's **(8)**.. .

3   **Read the text below and complete it with words from the list. Change the form where necessary.**

consume contribute destroy exhaust fuels increase
inefficiency means renewable rise tackle

Transport fuels

In the last 50 years, the number of cars on British roads has **(1)**.................... from two million to over 20 million, and this figure continues to **(2)**.................... . Even after a century of engineering, the conventional car is incredibly **(3)**.................... . Almost 80% of the fuel energy a normal car **(4)**.................... is lost as engine heat and **(5)**.................... fumes , so that only 20% is actually used to move the car.

Cars and lorries cause noise, pollution, harm to health, and the **(6)**.................... of habitats. They also **(7)**.................... to global warming.

These problems can really only be **(8)**.................... in two ways. Firstly, by using cars and lorries less and looking at alternative **(9)**.................... of transport such as trains, buses, trams, bicycles and of course our feet! Secondly, by moving towards alternative **(10)**.................... . Amongst possible solutions are biodiesel, made from plant or animal oils, as well as using electricity from **(11)**.................... sources to power electric motors.

Language development
Conditionals
▶ CB page 83, GR page 180

Review of conditionals

1 **Put the verbs into the most suitable tense.**
1 Imagine you .... (*walk*) in the mountains and there .... (*be*) suddenly a thunderstorm – .... (*you know*) what to do and how to avoid being struck by lightning?
2 As long as you .... (*can see*) lightning and hear thunder, you .... (*be*) at risk.
3 Lightning strikes are rare, but you .... (*have*) a much better chance of survival if you .... (*crouch*) down.
4 The last person to be killed by lightning was standing under a tree. It's possible that if he .... (*not stand*) under the tree, he .... (*survive*).
5 Another recent victim probably .... (*not injure*) if he .... (*not carry*) an umbrella.

Mixed conditionals

2 **Rewrite the sentences using a mixed conditional.**
0 I'm lost and I can't find my way home.
If I <u>wasn't lost, I would be able to find</u> my way home
1 I didn't light a fire because I don't know how to.
If I .... one.
2 I understand how the economy works because I studied economics at university.
If .... the economy works.
3 We don't know where to look for her because she didn't tell us where she was going.
If she .... look for her.
4 We're in danger now because we didn't take sensible safety precautions.
If we .... in danger now.
5 I was bitten by a snake because I work in a zoo.
If .... by a snake.
6 I can't show you my essay because I handed it in this morning.
If .... show it to you.
7 It didn't snow last night, so it's not freezing on the mountain today.
If it .... freezing on the mountain today.
8 I don't think he's got his phone with him because he hasn't called me to say he was going to be late.
If he .... going to be late.

Alternatives to *if*

3 **Underline the correct alternative.**
1 Please do not hesitate to contact me .... you require further information.
A should   B whether   C as long as   D providing
2 .... we got there earlier, we would have got tickets.
A Provided   B Had   C Imagine   D Should
3 I don't mind babysitting, ... the children are in bed and asleep.
A unless   B but for   C providing   D otherwise
4 I'm going to this conference .... the company pays for me or not.
A whether   B unless   C as long as
D provided that
5 .... you hold a snake by its head, it can't bite you.
A Unless   B As long as   C Were   D Supposing
6 I'm sure the woman would have died .... the help of a man who was passing and knew what to do.
A but for   B whether   C providing   D otherwise
7 .... the electricity supply to fail, the machines would automatically switch off.
A Should   B Provided   C As long as   D Were

4 **Decide which of the following sentences are correct, and correct those that aren't.**
1 If you want to avoid pesticides, you would eat organic food.
2 If the company didn't dump chemical waste in the river, the fish won't have been killed off.
3 Unless we don't stop burning oil, we'll destroy the ozone layer.
4 If you won't help us, I'll find someone who will!
5 If the government will change the law, companies would have to stop dumping waste.
6 If it will make you happy, I'll recycle all these magazines.
7 I'd be grateful if you will investigate the issue of water quality soon.

English in Use
Error correction (spelling and punctuation)
(Paper 3 Part 3) ▶ ER page 169

1 Read the title of the text to identify the topic. Then read the whole text quickly for general understanding, ignoring the mistakes for the moment.
   1 What does the writer think of umbrellas?
   2 What reasons does he give for this opinion?
   3 Is the style of the text humorous or serious?

2 Read the text again, sentence by sentence, and complete the task. Use the Help clues if necessary.

3 When you've finished, read the whole text again to check it makes complete sense.

TIP

Spelling errors are more likely to be found in longer words related to the topic, so check things like double consonants, vowels and words with prefixes and suffixes. You need to check the spelling of all the words in the text, but if you have already found a punctuation mistake in a line, and you are sure about it, then that line will not also contain a spelling error.

HELP
➤ **Question 1**
   A punctuation mark is missing in this line.
➤ **Question 5**
   Check the spelling of the words in this line.
➤ **Questions 10–15**
   One of these lines is correct. Do you know which one?

In most lines of the following text, there is **either** a spelling **or** a punctuation error. For each numbered line **1–16**, write the correctly spelt word or show the correct punctuation. **Some** lines are correct. Indicate these lines with a tick (✓) in the box. The exercise begins with three examples **(0)**, **(00)** and **(000)**.

Useless things, umbrellas

If there's one thing I dislike about living in London, it's when	**0** ✓
whether forecasters, after predicting showers, add with a smile:	**00** weather
'So dont forget your umbrellas.' But they haven't said it this	**000** don't
week for the very good reason that its been both wet and windy,	**1**
and umbrellas are useless in a high wind. Today, you can see	**2**
people all over the city who look, as if they are being pulled along	**3**
by there umbrellas. You see them twisting and turning as if	**4**
strugling to control some large ill-behaved bird. Then suddenly,	**5**
the umbrella blows inside out, after which it is useless, either	**6**
because the material is torn or the fraime is broken. Another	**7**
drawback of umbrella's is that no object is so frequently left	**8**
in public places: 12,000 a year on the London Underground	**9**
alone, according to a radio report broadcast this week. 'you	**10**
used to get a lot of very nice golfing umbrellas,' an enployee	**11**
told the reporter, but now they're mostly dumpy, folding ones.'	**12**
These are, of course, more convinient, because they fit into a bag,	**13**
but they are no good in the wind. I cant help but think that if we	**14**
can invent ingenious things like the mobile phone, someone	**15**
should've though up a gadget to replace the umbrella by now.	**16**

Language development
Can you find an example of a mixed conditional in the text?

Reading
Multiple-choice questions (Paper 1 Part 3)
▶ ER pages 168

1 Read the title of the text and the subheading.
   1 What is meant by the phrase *throwaway society*?
   2 What attitude do you think the artist will have towards the *throwaway society*?
   3 What type of art do you think the artist will be working in?
      a) portraits   b) abstract sculpture
      c) modern art installations

2 Read the text quickly to check whether your predictions about the artist were correct.

3 Read all the questions and highlight the key words in each question. The first two have been done for you. The questions follow the same order as the text, and there is one piece of text for each question.

4 a Read question 1. How do you know how to locate the relevant piece of text?

   b Read this piece of text carefully. Look back at the question and think of your own answer. Now read the options – which one is closest to your own answer?

   c Read the paragraph again carefully to check that your answer is right and that the other options are definitely wrong.

5 Now continue to answer the rest of the questions. Always read the section of text carefully, to find your own answer to the question, then find the option which is closest in meaning to your own answer.

Read the following magazine article about an artist and answer questions **1–6**. Mark the letter **A**, **B**, **C** or **D**. Give only one answer to each question.

GARBAGE GURU

We live in an increasingly throwaway society. I meet an artist who's making a material difference.

Steve Bradley freely admits his work is garbage. 'It's true,' he says. 'My work is rubbish.' As an environmental artist, Steve's spent most of his working life picking up the things that other people have thrown
5 away, and devising new ways to use art and humour to get us thinking about the environment. His work has been concerned with what our attitudes to rubbish and the environment say about our society. But these aren't abstract gallery pieces for people in smart suits to
10 spend a fortune on. Steve believes in taking art to the people: a market stall in the city of Hull; a window on a street in downtown Tallahassee, Florida; and now, the Visitors' Centre in an English National Park where we meet.

15 I'd read about Steve in a tabloid newspaper. He explains the project that had earned this notoriety: 'In Hull, I picked up used lottery scratchcards off the streets and sold them on a market stall, three for 50p. Of course, they were worthless, and that was the whole
20 point. Kids wanted to know what I was doing, and I'd explain the disappearing act to them, how something could be worth a pound (the cost of a scratchcard), then worth nothing. It was a ploy, you know, to get them thinking about the value of things. You look at any
25 drinks can, or a bottle; the material you throw away is often worth more than the product you have paid for and consumed!'

'When I called the National Park authorities for permission to pick up rubbish in a famous beauty spot
30 and do something unspecified but vaguely arty next to the Visitors' Centre, they were understandably wary that I might give people the impression that our National Parks are filthy. But the truth is, the problem of litter isn't confined to the National Parks. Litter costs
35 taxpayers £410 million a year, or at least that's what it costs local government authorities to clean up across the UK. However, on private land – such as farmland – the cost of clearing litter is met by the landowner, so the real cost is even higher. The National Park has now

40 removed all bins from car parks and laybys, because it encourages people to take their litter home rather than leave it for overstretched local authorities to deal with.

But there's still plenty to be found – Steve and I are filling large black bin-liners with the stuff. He notices
45 that most crisp packets have been obsessively folded into tiny origami-like structures, or tied into a knot: 'I've seen this in a few places; I call it pre-litter anxiety. There's obviously a time lapse between consuming the contents and discarding the waste ... it's really rather
50 creative behaviour.'

In the grounds of the Visitors' Centre, Steve sets up the canvas where he'll display the litter we've just collected. A garden net is strung up between three trees and pegged to the ground by one corner. After
55 about an hour, a coachload of would-be art critics arrive, invited over for the occasion from a local school. They're intrigued and eager to join in. They tie rubbish to the net and surround Steve with cheeky questions until they're chivvied back onto the coaches
60 by their long-suffering teachers. Steve's in his element as he adopts the role of lively, gesticulating artiste. 'So, Steve,' I say, surveying the scraps of debris, drinks bottles and sweet wrappers which have been retrieved and recruited into a new existence as art, rather than
65 litter: 'What does it all mean?' Refreshingly, he's more interested in what the kids made of it than what he, as the artist, wants the work to say: 'I'm not looking for people to see anything specific in my work. If pressed, I'd want the audience to be surprised, then laugh; but
70 any emotion or reaction is good. It's about raising their awareness of the environment they live, work and play in.'

After spending the day with Steve, I've succumbed ever so slightly to garbage fever. As we untie the net, I feel
75 a tinge of regret at destroying our original piece; this is my first venture into the world of modern art. From rubbish to litter to art, then back to rubbish, our installation, entitled 'Net Deposit', is rolled into a bin-liner to be thrown away (again) when we get home.
80 Everyone's got their own reasons for hating litter, but until now I've always kept my dislike of detritus quiet. Who cares about a few crisp packets? Well, in his classic book *My First Summer in the Sierra*, published in 1911, the Scottish nature lover John Muir came to
85 the conclusion that: 'when we try to pick out anything by itself, we find it hitched to everything else in the universe.' In a nutshell, and about 70 years before a single Greenpeace calendar was sold, he'd summed up the essence of ecology; that everything matters, even
90 if some things matter more than others. I'm guessing, but I suspect John Muir would never have dropped his crisp packet at a beauty spot.

1 In the first paragraph, we learn that Steve Bradley's art
   A has not been well received in some circles.
   B is not based on an entirely original concept.
   C is intended to raise awareness of certain issues.
   D has been taken quite seriously by some buyers.

2 What was the main aim of Steve's project in Hull?
   A He wanted to get press coverage for his activities.
   B He was trying to raise money for environmental causes.
   C He wanted to encourage young people to clean up their area.
   D He was trying to draw attention to the way resources are wasted.

3 When Steve approached a National Park for permission to create a work of art there, the authorities
   A assumed he would be critical of their litter policy.
   B were concerned that he might attract negative publicity.
   C felt that his activities would be more appropriate elsewhere.
   D were worried that people would see this as a waste of public money.

4 To Steve, what does the example of the folded crisp packets suggest?
   A People feel guilty about the places where they drop litter.
   B Some people may actually discard litter accidentally.
   C He's not the only person to be artistic with litter.
   D Litter is not only dropped by thoughtless people.

5 When the schoolchildren arrive at the Visitors' Centre, the writer observes that Steve
   A clearly enjoys the performance aspect of his work.
   B doesn't really have the approval of their teachers.
   C is surprised by the children's reaction to his work.
   D gets pleasure from explaining the meaning of his art.

6 At the end of the article, the writer quotes John Muir in order to
   A illustrate how her own views have changed through meeting Steve.
   B question some of the assumptions that we may have about ecology.
   C demonstrate that there has long been a link between art and ecology.
   D underline her view that the work Steve does is actually of great value.

Writing Notes and emails (Paper 2 Part 1)

▶ CB pages 84–85, WR pages 195–197

Exam strategy

In the exam, you may have to write more than one note, memo or email. Read the information from all the input texts carefully before you start to plan your answer. Make sure that you include all the relevant points from the notes you are given, and that you organise your points logically.

1 Look at the Part 1 task below and answer these questions.
   1 Who wrote the article?
   2 Who must you write an email to?

Your friend Chiara was involved in a clean-up campaign at her college, organised by the Student Union. You want to organise a similar campaign at your college. Chiara has sent you a copy of their advertising poster, notes from their planning meeting, and an extract from an article she wrote for her college newspaper after their clean-up event. Read the poster, the meeting notes and extract from her article. Using the information, write

- an email to your own Student Union President, explaining what happened at Chiara's college, why it would be a good thing to do at your college and what work it would involve.
- a note to your friend Jon inviting him to help you and explaining what you would like him to do.

Write your **email** in approximately 200 words and your **note** in approximately 50 words.

2 Read all the notes and underline the points that you should include in the email.

3 Read the email written by a student in answer to the task. It is too short because information is missing. Underline the parts of the task that have been left out.

Hi Cris,

I am writing to tell you about a special event that was organised at East College and was extremely successful.

It was a clean-up day, aimed at solving problems of litter in the college. The day started with volunteers meeting up outside the Union building – they picked up litter around the grounds and gave out leaflets to other students encouraging them to be tidier. They all had a free meal afterwards, and what was so good about the day was the impact it seems to have had on the college afterwards. Students have become a lot more aware of the importance of keeping the campus clean. They also tried imposing fines for dropping litter, which was not very successful.

I think we should do the same thing here. We would need to organise some publicity (posters and leaflets) and some sort of reward for volunteers. At East College they provided a free meal, but I think that would be really difficult to organise. We could give volunteers a free ticket to the next disco instead.

Can we meet to talk about it? What about next Saturday?

Best wishes

Sam

4 Decide where the missing information should go in the email and write sentences that you can insert.

5 Now write the note to Jon. Remember to include all the information you need from the input texts, and to use an informal style.

Clean-up-the-campus day!

Saturday June 14th
Come and join us.
We need volunteers to:
- pick up litter
- give out leaflets
- make a difference to our environment

Have fun, too! Free supper in the evening for all volunteers. Email Chiara for more info, or meet outside the Union building at 10.

- Must provide cleaning materials
- Give volunteers something as reward
- Need lots of advertising (leaflets?) (Ask Jon)
- Students need to feel proud of campus
- One-day event only
- Someone to design a poster (Jon? A day's work?)

On the positive side, we were inundated with volunteers only too keen to clean up the college grounds, although they were relieved that we gave them rubber gloves. The high spot was the free buffet supper in the evening, but since then we have seen a radical change in the attitude of students. They are more aware of the need to keep our campus clean, and although the imposition of fines for dropping litter turned out to be unpopular, the policy of no-smoking on the campus has been a roaring success.

A Health and fitness

English in Use
Word formation (Paper 3 Part 4)
▶ CB page 90, ER page 170

1 Read the title of the first text to identify the topic. Then read the text through quickly for general understanding, ignoring the gaps for the moment.

2 Read the text again carefully and try to decide what type of word will fit in each gap. Then fill in the gaps, using the Help clues if necessary.

3 Read through the text again when you've finished and check that the words you've written fit in with the overall meaning of the text and are spelled correctly.

4 Repeat the procedure for the second text.

HELP
➤ **Question 2**
Which suffix is added to this verb to create the adjective? Read the rest of the sentence – does this word need a negative prefix?

➤ **Question 7**
This noun requires two suffixes – the first creates a verb from the noun, and the second turns that into an adjective.

➤ **Questions 10–15**
One of these items requires a negative prefix. Do you know which? You have to read the surrounding text very carefully to be sure.

➤ **Question 11**
Add a suffix to this verb to make the noun. Two nouns are possible; this one is used to talk about people rather than events. Check if it needs to be singular or plural in this context.

For questions **1–15**, read the two texts below. Use the words in the boxes to the right of the texts to form **one** word that fits in the same numbered space in the text. The exercise begins with an example **(0)**.

NEWSPAPER FEATURE

No cosmetic surgery for Catwoman

In the film *Catwoman*, the actress Halle Berry plays a woman who works for a cosmetics firm which is putting a new 'miracle' cream into (0)*production* . The company claims that the cream will slow down the process of (1)..................... . In the film, our hero discovers that using the cream may actually lead to (2)..................... side effects and so decides to 'blow the whistle' on her employers by telling the world about the dangers.

And yesterday, at a London press (3)..................... , the film star herself revealed that she was equally (4)..................... about the issue. She spoke out against the social (5)..................... that lead women to go to such (6)..................... in an attempt to look younger. As she said, 'I see women in their thirties getting plastic surgery. There is this plastic copycat look that is evolving, and that's (7)..................... to me. I feel sad that's what society is doing to women.'

(0)	**PRODUCE**
(1)	AGE
(2)	PLEASE
(3)	CONFER
(4)	PASSION
(5)	PRESS
(6)	LONG
(7)	FRIGHT

EDITORIAL FROM A SCIENTIFIC JOURNAL

Science matters

The scene is the 2020 Olympic Games. All eyes are on a 20-year-old athlete who runs like the wind. He was born with an (8)..................... genetic advantage: enormous muscles. His body's natural brake on muscle development simply doesn't work. (9)..................... who have studied the rules can find no reason to (10)..................... him. He has taken no drugs; his is a natural advantage. Officials are faced with a dilemma. Should the rules against doping be relaxed to give his less genetically endowed (11)..................... more of a fair chance?

The Olympic scenario is (12)..................... , but the person is not. He's a real four-year-old German boy who is reportedly able to hold two 6.6lb weights with his arms extended (13)..................... , a feat beyond many adults. He is the human equivalent of the so-called mighty mice, whose muscle power was genetically enhanced by scientists searching for a new form of (14)..................... for muscular diseases. It didn't take people long to see the sporting potential of such genetic (15)..................... , however.

(8)	ORDINARY
(9)	LAW
(10)	QUALIFY
(11)	COMPETE
(12)	HYPOTHESIS
(13)	HORIZONTAL
(14)	TREAT
(15)	MODIFY

Language development
Emphasis
▶ CB page 93, GR page 181

Emphasis with *what, the thing that,* etc.

1 Complete the sentences with the words or phrases from the box.

What   The reason   The person who
The place where   The thing that

1 .... deals with all the accounts is Mr Johnson.
2 .... I enjoy is just sitting relaxing by the pool.
3 .... we're late is that all the trains were delayed because of a bomb scare.
4 .... you should do now is write to the school asking for an apology.
5 .... the accident happened is just behind the sports centre.

2 Rewrite each sentence to emphasise the words in italics, using the words given.

1 All the teenagers usually hang out in *the park*. (The place …)

....

2 I was so angry with her because *she had promised to be home by nine o'clock*. (The reason …)

....

3 *His ability to score goals from outside the penalty area* is so impressive. (The thing …)

....

4 *Her habit of leaving her things all over the house* drives me mad! (What …)

....

5 They're due to arrive at *six o'clock*. (The time …)

....

6 You need to talk to *your tutor* about this. (The person …)

....

3 Rewrite each sentence to emphasise the words in italics, using *What, The person, The reason,* etc.

1 She dialled 999 because *she panicked*.

....

2 We usually meet in *the café on the High Street*.

....

3 The aid agencies are trying to help *the refugees*.

....

4 *France* has the best health service in Europe.

....

5 I would really like *to train as a doctor*.

....

6 Our sales are highest in *August*.

....

Emphasis with *It* and *be*

4 Read the following text, then correct the sentences below.

> Louis Pasteur, the French chemist and founder of the science of microbiology, discovered that the process of fermentation is caused by micro-organisms and that heating can prevent it. The heat treatment became known as pasteurisation, and it is now routinely used to treat milk for domestic consumption. Later, he developed the 'germ theory of disease', which was probably the most important medical discovery of all time, as it provided both an understanding of the cause of disease as well as the means to prevent it. In 1885, he created the first vaccine for rabies.

1 Fleming discovered the process of fermentation.
No, it was ....
2 Pasteur founded the science of molecular biology.
No, it was ....
3 Fermentation is now routinely used to treat milk for domestic consumption.
No, it is ....
4 Pasteurisation was Pasteur's most important medical discovery.
No, it was ....
5 He created a vaccine for rabies in 1865.
No, it was ....

5 Rewrite the sentences using an *it*-clause to emphasise the words in italics.

1 I developed a bad allergic reaction *last Wednesday*.

....

2 I first felt ill *on the way home*.

....

3 The following morning I went back to bed *because I felt so lousy*.

....

4 The cough was bad but *the headache* was the real problem.

....

5 I *only* discovered the cause *when I saw the doctor*.

....

6 I felt well enough to go back to work *on Monday*.

....

7 *Someone at work* suggested what might have caused the problem.

....

8 The problem was caused by *breathing in paint fumes*.

....

English in Use
Gapped text (Paper 3 Part 6)

▶ ER page 170

1 a Read the title of the text and look at the picture. What do you think the text is going to be about?

   b Read the whole text quickly, ignoring the gaps for the moment, to find out if you were right.
      1 What would this new form of medical treatment achieve?
      2 What would it mean for plastic surgery?

2 Read the text again carefully and do the task, using the Help clues if necessary. Remember that there are three phrases that do not fit into the text at all.

3 Read through the text again when you've finished and check that the answers you have chosen fit in with the overall meaning of the text.

HELP
➤ Question 1
   Look for a phrase that relates to a period of time. The sentence after the gap contains *by prolonging this process*, so the process must take place over time.
➤ Question 2
   Look for a phrase that links with *to maintain that appearance of youthfulness*.
➤ Question 3
   Look at the two phrases that begin with a *to*-infinitive. Which of them makes sense after the verb *prepared* in the text?

For questions **1–6**, read the following text and then choose from the list **A–I** given below the best phrase to fill each of the spaces. Each correct phrase may only be used once. **Some of the suggested answers do not fit at all**.

Maintaining a youthful appearance

A breakthrough in the area of human cell research has led scientists to believe that they could have discovered how to slow down or even stop the ageing process. The human body is made up of millions of cells, which normally divide and multiply (1)........ . What scientists hope is that by prolonging this process, it may be possible to maintain that appearance of youthfulness (2)........ . It would also avoid the need for cosmetic surgery, an expensive and risky process which is growing in popularity. Many people are resorting to a variety of surgical procedures because they are not prepared (3)........ .

Concerns about their appearance can often have a negative effect on many aspects of a person's life, especially if they believe their body makes them look older than they actually feel. It is for this reason that a facelift is one of the most frequently performed cosmetic operations, (4)........ .

The application of this new research could be as straightforward as an injection and, if successful, would offer a far safer way (5)........ . 'Stopping the clock' in this way could mean that the skin on many parts of the human body would remain largely unaffected by any obvious signs of age. Although the research has so far been mainly laboratory based, there seems no reason why something that works in a test tube should not be equally successful (6)........ .

A although it does not always have satisfactory results.
B by the time necessary to recover from the procedure.
C which is so sought after in contemporary society.
D but they are very costly.
E for only a limited period during a lifetime.
F when used as a form of medical treatment.
G to let nature take its course.
H to create a young image.
I when the results have been confirmed.

Language development
Look at the sentences in the text. Which ones use cleft sentences to emphasise one particular part of the sentence? Underline them.

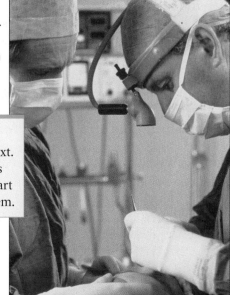

Writing
Cohesion
▶ CB page 94, WR page 200

Cohesion

1 Complete the text with cohesive devices from the list.
although   and   instead   or   others
rather than   these   too   whereas

The last few years have seen a rise in the popularity of alternative therapies. **(1)**......................... do not use synthetic drugs **(2)**......................... surgery. **(3)**......................... , the emphasis is on maintaining health **(4)**......................... dealing with the causes of illnesses **(5)**......................... their symptoms. **(6)**......................... some treatments are accepted by orthodox doctors, **(7)**......................... are rejected as ineffective. Acupuncture is widely accepted, and homoeopathy is **(8)**......................... . In time, more will become accepted, **(9)**......................... it's hard to say which.

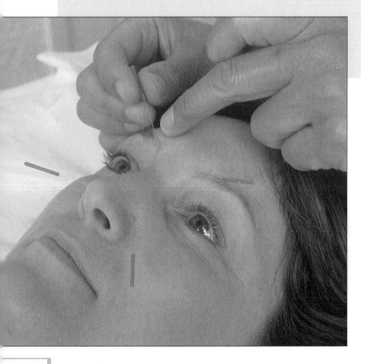

Substitution and omission

2 For each sentence, choose which option works best to make the sentence cohesive and natural. A dash (–) means that the sentence is already cohesive.
1 Acupuncture is very effective and shiatsu ....
   A is very effective too   B is too   C too
2 After my friend recommended the massage, I had ....
   A one too   B too   C the massage
3 I went to the same therapist that ....
   A my friend did   B my friend went   C my friend
4 I tried Indian head massage and reiki, but .... for me.
   A they neither worked   B both didn't work
   C neither of them worked
5 I find that shiatsu works much better than aromatherapy ....
   A works   B –   C is
6 I rang to make an appointment and .... for tomorrow.
   A made one   B made an appointment   C that's
7 I was told I'd have to take all my clothes off, but I wouldn't ....
   A take my clothes off   B take off   C do that
8 The treatment was expensive, but .... worth it.
   A it's   B it was   C the treatment was
9 I ended up having acupuncture, although I hadn't intended ....
   A to have   B to   C to do
10 Jenny said it was a fantastic treatment, but she didn't say ....
   A why it was fantastic   B why
   C why she thought it
11 I'd like a massage. I've heard that certain types .... are more suitable than others.
   A –   B of massage   C of it
12 I spoke to a therapist .... said she could help me.
   A . The therapist   B , who   C and

3 Complete the sentences. Use one suitable word in each gap.
1 I've just heard that there's an open day on Saturday at the alternative health clinic in town. You know, the .... on Malvern Road.
2 'Would you like to come to the cinema with us tonight?' 'Yes, I'd love .... ?
3 Simon says he's going to resign from his job, but he always says .... when he's had a bad day.
4 She always says she'll help us clear up at the end of the evening, but she never ....
5 'I really enjoyed that film.' 'So .... I.'
6 Are you coming to the party on Saturday? If .... , don't forget to bring a bottle with you.

7 Annie and James need to know that we've changed the date of the trip, so I'll phone them .... tonight.

8 My car is being repaired at the moment, so do you mind taking us in .... ?

9 'We're meeting in the Black Bull pub in town at eight o'clock.' 'OK, I'll see you ....'

10 Phil is really into alternative therapies. You know, aromatherapy and other .... things.

4 **Rewrite the following text to make it more cohesive either by deleting unnecessary words or by using substitution.**

Aromatherapy uses fragrant oils. The oils are rubbed into the body. Aromatherapy is good for physical disorders and for emotional disorders as it works on a physical level and on an emotional level. You can have a whole course of treatments, but you don't have to have a whole course of treatments. Just one treatment is enough to feel some benefit. If relaxation is the aim, try aromatherapy; if it is not the aim, try something else.

....
....
....
....
....
....
....
....
....
....
....
....
....
....

Linking devices

5 **For each sentence, mark the two options that are possible.**

1 I think that your diet lacks fibre. .... , I am recommending that you eat more fruit.
A Consequently   B Furthermore   C That is why
D Nonetheless

2 Exercise is certainly a good thing for everyone. .... , you should never overdo it.
A In addition   B Nevertheless   C Furthermore
D Even so

3 I'm going to show you how to use the exercise ball. .... , you can have a go with it on your own.
A In the meantime   B Afterwards   C Later
D In the end

4 That's about all I've got to say about exercising. .... , I'd just like to remind you that exercise is meant to be fun, so try to enjoy it.
A Lastly   B Later   C Finally   D In the end

5 I spent ages looking for the right running shoes. I .... found a pair just like my old ones.
A eventually   B finally   C lastly   D in the end

6 I need to change my diet. I really should do some exercise ....
A besides   B moreover   C too   D as well

7 Running is a great way to get fit. .... , it can be very bad for your joints.
A Consequently   B On the other hand
C Meanwhile   D However

8 The club insists that all members have an induction before using the equipment. .... , the club is not responsible for injuries caused by incorrect use of the equipment.
A Besides   B That's why   C Furthermore
D Moreover

6 **Use the underlined conjunctions to help match the sentence halves.**

1 I think you should take vitamin C
2 You won't need to take iron tablets
3 I'm going to the health-food shop
4 Take one of these energy boosters
5 I eat a spoonful of yeast every morning
6 I've been taking multi-vitamins for years
7 You don't need expensive diet supplements
8 I got two of everything

a as soon as you start feeling tired.
b although I don't really know if they do any good.
c provided you eat a healthy balanced diet.
d in addition to the iron tablets.
e despite the fact that it tastes revolting.
f unless you are anaemic (short of iron).
g since they were on special offer.
h to get some brown rice.

Listening
Sentence completion (Paper 4 Part 1)

▶ ER pages 170–171

1 Read the instructions for the exam task below. Then read the sentences and think about the topic and what you expect to hear. Can you predict the type of information you will be listening for in each item? For example:
- Question 1: Is this likely to be:
  a) an activity? b) an object?
  c) a person?
- Question 2: What is a *term*?
- Question 3: Is this word likely to be:
  a) a verb? b) a noun? c) an adjective?
- Question 4: Where could someone borrow money from?

2 ◯ Listen to the recording once and complete the sentences. Use the Help clues if necessary.

3 Listen again to check and complete your answers. Remember to check your spelling.

HELP
➤ Question 2
Judy signals that she is going to use a term when she says *what people call.* Listen out for this phrase – the answer comes after it.
➤ Question 3
You are listening for the type of holiday Judy went on – in this case, it is an activity.
➤ Question 5
You are listening for a noun – something that Judy was using – but listen for a phrase that indicates her friends were *surprised* – the answer will come soon after that phrase.

4 Look at the following wrong answers that students gave to some of the questions. Listen again and decide why they are not correct.
1 oils
2 health fanatic
7 perfume
8 *The Easy Way to Health*

You will hear a woman called Judy Simpson, who is a complementary therapist, giving a talk about her life and work. For questions **1–8**, complete the sentences. **You will hear the recording twice**.

> ## Complementary therapist
>
> As an example of the work she does, Judy mentions a treatment which uses [＿＿＿＿ 1] at varying temperatures.
>
> Judy uses the term '[＿＿＿＿ 2]' to describe herself as she was in her twenties.
>
> It was during a [＿＿＿＿ 3] holiday that Judy made the decision to go self-employed.
>
> Judy borrowed money from her [＿＿＿＿ 4] to finance her training as a complementary therapist.
>
> Judy's friends were surprised to hear that she was using a [＿＿＿＿ 5] as part of her fitness programme.
>
> Last year, Judy launched an unsuccessful online business selling [＿＿＿＿ 6]
>
> Judy is currently planning to open a [＿＿＿＿ 7] of her own.
>
> Judy recommends reading her book which is entitled [＿＿＿＿ 8]

5 a Match the nouns in A and B to form compound nouns.

A	B		
1 health	a style	....	....
2 redundancy	b levels	....	....
3 energy	c fanatic	....	....
4 life	d payout	....	....

b Match the compounds in Exercise 5a to the definitions below.
1 an amount of money paid to someone when they are asked to leave their job
2 someone who is obsessed with staying healthy
3 the amount of energy that you have
4 the way that someone lives their life

B Unveiling the past

Language development
Verb complementation
▶ CB page 99, GR page 182

Verbs + -ing, to-infinitive or infinitive without to

1 Read the text and put the verb in brackets into the correct form.

A few years ago I spent a day **(1)**_____ (work) on an archaeological dig behind an old house. The location was believed **(2)**_____ (be) the site of an old Roman bathhouse.

First, I helped the archaeologists **(3)**_____ (clear) the site, then we began **(4)**_____ (dig). They instructed me **(5)**_____ (remove) the soil in 2cm layers. This involved **(6)**_____ (scratch) the earth very carefully with a tool no bigger than a small spoon. I suggested **(7)**_____ (use) something bigger but they didn't appreciate my **(8)**_____ (say) that, even though they seemed **(9)**_____ (think) that the ruins were at least a metre down.

I watched one person **(10)**_____ (dig) up a skeleton, but it turned out **(11)**_____ (be) a pet cat that someone had buried in the garden. That proved **(12)**_____ (be) the high point of the day.

2 Complete the sentences using the words in brackets. You may need to add a preposition.

1 The teacher asked _____ .
   (me / wait outside)
2 My friends warned _____ .
   (me / not trust / her)
3 I arranged _____
   _____ .
   (some friends / help / me / move house)
4 My parents refused _____ .
   (let / me / stay out late)
5 We all had to wait _____
   _____ .
   (Jane / finish / her meal)
6 He wanted _____ .
   (her / go / with him)

Verb + -ing form / to-infinitive with a change in meaning

3 Underline the most appropriate verb forms in italics. In some cases, both are possible.

1 a Most teachers don't allow *to eat / eating* in the classrooms.
   b The school doesn't allow students *to take / taking* books home.
2 a My grandfather teaches *to swim / swimming* in the local swimming pool.
   b My grandfather taught me *to swim / swimming* in a lake near our house.
3 a The museum guide advised us *to start / starting* in the Renaissance section.
   b The doctor advised against *to travel / travelling* so soon after the operation.
4 a I remember *him buying / him to buy* that watch. He got it in London.
   b I must remember *to buy him / buying him* a birthday present.
5 a I hate *to say / saying* this, but I think it was your fault.
   b I've always hated *to get / getting* my hair wet.

4 Complete the sentences using an appropriate verb from the list in the correct form.
arrive   ask   give up   inform   iron
pick up   read   show   study   tell

1 Unfortunately I stopped _____ history books when I left school.
2 On Sunday evening I like _____ all my shirts, ready for the week ahead.
3 The management regrets _____ visitors that photography is not permitted in the museum.
4 Doing a Masters in Archaeology means _____ for another two years.
5 Jackie forgot _____ me that the museum is closed on Mondays!
6 My brother really regrets _____ Latin when he changed schools.
7 On the way home, I stopped _____ some information from the library.
8 I've been meaning _____ you about your trip to Pompeii for ages.
9 I'll never forget _____ in Venice on the Orient Express.
10 Mum likes _____ people around the old town, pretending to be a guide.

English in Use
Register transfer (Paper 3 Part 5)

▶ ER page 170

1 Read the job information sheet quickly for general understanding. Now read the email quickly, ignoring the gaps for the moment. Answer these questions.
1 Who is the training for?
2 Why is Lisa sending an email to Toni?
3 How is the style of the two texts different?

2 a Look at the words and phrases in bold on the job information sheet. Find and mark the same information in the email.

b Now answer these questions to help you complete gaps 1 and 2.
1 Look at question 1. The correct answer is a verb, followed by *to* with the same meaning as *compulsory*. Which verb is correct?
a) must
b) need
c) got
2 Look at question 2. The correct answer is an informal phrase which means *payment is made*. Which is it?
a) get paid
b) make money
c) cash in

3 Complete the task using the same techniques.

Language development

How many linking devices can you find in these two texts? Underline them.

For questions **1–13**, read the information sheet produced by a museum for trainee guides. Use the information in it to complete the numbered gaps in the informal email. The words you need **do not occur** in the information sheet. **Use no more than two words for each gap.** The exercise begins with an example **(0)**.

INFORMATION SHEET

MUSEUM OF NATURAL HISTORY
GUIDE
Job Information

The training takes place on three **consecutive** Saturdays beginning 7th March. **Attendance** at all three training sessions is compulsory. Additional payment is made for this, however, over and above the agreed salary.

Training Day Programme:

a.m. – Lectures are given covering the **significant aspects** of natural history relating to the exhibitions in the current programme. A full-colour brochure is supplied on loan to trainees to enable them to familiarise themselves with the museum layout.

p.m. – Each trainee will have the opportunity to observe an experienced guide at work with museum visitors.

An information sheet is supplied two weeks prior to the training. Trainees are expected to use this to revise their knowledge of natural history.

On completion of the final afternoon session, each trainee will give a presentation (maximum length 10 minutes) on a topic of their choice related to natural history.

EMAIL

Toni,
I've got the info about the job at the Museum of Natural History. They're running training sessions – three Saturdays in
(0) ___a row___ in March – and you've (1) _____ go to all of them. You do (2) _____ for these, though, on (3) _____ the normal salary. At the sessions, there are lectures where they give you information about the main things which are on (4) _____ in the museum at (5) _____ . You also get a brochure so that you can get (6) _____ of how the museum is organised. Then, in the afternoons, you get (7) _____ to watch an experienced guide working with visitors.
You're also given an info sheet, two weeks (8) _____ the training sessions, which you are (9) _____ use to (10) _____ up your knowledge of natural history. In the last session, you give a presentation, which lasts (11) _____ than ten minutes. You can choose any topic (12) _____ as it has something (13) _____ with natural history.
Love Lisa

Writing
Guidebook entry (Paper 2 Part 2)

▶ CB pages 100–101, WR page 194

Exam strategy

When you write an informational text, your writing may be purely factual, but sometimes you may need to make it more interesting to persuade the reader about something. Think about your target reader and decide which approach is required before you plan and write your answer.

1 Look at the two tasks below and answer the questions.
   1 Which reader (A or B):
      a) is aged 30–40?   b) is aged 18–25?
   2 Which reader (A, B or both) will be interested in:
      a) beaches? c) safety?   e) nightclubs?
      b) pubs?   d) museums? f) shops?
   3 Which text (A or B) should be:
      a) informative and exciting to read?
      b) informative and gently persuasive?

A

Your local tourist authority wants to attract more family visitors to the town, and is planning to publish a special page advertising the town in the general guidebook to the whole region. You have been asked to write this page. You should say why the town would be interesting for families to visit, what they can do there and give some practical advice on finding places to stay.

Write your **entry for the guidebook** in approximately 250 words.

B

You have been asked to contribute a page in a brochure advertising things for young people to do in your town. You should explain what facilities there are for young people and describe what they can do there. You should also include information on cafés and restaurants and easy ways of getting round the town.

Write your **entry for the guidebook** in approximately 250 words.

2 Look at a student's incomplete answer to Task A. The writer has some problems with cohesion and repetition.

   a Correct three reference words.

   b Delete one repetitive sentence in each of the first two paragraphs.

Ⓐ
Come to sunny Compton!

There are many reasons why Compton should feature on your list of places to visit in this region, and not the least of this is its family orientation. It's a great place for families to spend time together. Families will have a good time here and there are some really interesting places for him to visit.

Known locally as the jewel of the coast, its golden sandy beaches are delightful and are also extremely safe for small children. The beaches are beautiful and not dangerous. Compton also has a lifeguard station within easy reach.

The town has something for everyone. For the best view of the picturesque old buildings, it's a good idea to take the sightseeing bus tour – it takes two hours and is well worth it.

- Museum of the history of Compton
- Zoo
- Castle with beautiful gardens and play area
- Accommodation – lots of small hotels ideal for families

3 Now look at a student's incomplete answer to Task B, which is informative, but not very interesting or exciting to read.

   a Add these adjectives to the text to replace *nice* and make the text more interesting to read:
      lively   thriving   trendy   exclusive

   b Insert the following rhetorical questions into the best places in the text, to involve the reader more.
      What's the town like?
      So what is there to do in the evenings?

Ⓑ
Compton is a nice place to have fun with friends – it's a nice town with lots going on.

The town itself is interesting, with good shops – these include not only extremely nice boutiques selling expensive designer clothes but also cheaper chain stores. You won't have any trouble finding what you want in Compton, and you can be sure of finding the most up-to-date merchandise there.

Compton has a good night-life, too, including nice clubs and a cinema complex which shows the latest films.

- Lots of cafés/restaurants
- Friendly pubs/nightclubs
- Good public transport, even late at night

4 Now complete the answer to either Task A or Task B, using the student's notes.

Reading

Gapped text (Paper 1 Part 2)

▶ ER page 168

1 Read the title and subtitle of the text, to identify the topic of the text. Then read the base text quickly, ignoring the gaps for the moment. Answer these questions to check your comprehension.

1 It had been generally believed by scientists that Tyrannosaurus Rex
a) was a predator, which killed other animals for food.
b) ate the dead remains of other animals.
c) ate only plants.

2 Why have Jack Horner's ideas caused a lot of disagreement?

3 What three pieces of evidence does Jack Horner give for his theory?

2 a Look at question 1.
- Read the text before and after the gap. Use the highlighted words and phrases to help you choose which option A–G fits the gap.
- Now read option D. Find the words and a phrase that relate to the first paragraph, showing that Horner is prepared to argue with conviction.

b Read the options A–G and underline words and phrases that might help you to match them to the text.

3 Now look at questions 2–6 and follow the same procedure. Words have been highlighted around questions 2 and 3 to help you.

4 When you have finished the task, read the whole text through to check it makes sense.

5 a Scan the text to find these words and any related forms.
1 controversy
2 predator
3 carnivore
4 scavenger
5 herbivore

b Use your dictionary to complete a word family for each item in Exercise 5a in your vocabulary notebook.

For questions **1–6**, you must choose which of the paragraphs **A–G** fit into the numbered gaps in the following magazine article. There is one extra paragraph which does not fit in any of the gaps.

DIGGING FOR DINOSAURS

Jack Horner's ideas about the dinosaur, Tyrannosaurus Rex, have created some controversy. Lucy Winston meets him to discover why.

Jack Horner, one of the world's most prominent dinosaur experts, looks very North American, in a grey-blue, short-sleeved shirt and blue jeans. His bald crown is fringed by longish grey hair, and creases crinkle the corners of his
5 eyes from years of squinting at the sun. He has a humorous, wry smile, but beneath this unassuming exterior is someone prepared to argue his point with conviction and intelligence.

| 1 | |

He's talking about the controversial theory he's been
10 working on for the last ten years – that Tyrannosaurus Rex, the predatory king of the prehistoric world, was in fact a scavenger more akin to a vulture; the big black bird that feeds on the dead flesh of larger wild animals. It's an idea that has met with considerable scepticism over the
15 years, but it has recently been gathering momentum.

| 2 | |

Jack Horner is not your typical academically gifted palaeontologist. Growing up with dyslexia, he struggled hard at school. 'I liked digging in the dirt when I was a little kid, and discovering things,' he remembers. 'I came
20 across my first piece of dinosaur bone sticking out of the rock when I was only eight, and I've kept it,' he adds with a laugh. Much to his surprise, a high-school project on dinosaurs led to his being offered a place at university to study palaeontology. Yet, after persevering with his
25 studies for four years, he decided he had taken all the courses he needed to be a palaeontologist, so left without a degree.

| 3 | |

I challenge him, saying that Tyrannosaurus Rex does share certain characteristics with predatory reptiles, and he
30 looks at me appraisingly. 'Like what?' he questions. 'Well, it's got a big mouth full of sharp teeth,' I reply. 'No, it hasn't,' he counters. 'It's got a mouth full of blunt teeth. There's a big difference.'

I try again: 'What about its big hind legs?'

35 'Yes, Tyrannosaurus Rex has big hind legs,' he concedes. 'So? That doesn't mean he can run fast.' Humans and other animals that are adapted for walking have longer thigh bones and shorter shin bones. On the other hand, fast-running animals such as the cheetah have short
40 thigh bones and long shin bones. Based on this, the leg bones of all known predatory dinosaurs seem to be designed for running after their prey. Tyrannosaurus Rex was, he believes, a walker.

4	

'Scavengers are much more common than predators, but
45 still less common than their prey.' Horner explains. 'If you look at how many meat eaters there were and how many prey animals, then you add up the huge numbers of Tyrannosaurus Rex, being the most common meat-eating dinosaur, compared with the scarcity of the
50 herbivorous dinosaurs, the numerical proportions are similar to those you find in some African national parks where the flocks of vultures wait to feed on animals killed by hyenas.'

5	

'Each of these points is based on scientific data that can
55 be falsified,' he concedes. 'Yes, one is a mammal and the other a bird, and somebody else could study this and find out that there's something weird going on. But nobody has done it yet.'

6	

'Just because Tyrannosaurus Rex had vicious-looking
60 teeth and looked intimidating, doesn't make it a lethal predator by default. This is the first hypothesis to be based on science. So I'm not going against the grain. Science is about evidence, not egos.'

A Horner frequently likens Tyrannosaurus Rex to these scavenging birds, and he recently scanned the brain of one in search of evidence to support his theory. He compared the size of its olfactory lobes, the parts used for scent detection, with those of a bloodhound. This dog has a highly sensitive localised sense of smell, but can't smell over large distances. Vultures, on the other hand, can sniff out a dead animal several miles away. He found the vulture had enormous olfactory lobes in its brain, as did the Tyrannosaurus Rex, but the bloodhound did not.

B Ironically, Horner has now become one of the world's foremost dinosaur experts. He found the first dinosaur eggs in the world, and it was he who discovered the largest, oldest and most complete Tyrannosaurus Rex skeleton. Yet the more he has learned, the more he has become convinced that, far from hunting its own food, Tyrannosaurus Rex survived on the scavenged meat of animals killed by other predators.

C As a result, he was later appointed as the scientific consultant for the *Jurassic Park* films, a position Horner views with amusement. The whole theme of the blockbuster films seems contrary to his personal theory of Tyrannosaurus Rex as a scavenger, and I questioned his reaction. 'I was glad that the lead character did not get eaten by the dinosaurs,' is all he'd say.

D 'When you do historical science, you come up with a supposition,' he says in a pleasant Montana drawl. 'But each piece of information should be backed up by a body of evidence. You can't just overturn a hypothesis with one piece of information, when there exists a large body of data that supports something else.'

E 'I admit that comparing only two different species is not the strongest possible hypothesis, and obviously it could be more rigorous, but in the absence of a more wide-reaching study, it's going to stand,' he states firmly. His main argument for those who think Tyrannosaurus Rex could have been a predator is that you still need some evidence of this, and he remains adamant that there is none.

F It has now reached the point where a leading natural history museum in the UK has put together an exhibition presenting evidence to support the argument and is inviting people to make up their minds. Tyrannosaurus Rex can now be viewed in a new light, as a scavenger, compared with the more popular view of it as a predator.

G By far the most convincing evidence, however, Horner maintains, is what he terms the 'biomass' of Tyrannosaurus Rex compared with that of other dinosaurs of its era. By calculating this biomass, or the proportion of dinosaurs over a given area, it's possible to work out how many of each type existed.

A | Against the odds

English in Use
Lexical cloze (Paper 3 Part 1)

▶ CB page 106, ER page 169

1   Read the title of the text, then read the whole text quickly for general understanding, ignoring the gaps for the moment.
  1 Where did the family sail to?
  2 Which family members continued to work during their trip?

2   Read the text again carefully and try to predict what each answer will be. Then look at the options **A–D** and complete the task. Use the Help clues if necessary.

3   Read through the text again when you've finished to check your answers.

HELP
➤ **Question 2**
  Which verb completes the expression with *out of their system*?
➤ **Question 8**
  Read the whole sentence carefully. Only one of the options creates meaning in the context.
➤ **Question 14**
  Only one of the options combines with *out* to make a phrasal verb.

For questions **1–15**, read the article below and decide which answer **A**, **B**, **C** or **D** best fits each space. The exercise begins with an example **(0)**.

A family gap year

When Jonathan and Claire Spencer, **(0)** .A.. by their two children aged eight and 11, set off on a 17,000-mile voyage from England to Australia in their 51-foot yacht *Attitude*, Jonathan **(1)**........ the year-long voyage as 'the gentlest way of having an extreme experience'. But the couple were not trying to **(2)**........ anything out of their system, and certainly didn't see the trip as something which had to be achieved at all **(3)**........ . Indeed, in spite of the enormity of their adventure, the Spencers were in no **(4)**........ dropping out. Both are **(5)**........ sailors, and regarded their adventure as a career break, as a kind of family gap year.

Claire had been **(6)**........ a year's unpaid leave from her job, and the family rented out their home in London. Meanwhile, arrangements were made for the children to return to school after a year's **(7)**........ ; this had the school's blessing, **(8)**........ a private tutor was employed to keep them up to **(9)**........ with the curriculum.

The strangest **(10)**........ of the trip, however, was that Jonathan, the managing director of a property company, was able to take his job with him. He worked out a way of **(11)**........ his duties without actually **(12)**........ foot in the office. As you might imagine, the arrangement was **(13)**........ dependent on technology, and the cabin on *Attitude* was **(14)**........ out with a communications satellite which **(15)**........ him to keep in phone and email contact with his workplace. Could this be the gap year of the future?

	A	B	C	D
0	accompanied	escorted	supplemented	attended
1	expressed	described	explained	outlined
2	let	take	remove	get
3	costs	events	accounts	lengths
4	manner	fashion	sense	point
5	fond	keen	eager	doting
6	granted	conferred	consented	yielded
7	omission	truancy	absence	default
8	so that	as well as	even if	as long as
9	pace	speed	rate	stride
10	aspect	issue	matter	angle
11	functioning	achieving	fulfilling	satisfying
12	placing	setting	putting	stepping
13	principally	extensively	decisively	entirely
14	stocked	equipped	fitted	furnished
15	enabled	enforced	ensured	engaged

Language development
Spelling
▶ CB page 108, WR page 202

Spelling changes

1 Complete the sentences with the correct form of the words in brackets.
   1 We have had a lot of .... about our new product range. (*enquiry*)
   2 Watching the artist at work was a deeply .... experience. (*satisfy*)
   3 The only .... character in the whole book is the detective's wife. (*like*)
   4 The island of Java has a number of .... that could erupt at any moment. (*volcano*)
   5 His room was like a library with .... of books on every wall. (*shelf*)
   6 I have no .... in recommending Juan as an honest and reliable employee. (*hesitate*)
   7 Flooding on this area of the coast is a common .... (*occur*)
   8 I'd .... you to be more careful with your money in future. (*advice*)
   9 I was .... to ask Kevin where he'd been, but I resisted the temptation. (*die*)
   10 When I was younger I .... to go out with friends, but now my .... would be to spend time at home. (*prefer*)

Endings often misspelt

2 Add the missing letter(s) to complete the words in these sentences.
   1 Crossing the Atlantic in a canoe would be virtually imposs__ble.
   2 To ski down Everest is a remark__ble thing to attempt.
   3 The government minister was embar__a__sed by the stories in the press.
   4 You should not exc__ __d the speed limit.
   5 If you wish to take up the place, you will have to write a letter of accept__nce.
   6 Some of the excuses James came out with were unbeliev__ble.
   7 It is incred__ble that he managed to survive at sea for so long.
   8 After the earthquake, I wanted to help, so I volunt__ __red my services as a driver.

Commonly misspelt words

3 Complete the nouns in these sentences. Some of the letters have been given.
   1 In order to exchange goods in a shop, you need your r__ __ __ __ __ __ __ __ .
   2 Hard work and preparation are no g__ __rant__ __ of suc__ __ __ __ __ .
   3 Another word for your job is your o__ __ __ __ __ __ __ __ __ __ __ .
   4 Winning a medal gives someone a great sense of ach__ __ __ __ __ment.
   5 Looking at your injuries, I think you should seek im__ __ __ __ __ __ __ __ medical attention.
   6 Lost in the fog, I was sep__ __ __ __ __ __ __ from the rest of the group.
   7 I'm not sure how big the room is exactly, but it's a __ __ __ __ __ __ __ __ __ __ __ __ __y 15 metres^2.
   8 If you let me think about it, I'll give you a de__ __ __ __ __ __ __n in a few minutes.
   9 Just because the restaurant is expensive, it isn't nec__ __ __ __ __ __ __ __ __ __ the best.
   10 After lunch, we went for a le__sure__ __ stroll.

4 It is important to check your work for spelling mistakes. There are 24 mistakes in this letter. Read it carefully to find and correct all the mistakes.

Dear Sir/Maddam

I am writting to complaine about the service I recieved in your restaurant last night. Generaly the food was poor and the service was awfull.

The potatos were nearly raw, and the source that the chicken was cooked in was much saltyer than was neccessary.

The waiter kept droping thinks, including two knifes, which he then put back on the table for us to use.

In additton, we were forced to wait nearly an hour between the main course and the desert. When we pointed this out to your staff, they became rude and aggresive.

I don't think you realise how much distres this causes to a person like myself who allways trys to maintain the highest standads in all aspects of my live.

I look forward to hearing your explainations and how you propose to compensate us.

Yours sincerly

D. Smith

English in Use
Word formation
(Paper 3 Part 4)

▶ ER page 170

1 Read the title of the first text and think about what you are going to read. Then read the rest of the first text quickly for general understanding, ignoring the gaps for the moment.

2 Read the text again carefully and try to decide what kind of word will fit in each gap. Then fill in the gaps using the Help clues if necessary.

3 Read through the text again when you've finished and check that the words you've written fit in with the overall meaning of the text and are spelled correctly.

4 Repeat the procedure for the second text.

HELP

▶ Question 2
Which suffix is added to this noun to create the adjective? Are there any spelling changes?

▶ Question 5
This adjective requires a suffix to make it into a noun.

▶ Question 8
Add a prefix to this adjective to make a verb meaning *to get over*.

▶ Questions 10–15
One of these items requires a plural noun. Do you know which? You have to read the surrounding text very carefully to be sure.

For questions **1–15**, read the two texts below. Use the words in the boxes to the right of the texts to form **one** word that fits in the same numbered space in the text. The exercise begins with an example (**0**).

EXTRACT FROM A WEBSITE

Taking a balloon to the edge of space

There is nothing in Colin Prescot's outward (**0**)*appearance* to suggest that he is the type of person who craves the thrill and (**1**)..................... of extremely (**2**)..................... situations. But this laid-back middle-aged man is setting out to break the world ballooning altitude record of 31,000 metres, by travelling to the very edge of space. Sitting on a chair fastened to an open platform, Colin will be suspended below an enormous helium balloon for his (**3**)..................... to the edge of the stratosphere. Although it sounds like a pretty (**4**)..................... prospect, and he will have to wear a spacesuit in order to survive the experience, Colin insists that (**5**)..................... is always his first priority on all balloon trips. Nevertheless, he admits to getting a boost of adrenalin every time he goes up in a balloon, and feels that he is at his most (**6**)..................... in situations that call for such a high level of (**7**) ....

(**0**) **APPEAR**
(**1**) EXCITE
(**2**) RISK
(**3**) FLY
(**4**) FRIGHT
(**5**) SAFE
(**6**) EFFECT
(**7**) CONCENTRATE

NEWSPAPER REPORT

Iron men let off steam

If you've tried bungee jumping and paragliding and still haven't (**8**)..................... the urge to prove yourself by taking part in (**9**)..................... challenging activities, then extreme ironing could be the thing for you. (**10**)..................... describe themselves as 'ironists' and like to climb mountains, go surfing or trek cross-country, doing their ironing along the way. It all started in 1997, when Philip Shaw, a mountaineering (**11**)..................... from Leicester, decided to iron his shirts in the garden on a hot day. His flatmate (**12**)..................... described this as 'extreme ironing' and the idea of the spoof sport was born. The sport's worldwide (**13**)..................... body, the Extreme Ironing Bureau, has received 20,000 hits on its website, and future expeditions include hang-gliding ironing and white-water ironing. For ironists, who are now earning the grudging respect of mainstream extreme-sports fans, the (**14**)..................... for the sport comes from the chance to combine the thrill of an extreme outdoor activity with the (**15**)..................... of a well-pressed shirt.

(**8**) COME
(**9**) PHYSICAL
(**10**) PARTICIPATE
(**11**) ENTHUSE
(**12**) JOKING
(**13**) GOVERN
(**14**) MOTIVATE
(**15**) SATISFY

Language development

Look through the text again and make a note of all the words that are spelled with a double letter. Make sure you remember to spell them correctly.

Writing
Paraphrasing
▶ CB page 110

Exam strategy

In Paper 2 Part 1, you have to paraphrase words and phrases from the input texts so that the ideas are the same, but the language is different. Sometimes you have to change the register, to express the ideas in a more formal or more informal way. You also have to use this skill in Paper 3 Part 5 (register transfer).

Using synonyms

1 One way to paraphrase is to use synonyms. For each of the words below, cross out the word (A–D) which is not a synonym.

Adjectives

1 expensive   A pricey   B dear
                C costly   D fortunate

2 important   A necessary   B convinced
                C required   D essential

3 unusual   A bizarre   B weird
                C outstanding   D strange

4 boring   A prestigious   B dull
                C tedious   D dreary

5 ordinary   A standard   B run-of-the-mill
                C genuine   D typical

Nouns

6 solution   A answer   B verge
                C remedy   D way out

7 problem   A frenzy   B hiccup
                C difficulty   D hassle

8 effect   A consequence   B implication
                C attribute   D end result

9 plan   A vision   B timetable
                C schedule   D programme

10 reason   A explanation   B motive
                C pretension   D justification

Verbs

11 employ   A hire   B order
                C take on   D contract

12 find out   A check out   B investigate
                C accuse   D ascertain

13 repay   A reimburse   B pay back
                C refund   D repair

14 prevent   A seize   B impede
                C thwart   D obstruct

15 solve   A put right   B conceive
                C remedy   D sort out

Using opposites

2 Complete the second sentence of each pair so that it paraphrases the first.

0 The family is poor.
   The family is not well-off.

1 The food is cheap.
   The food doesn't .... much.

2 I refuse to take part in the discussion.
   I'm not .... to take part in the discussion.

3 We reject the suggestion that the facilities are underused.
   We don't .... the suggestion that the facilities are underused.

4 Students here are quite poor.   .
   Students here are not .... of money.

5 The residents are very unhappy about the proposals.
   The residents are far from .... about the proposals.

6 It's well known that the centre is going to close.
   It's no .... that the centre is going to close.

7 For us, the closure of the factory is very serious.
   For us, the closure of the factory is no ....
   matter.

8 The principal's suggestions are totally predictable.
   The principal's suggestions come as no .... to us.

Changing the form

3 Complete the second sentence so that it paraphrases the first.

0 You are more likely to succeed if you have help.
   You are more likely to be successful...... if you have help.

1 You may be surprised by this.
   This may come as a .... to you.

2 I've decided to sell my car.
   I've decided to put my car up for ....

3 I'd like to apologise to you.
   I'd like to offer you my ....

4 It's more suitable for children.
   It would .... children.

5 It showed how generous people can be.
   It showed the .... that some people have.

6 I was assisted by some passers-by.
   Some passers-by came to my ....

7 He is a person I can trust.
   He is a totally .... person.

8 The manager still insists on staff wearing uniforms.
   The manager is still .... on staff wearing uniforms.

Listening
Note completion (Paper 4 Part 2)
▶ ER pages 170–171

1   Read the instructions for the exam task. Then
    read the notes and think about the topic. What
    do you expect to hear? Can you predict the type
    of information you will be listening for in each
    item? For example:
    • Question 1: Is this likely to be:
      a) a large number?   b) a small number?
    • Question 2: Is this word likely to be:
      a) a verb?   b) a noun?   c) an adjective?
    • Question 6: Is this word likely to be:
      a) a pleasure?   b) a necessity?   c) a habit?

2   🎧 Listen to the recording once, and complete
    the notes. Use the Help clues if necessary.

HELP
➤ Question 1
  Be careful. Three distances are mentioned. How far
  did he run in 48 hours?
➤ Question 2
  We hear the general term and also some examples
  of what he studied. It's the general term which is
  needed here.
➤ Question 7
  You are listening for a superlative – think of the
  adjectives that would fit this context.

3   Look at the wrong answers that students gave to
    some of the questions. Listen again and decide
    why they are not correct.
    2 elephants
    3 medicines and mountainers
    4 1978

4   Match these nouns from the text to their
    definitions.
    1 dehydration   a having to manage without
    2 a feat   something
    3 a leak   b suffering from a lack of
    4 an entry   water
    5 deprivation   c a mention of something in
                        a reference book
                     d a remarkable achievement
                     e water getting in or out of
                        something by accident

You will hear a radio announcement about a new documentary
series called *Feats of Endurance* that will be broadcast soon.
For questions **1–8**, complete the notes. Listen very carefully as
you will hear the recording ONCE only.

FEATS OF ENDURANCE

First programme: Pheidippides
• world's first marathon runner
• ran a distance of | 1 | | in 48 hours.

Second programme: J. Michael Fay
• did research into | 2 | | in Africa
• walked 3,200 kilometres in 465 days.

Third programme: Reinhold Messner
• went up Mount Everest without oxygen
      (proved both | 3 | *and* | wrong).
• went up again in the year | 4 | |

                              – this time alone!

Fourth programme: Two cases of deprivation:
Steven Callahan
• 76 days alone at sea (despite facing
  | 5 | |, dehydration and a leaking life-raft).

Randy Gardner
• over 11 days without | 6 | |

Final programme: Paddy Doyle
• said to be the | 7 | | man in the world.
• has had a total of | 8 | |
            entries in *Guinness Book of Records*.

B Kicking the habit

Vocabulary
Obsessions
▶ CB page 111

1 a Match each verb with the phrase that creates a common expression.

1	to conceal	a	over your life
2	to tear	b	yourself something
3	to take	c	something for the sake of it
4	to do	d	something from someone
5	to feel	e	short of something
6	to tell	f	nervous without something
7	to fool	g	yourself away from something
8	to not be	h	yourself

b Rewrite the following sentences using the correct form of expressions from Exercise 1a.

1 I used to buy shoes in the sales, *even though I didn't need them.*

....

2 The exhibition was excellent, so *it was hard for me to leave* and get the train home.

....

3 I keep *trying to make myself believe* there was nothing I could have done to help.

....

4 You can never get served, even though *the shop has plenty of staff.*

....

5 Although Alice was pregnant, *her friends didn't know her secret.*

....

6 She pretended that she was in control of the situation, but *she knew it was not true.*

....

7 I'd *be worried if I didn't have* my address book with me when I went out.

....

8 I spent so much time playing and thinking about chess that *it controlled my life.*

....

2 In each sentence, choose the correct word to complete the underlined expression.

1 I first went to play bingo for a joke, but it wasn't long before I'd got the *germ / infection / bug*, and now I play every week.

2 At first I wasn't much of a soap opera fan, but after a while, I <u>was *hooked / trapped / caught.*</u>

3 Gus is a bit of <u>a fitness *fellow / freak / fan*</u> and goes to the gym at least four times a week.

4 When my friends surprised me, I was feeling angry and <u>was in no *feeling / sense / mood* for</u> a joke.

5 For years I had put sugar in my tea, so it was hard to *break / crack / snap* the habit.

6 After a hard day at work, I like to come home and *fall / collapse / plunge* in front of the TV.

7 <u>Given a *dilemma / decision / choice* between</u> bingo or cards, I'd much rather play bingo.

8 The bus is quick and cheap. Taking a taxi is simply *throwing / passing / sending* money away.

9 Sometimes I log on just to check my email, but <u>one thing *brings / leads / comes* to another</u>, and before I know it I've been there five hours.

10 I didn't intend to join the drama society, I just seemed <u>to get *pulled / blown / sucked* in</u>.

3 Complete the text with a suitable word in each gap.

My obsession with DIY started a few years ago when I needed to get a wall painted before I had new carpets fitted. Unable to find a decorator, I decided to do it myself. Within a few weeks, I'd **(1)**.................... the bug. When I wasn't working on the house, nothing could **(2)**.................... me away from the makeover shows on TV.

The thing about DIY is that it's easy to get sucked **(3)**.................... . For example, you see a nasty mark on a wall, and one thing leads to **(4)**.................... , and before you know it the whole room needs redoing. I wouldn't call myself obsessive, but **(5)**.................... the choice between going away for a week's holiday and spending a week at home decorating the spare room, I'd much rather do the latter. Once I replaced the glass in a window just for the **(6)**.................... of it.

It's not that I was **(7)**.................... of money. In fact, I spent a fortune on fancy tools, but I **(8)**.................... myself that it was all right because of the money I was saving not getting people in to do jobs. I also thought of myself as a bit of a craftsman, but in actual fact I was just fooling **(9)**.................... .

Eventually, my wife realised it had taken **(10)**.................... my life and she moved out. Sadly, when we split up, we had to sell the house, so I lost all my hard work. Perhaps I should have had a solicitor at the divorce hearing instead of trying to do it myself!

Language development
Unreal tenses
▶ CB page 115, GR page 183

wish/if only

1 Read the text and complete the gaps with an appropriate auxiliary verb.

My boyfriend spends hours every day on the computer. I hate the computer, and I wish he **(1)**........................ spend so much time on it every day. He's tried to break the habit, but he says he can't. If only he **(2)**........................ break the habit, then we'd be able to spend our evenings together. He keeps saying he'll restrict himself to an hour a day, and I wish he **(3)**........................ do that. If only he **(4)**........................ pay as much attention to me as he does to that machine of his! He upgraded it last month to a more powerful machine, and I really wish he **(5)**........................ , because now he's even more obsessed with it than before.

2 Correct the mistakes in these sentences.
1 I wish that chocolate doesn't bring me out in a rash.
2 I wish I would remember where I've put my keys.
3 He talks as though he would earn a huge salary, but I know he doesn't.
4 I'd sooner spent my money on clothes than food.
5 If only travel would cost less, I'd travel a lot more.
6 It's time we stop messing around and start work.
7 I'd rather you speak to James because you know him better than I do.
8 I wish I didn't spend all my money yesterday, then I would still have some in my bank account.

3 Rewrite these statements using *I wish* or *If only*.
1 I'd like to be fitter.
   I wish ....
2 Not having my phone with me is very inconvenient.
   If only ....
3 I can't find a job that I really enjoy.
   I wish ....
4 I regret not studying French at school.
   If only ....
5 I worry about my daughter because she never tells me where she's going.
   If only ....
6 It's a pity that I left my sunglasses on the beach.
   I wish ....
7 I'd really like it if someone invented decent clothes that didn't need ironing.
   If only ....
8 I was stupid to call the shop assistant dishonest.
   I wish ....

9 These aeroplane seats are very uncomfortable – wider ones would be better.
   I wish ....
10 It's a shame that my parents couldn't come to the wedding.
   If only ....

Other expressions

4 Rewrite the sentences using expressions from the list. Use each expression once only.
   It's high time   He'd sooner   Suppose   as if it   Supposing   I'd rather   It's time I   as though he

1 He talks to his dog in the same way as he talks to a human being.
   ....
2 Please don't wear your shoes in the house.
   ....
3 If you moved house, where would you go?
   ....
4 He thinks that moving is more hassle than staying where he is.
   ....
5 I really ought to settle down and get a place of my own now.
   ....
6 I've lived here six months, but it feels like longer.
   ....
7 We should have had this room redecorated ages ago.
   ....
8 Could you afford to stay if the rent went up?
   ....

5 Rewrite the sentences using the words in brackets.
1 She talks to me in the way that my mother would. (*though*) ....
2 I'd like you to drive, if that's OK. (*sooner*)
   ....
3 We really should go to bed now. (*time*)
   ....
4 I don't want you to tell me how the film ends. (*rather*) ....
5 If the information turns out to be wrong, what will you do? (*supposing*)
   ....
6 She looked like someone who had been crying. (*as if*)
   ....
7 What if she had drowned? How would you have felt? (*suppose*) ....
8 You really should get a job and become independent. (*high time*) ....

English in Use
Error correction (extra word) (Paper 3 Part 3)
▶ ER page 169

1 Read the title of the text to identify the topic. Then read the whole text quickly for general understanding, ignoring the mistakes for the moment.

  1 When did the writer drink more coffee?
    a) during the week
    b) at the weekend
  2 What symptoms did she suffer when she drank less coffee?
  3 Does she feel better now that she has given up coffee?

2 Read the text again, sentence by sentence, and complete the task. Use the Help clues if necessary. Remember that punctuation relies on the whole sentence, not just the line.

3 When you've finished, read the whole text again to check it makes complete sense.

In **most** lines of the following text, there is **one** unnecessary word. It is either grammatically incorrect or does not fit in with the sense of the text. For each numbered line (**1–16**), find this word and write it in the box. **Some** lines are correct. Indicate these lines with a tick (✓) in the box. The exercise begins with two examples **(0)** and **(00)**.

Can you be addicted to coffee?

Until recently, I was a coffee addict. Coffee was part of my daily	**0**	✓
life. Looking back, I can see I relied on a regular dose for to get me	**00**	for
through in the day. After the first cup at breakfast, I'd feel invigorated	**1**	
and ready to face the world; but unless I had another mid-morning,	**2**	
my energy level would slump and I'd have become irritable. Then one	**3**	
day my boss mentioned me that he'd given up coffee. I nodded politely,	**4**	
but the very thought of skipping just one of my daily coffees made	**5**	
me feel uneasy. It suddenly occurred to me that if I might be dependent	**6**	
on the stuff. The same dictionary definition of an addiction is 'taking a	**7**	
drug excessively and being unable to cease doing so without adverse	**8**	
effects'. If I was looking up for evidence of the latter, it wasn't hard to	**9**	
find. Like many people, I sipped of coffee all through the working day,	**10**	
only to find that at weekends, when I consumed less, I ended them up	**11**	
with a massive headache. I tried vainly to give up on several those	**12**	
occasions, but within the two days was back on it again. Eventually	**13**	
I discovered that it takes a fully couple of weeks to get the caffeine	**14**	
out of your system. But it's worth persevering, because providing	**15**	
you can break the habit completely, and you'll really feel the benefits.	**16**	

HELP
➤ Question 1
  Check the prepositions on this line.
➤ Question 3
  Is the tense correct in this line?
➤ Questions 10–16
  One of these lines is correct. Do you know which one?

Language development

Look at all the verbs in the text. Which sentences include hypothetical tenses? Underline them.

Reading

Multiple matching (Paper 1 Part 4)

▶ ER page 168

1 Read the title and the subtitle of the text opposite. What do the five people have in common? Make a list of the types of personal ambitions that you think the five people might have.

2 Read the text quickly to find out about the ambitions of each person. Were your predictions correct?

3 a Read the instructions for the exam task below, then read all the questions and highlight the key words. The first two have been done for you.

   b Read section A (about Hannah Woodford) carefully and mark any sections of text that contain similar ideas or information to the questions 1–19. For example, look at question 11. Find the idiomatic phrase in section A of the text that means *taking on too much responsibility*. You have now found one question which matches option A. There are two more. Can you find them?

   c Now read section B (about Tamsin Jackson). Look at question 1 and find the phrase in the text that matches *soon able to get on with.*

4 Now complete the task.

5 Skim the text to find the idiomatic phrases in A below. Think about the meaning in the context of the text, then find the best paraphrase in B.

A
1 get something up and running
2 set foot somewhere
3 come up with something
4 take up an offer
5 the odds are stacked against someone
6 give someone a push
7 point someone in the direction of
8 have all your eggs in one basket

B
a to accept something
b to depend totally on one thing
c to enter/arrive somewhere
d to have an unexpected idea
e to encourage/motivate someone
f to make a useful suggestion about how to get something
g to start a business
h someone is very unlikely to succeed

Answer questions **1–19** by referring to the magazine article about people who have realised a personal ambition. Choose your answers from the sections **(A–E)**. Some of the choices may be required more than once.

Which person

was soon able to get on with their new neighbours?	**1** ....
did not allow family criticism to divert them from their chosen course of action?	**2** .... **3** ....
was unwilling to make a total commitment to a project in its initial stages?	**4** ....
has discovered personal qualities that they were unaware of?	**5** ....
required the practical assistance of business contacts in their field?	**6** ....
was determined to succeed in their objective despite a lack of funds?	**7** ....
is convinced that they will enjoy lasting job satisfaction?	**8** .... **9** ....
says they were searching for more flexibility in their daily life?	**10** ....
realised they had taken on too much responsibility too quickly?	**11** ....
benefited from a shared family interest?	**12** ....
took steps to remedy a lack of experience of dealing with business finances?	**13** ....
appreciates that a strong personal relationship helped in seeing a project through?	**14** ....
received encouragement from a colleague to launch a project?	**15** ....
was surprised when a risky business venture began to succeed?	**16** ....
realised the value of working as a part of a team in order to achieve their objectives?	**17** ....
admits that the extent of their financial commitments made them feel insecure?	**18** ....
has no particular wish to make huge profits?	**19** ....

DON'T JUST DREAM IT ... DO IT!

Why do some people suddenly decide to take a risk in their lives and follow their personal ambition, when most of their friends are quite content to play it safe? We talk to five people who followed their dream.

A Hannah Woodford

I'd always loved the elegant lines of the beautiful 18th-century building in which I'd rented a room for my work as a freelance lecturer in interior design. As a way of covering my costs, I'd hire it out on an occasional
5 basis as a meeting room. People loved it, and I realised I'd stumbled across a possible business venture. The market was flooded with white-walled conference centres, but there was clearly a demand for something more sumptuous. I realised I could offer my room, and
10 others like it, as a practical, yet impressive location for top-level corporate events. There were several other rooms on offer in the same building, and being a designer, I had a clear vision of the conference centre I could create, but had to draw on the experience of
15 people I knew from the world of art and design in order to get it up and running. The project rapidly took off, and within months I'd taken over the whole building. I quickly realised that, although I knew the demand was there, professionally I had bitten off far more than I could chew
20 with this venture. The rent I was paying was astronomical, and I began to feel very exposed. Unless I sought proper guidance, I knew I'd be in trouble. Much to my parents' relief, I invested in a comprehensive business course, which enabled me to get a better grasp
25 of accounts. I'm now gaining a nationwide reputation in the corporate world – looking back, it was certainly worth the risk!

B Tamsin Jackson

Together with my husband, I was searching for an escape from the rat race, and when I heard about a
30 small 'eco-village' – a community that is entirely self-sufficient in everything from food to energy – located on the west coast of Scotland, it sounded exactly what we were looking for. The community lives rent-free on an island in return for caring for the environment. I knew
35 from the first moment we set foot on the island that it was simply meant to be, and we hit it off with the locals in no time. We wasted no time in abandoning our careers and selling our house in London, much to the horror of my parents, then settling down to life in a small
40 cottage on the island. We knew that in order to succeed in our new life, we had to muck in with the others in the village, because we all shared the responsibility for preserving the unspoilt beauty of the island. Our lives have changed out of all recognition; instead of struggling
45 through traffic, I stroll down to tend the community organic garden, and we share all the household tasks. But the biggest change was the arrival of our son, Joshua, now 19 months old. I used to think I wasn't cut out to be a full-time mother. But here I can combine work
50 and childcare in a way that wouldn't have been possible before. It's a wonderful place to bring up children.

C Adrian Dexter

Hitting 30 signalled a major life-shift for me. After years of dividing myself between my home on the south-west coast of England and my family's delicatessen business in London, I
55 decided there must be more to life than work. I came up with the idea of a mail-order business selling speciality food hampers, because it wouldn't tie me down to working shop hours. I would deliver a beautifully presented basket of high-quality food to the doorsteps of the busy commuters, thereby
60 saving them the trouble of a time-consuming shopping trip. At first, I just took a deep breath and called all my acquaintances working in large companies to see if they wanted to buy my hampers as a corporate gift; to my amazement, several took me up on my offer. In fact, as far as the money side of the business
65 was concerned, I had very little idea what I was taking on, but it seems to be working. After all, I didn't go into this to make a fortune; it was more so that I could take control of my life, which I've certainly achieved.

D Jane Bartlett

Ever since we first met, my husband Peter and I had
70 talked about restoring an old house. After years of looking at derelict cottages, we'd begun to give up hope, until one day driving down a country lane, we caught sight of the castle and recognised it instinctively as the place where we were going to live. Even though the odds were stacked against us – given our
75 cottage-sized budget, and the fact that the castle turned out to be a crumbling ruin – from the moment we bought it, neither of us ever questioned what we'd taken on. The restoration was certainly a full-time job. If we'd listened to the pessimistic predictions of our relations, we'd never have carried on when
80 the rain was pouring through the ceiling. But Peter and I have always shared the same dream, and I couldn't have managed it without him. We've now opened the castle to the public, and our bed-and-breakfast business is growing, so I can't see us ever giving it up because we get so much out of it.

E Tim Manson

85 Although I trained as a lawyer, art has always been my passion. Travelling in Spain a few years ago, I noticed that wherever I went, there were wonderful original works of art for sale, not like the over-priced prints that are in the art galleries in the UK. I thought: 'What a brilliant concept! Why aren't we
90 doing this at home?' Back at work, I was lamenting the lack of exciting original art in Britain with Mark, my business partner, and he said: 'Just because somebody isn't doing something, doesn't necessarily mean it hasn't got potential.' That really gave me the push that I needed. I decided to try opening my
95 own art gallery to sell original art from up-and-coming artists, but what I lacked was financial backing. Luckily my father is a devoted art lover, and he was able to point me in the direction of some companies willing to invest in my project. So I took out a lease on a small gallery, largely using borrowed money. I
100 didn't want all my eggs in one basket, so I continued working as a lawyer during the week and was at the gallery at the weekends. Straightaway there was a huge response, and I'm now taking on work from artists all over the country. My business has doubled over the last 12 months, so I've recently
105 given up the law completely. I can honestly say that, although I work long hours, I don't think the thrill I get out of this business will ever wear off.

Writing
Letter and note (Paper 2 Part 1)

▶ CB pages 116–117, WR pages 195–197

Exam strategy

In a Part 1 task, don't 'lift' the words from the input texts. Keep the meaning, but use your own words wherever possible. Make sure that the words and expressions you use are in the correct register.

1 a Read the task on page 116 of the Coursebook again. Then read a student's answer on the right.

b The underlined phrases in the answer have been 'lifted' from the input text. Which could be replaced by items from this list?
In the first place   It was unsuccessful
reverse their decision   opposed the idea
without any warning

c Rewrite the remaining underlined phrases using your own words.

2 The writer could improve the answer by using more formal words. Find these expressions (1–6) in the text and replace them with the more formal words and phrases in the list below.
1 worried
2 forced through
3 say
4 tried
5 bring in
6 seem

appear   explain   introduce   implemented
concerned   attempted

3 Rewrite the answer with all the changes.

4 Now look at the second part of the task in the Coursebook, and at the student's note. Replace the underlined phrases, which were taken from the input text, with the more informal expressions from this list. There is one expression that you do not need to use.
drop a line to   giving you a hand with
you have in mind   replied   spell out
let you know what happens   come to terms with

LETTER

I am writing to complain about the suggested ban on smoking in public places. I work in Café Noir, a well-known restaurant popular with visitors in the centre of town.

I am very worried about this proposal, for a number of reasons. Firstly, I don't understand why this is being forced through (1) <u>at such short notice,</u> and why there has been no discussion – there is no time for anyone (2) <u>to get used to the idea.</u> And secondly, (3) <u>it is ridiculous</u> to suggest it in outdoor bars and restaurants – such an idea is (4) <u>totally unenforceable.</u>

To support my argument against the proposed ban, I would like to say what happened when the authorities tried to bring in a ban on smoking in my home town. (5) <u>It failed,</u> and the politicians had to (6) <u>change their minds.</u> (7) <u>For a start,</u> few people (8) <u>took any notice of the law.</u> Of course, most businesses (9) <u>were against it.</u> A small number of restaurants tried to implement a no-smoking policy, but (10) <u>half their customers disappeared overnight.</u> If the same thing happened here, (11) <u>I could lose my job.</u>

As a suggestion, (12) <u>why not encourage workplaces</u> to introduce specific non-smoking areas instead? This would seem to be a better solution.

NOTE

Sorry not to have <u>responded</u> to your email before – I can <u>provide a contribution to</u> your articles so let me know what <u>your ideas are.</u> I will <u>write to</u> the authorities and tell them about my home town – I'll <u>describe in detail</u> the effects of a smoking ban on businesses generally. I'll <u>inform you of the results.</u>

A A changing society

English in Use
Word formation (Paper 3 Part 4)
▶ CB page 122, ER page 170

1 Read the title of the first text to identify the topic. Then read the first text through quickly for general understanding, ignoring the gaps for the moment.

2 Read the text again carefully and complete the task, using the Help clues if necessary.

3 Read through the text again when you've finished to check your answers.

4 Repeat the procedure for the second text.

HELP
➤ Questions 1–5
One of these items requires a negative prefix. Read the surrounding text very carefully to be sure.

➤ Question 6
Is a noun or an adjective needed here? Read the sentence carefully.

➤ Question 11
You need to add both a prefix and a suffix to form an adjective that means *not nice to look at.*

➤ Question 12
You need to add a prefix to form a word which means *beginning.*

Language development
Read the text again. Underline all the adverbs ending in *-ly.* They all come from adjectives, but only one requires a spelling change. Which one?

For questions **1–15**, read the two texts below. Use the words in the boxes to the right of the texts to form **one** word that fits in the same numbered space in the text. The exercise begins with an example **(0)**.

REPORT IN AN ACADEMIC JOURNAL

What the world watches on TV

More than two billion people in developing countries now have access to (0) Western television. There are, however, few (1)................... statistics relating to television viewing in Africa and Asia. Far more is known about the programming strategies of international broadcasters, for example, than about what is actually watched or, more elusively, its impact. There is a (2)................... to assume that the poor, unlike the media-aware rich, are (3)................... influenced by what they see. But research has shown that across cultures, the (4)................... to the same programmes is as diverse as it is (5)................... , since apparently we all bring our own experience to bear on what we see. One study revealed that in rural Algeria, people watching the US soap opera *Dallas*, were not so much impressed by its capitalist values as by its (6)................... of a close-knit family and patriarchal world, something fast disappearing in their own culture, which they viewed through (7)................... eyes.

(0) WEST
(1) RELY
(2) TEND
(3) EASY
(4) RESPOND
(5) PREDICT
(6) REPRESENT
(7) NOSTALGIA

FEATURE IN A TRAVEL MAGAZINE

I witness the introduction of mobile phones in Bhutan

Bhutan's eccentricities have been (8)................... reported in the international press. In (9)................... to being one of the last countries to get television, smoking is illegal there, and there is a complete (10)................... of traffic lights since the population regards them as (11)................... . So, as one might expect, the introduction of mobile phones to Bhutan was a very organised affair. Far from being behind the times, the highly venerated King seems to have simply waited for the technology to be perfected abroad before importing it. From the (12)................... , everyone was clutching state-of-the-art handsets and the (13)................... ring-tone of all, a rather incongruous 'Merry Christmas', was to be heard everywhere. Once the free week's (14)................... on the largest mobile network ended for the country's 5,000 (15)................... , however, silence seemed to reign once more.

(8) WIDE
(9) ADD
(10) ABSENT
(11) SIGHT
(12) SET
(13) COMMON
(14) TRY
(15) SUBSCRIBE

Language development
Emphasis (inversion and fronting)
▶ CB page 125, GR page 183

Negative introductory expressions

1 **Decide whether the verb should be inverted or not and mark the correct option in each pair.**
   1 If I'm short of time, *I will / will I* stay up all night working.
   2 Only if I'm short of time, *I will / will I* stay up all night working.
   3 Rarely these days *I get / do I get* to bed before midnight.
   4 Sometimes these days *I get / do I get* to bed before midnight.
   5 Since I was a student, *I have / have I* lived alone.
   6 Not since I was a student *I have / have I* lived alone.
   7 Only after six months of study *I could / could I* speak Japanese.
   8 After only six months of study, *I could / could I* speak Japanese.
   9 Hardly *she had / had she* spoken when Jim arrived.
   10 *She had / Had she* hardly spoken when Jim arrived.

2 **Rewrite the following sentences beginning with one of the expressions in the list.**
   Not only … but also   Not since   No way
   Rarely   Not a   Only now   No sooner … than
   Under no circumstances

   1 The company will not give a refund without a receipt in any situation.
   2 The new computer system is both safer and more reliable.
   3 We hadn't been anywhere so interesting since we visited Nepal some years ago.
   4 We hardly ever come across such a hard-working student these days.
   5 We had only just started dinner when she suddenly said she had to leave.
   6 At the time, I didn't realise how dishonest she was, but I do now.
   7 We spent nothing, not even a penny, on food all the time we were there.
   8 I refuse to work on the afternoon of the Cup Final.

Emphasis through fronting parts of the sentence

3 **Rewrite these sentences, moving the underlined objects before the subjects.**
   1 It took <u>years</u> to complete the building of the tunnel.
   2 I'm going to enjoy <u>this</u>!
   3 We waited <u>weeks and weeks</u> with no news from them.
   4 Jerry's going to run a marathon? I'd like to see <u>that</u>!
   5 They say the health service is improving? I find <u>that</u> difficult to believe.

4 **Rewrite these sentences, putting the adverb/adverbial phrase of the second sentence in each case before the subject. Make any necessary changes. The adverb has been underlined in the first one for you.**
   1 The door suddenly opened, and Stella came <u>in</u>.
   2 I begged the boy to get help, and he ran off as fast as his legs would carry him.
   3 Hearing a noise, they opened the cellar door, and a black dog sprang out.
   4 There was a sudden gust of wind, and the balloon flew up into the treetops.
   5 There was an outhouse behind the main building. There was an old well in front of it.

5 **Rewrite these sentences beginning with *so* or *such* and making any necessary changes.**
   1 He was so tired that he could hardly walk.
   2 There was such danger in the streets that we dared not go out.
   3 Their anxiety was such that they did not sleep at all for three days.
   4 They were so confident of victory that they planned the celebrations before the election had taken place.
   5 His ability on the football field was such that no one could stop him scoring goals.

English in Use 2

Lexical cloze (Paper 3 Part 1)

▶ ER page 169

1 Read the title of the text below, then read the whole text quickly for general understanding, ignoring the gaps for the moment.
   1 What is *eBay*?
   2 How do you buy something on *eBay*?

2 Read the text again carefully and try to predict what each answer will be. Then look at the options **A–D** and complete the task. Use the Help clues if necessary.

3 Read through the text again when you've finished to check that the options you've chosen fit in with the overall meaning of the text.

HELP
➤ Question 1
   Only one of the options completes the expression with *by*.
➤ Question 2
   Which of these adverbs collocates with *regarded* to tell us that this opinion is commonly held?
➤ Question 12
   Which of these phrases captures the idea of *personal recommendations*?
➤ Question 15
   Does this adverb signal a reinforcement of the ideas in the preceding sentence, or a contrast to them?

> **Language development**
> Read the text again. Can you find two sentences which contain examples of fronting and inversion? Underline them.

For questions **1–15**, read the article below and decide which answer **A**, **B**, **C** or **D** best fits each space. The exercise begins with an example **(0)**.

The *eBay* Phenomenon

Located in an elegant 18th-century building in London is the nerve **(0)** .A... of one of the world's most prolific companies. It **(1)**........ by the name *eBay*. Not only has the company gone from Internet hobby site to potent economic force, with 95 million users in just ten years, it is **(2)**........ regarded as having altered the **(3)**........ of commercial life as we know it.

If you want to buy anything, from a nail file to an airliner, *eBay* is the Internet site to go to. A million items **(4)**........ for sale each day in what is **(5)**........ an online auction. If you like the description of an item, you **(6)**........ a bid within a given time limit; if you **(7)** .... to be the highest bidder, you become the **(8)**........ owner of the goods in question. But the most astounding factor behind *eBay* is not the range and value of the goods on **(9)**........ , but the fact that the whole business is **(10)**........ on mutual trust. Rarely do you find people so willing to buy unseen goods from an unknown source.

Part of the explanation for this **(11)**........ in the fact that 95% of *eBay* buyers and sellers are private individuals. The company has expanded through **(12)**........ recommendations rather than smart marketing, and there's a real **(13)**........ of community about it. What's more, using *eBay* **(14)**........ to that instinctive sense of satisfaction people get from the process of bargaining – and from actually getting a bargain at the end of it. **(15)**........ , it puts the fun back into shopping.

0	**A** centre	**B** heart	**C** focus	**D** middle
1	**A** calls	**B** goes	**C** knows	**D** greets
2	**A** largely	**B** deeply	**C** greatly	**D** widely
3	**A** course	**B** route	**C** flow	**D** trend
4	**A** arise	**B** emerge	**C** occur	**D** appear
5	**A** precisely	**B** effectively	**C** absolutely	**D** exactly
6	**A** cast	**B** put	**C** make	**D** have
7	**A** turn out	**B** check in	**C** show up	**D** send off
8	**A** proud	**B** conceited	**C** boastful	**D** vain
9	**A** issue	**B** supply	**C** question	**D** offer
10	**A** grounded	**B** based	**C** derived	**D** hinged
11	**A** finds	**B** draws	**C** lies	**D** comes
12	**A** matter-of-fact	**B** man-to-man	**C** tell-tale	**D** word-of-mouth
13	**A** sense	**B** feel	**C** touch	**D** mood
14	**A** entices	**B** attracts	**C** tempts	**D** appeals
15	**A** Otherwise	**B** In short	**C** Instead	**D** Despite that

Language development
Attitude clauses and phrases
▶ CB page 126, WR page 203

1 Underline the most appropriate word in italics.
 1 Many people think young men love gadgets. But *actually,* / *rightly,* it is women who now spend the most money on technology.
 2 *Not surprisingly,* / *Strangely,* the advent of TV has had a major impact on modern society.
 3 The 24/7 society has benefits, but *doubtless,* / *honestly,* who wants to go shopping at three in the morning?
 4 *Annoyingly,* / *As a matter of fact,* some of the original data from the study is missing, so we cannot draw firm conclusions.
 5 *Hopefully,* / *Obviously,* something must be done about the litter problem immediately before it gets out of hand.
 6 *Indeed,* / *Naturally,* everyone we interviewed in our survey said cheaper food would be a benefit.
 7 Because accommodation is so vital, the shortage of decent housing is, *arguably,* / *personally,* the most important issue facing the city at present.
 8 A lot of people complain that our facilities are too expensive, so *admittedly,* / *presumably,* if prices were reduced, more people would use them.

2 Complete each gap with a suitable expression from the list. Use each expression only once.
 frankly   funnily   granted   indeed   of course
 surely   understandably   worryingly

 1 You know we were talking about Sandra on Friday? Well, ... enough, I bumped into her on the street on Saturday!
 2 We don't mind at all if you join us. ...., we will be delighted.
 3 ...., the level of air pollution in the city is increasing every year.
 4 You must have heard of him, ... ? He's one of our best writers.
 5 Well, quite ...., I think he is overrated.
 6 They were pretty angry when they heard he had crashed the car, ... enough.
 7 Most people enjoy shopping, but .... there are exceptions to every rule.
 8 'Our products are the best on the market.'
 '....................., but they are also the most expensive, so not many people can afford them.'

3 Complete the expressions used for generalising with one word from the list.
 considered   generally   large   main   rule   whole

 1 .... speaking, we don't have much of a problem with crime in this area.
 2 All things ...., I think we made the right decision.
 3 On the ...., the children were very well behaved.
 4 By and ...., the event was a success.
 5 As a ...., I don't eat very much during the day.
 6 In the ...., the weather here is pretty good in summer.

4 Complete the expressions used for indicating an attitude or feelings with one word from the list.
 afraid   believe   far   honest   judging   speaking
 truth   turned

 1 Strictly ...., tomatoes are not vegetables but fruit.
 2 .... it or not, the figures show that crime is decreasing.
 3 To be ...., I didn't enjoy the party very much.
 4 As .... as I know, he's still living in Manchester.
 5 To tell the ...., we have no idea how the burglars got in.
 6 .... by his accent, he must come from the north of England.
 7 I completely forgot to tell them we'd be late, I'm ....
 8 I thought I was going to fail the test, but as it .... out, I did very well.

5 Complete the text by putting an appropriate word or expression from Exercises 1–4 in each gap. There may be more than one possibility.

 (1)....................., older people are more concerned about burglary than younger people. Yet, (2)....................., incidents of theft have not increased sharply in our neighbourhood in recent years. (3)..................... they do occur from time to time. (4)....................., a bag was stolen from the local library just last week. (5)....................., the incident was not a theft. (6)....................., the owner's friend had hidden the bag as a joke. But (7)....................., it seems that a lot of thefts take place during daylight hours, something you wouldn't necessarily expect. (8)....................., there is no one around to check who is entering the building at that time. (9)..................... the library should ensure that there is a receptionist on duty at all times?

Listening

Multiple matching (Paper 4 Part 4)

▶ ER pages 170–171

1 a Read the instructions for the task.

   b Read Task One carefully. Think about the vocabulary and expressions you would expect to hear connected with each of the social changes.

   c Read Task Two carefully and highlight the key words in the options. The first two have been done for you.

2 🎧 Listen to the recording twice. The first time you listen, do Task One. The second time, do Task Two. Use the Help clues if necessary. Remember that you are listening to understand the speakers' main points, attitudes and opinions.

HELP

➤ Question 1
   The speaker tells us that he now has to leave home early to *avoid the jams*. Which of the options A–H could this relate to? Listen to the rest of the text to hear confirmation of your chosen option.

➤ Question 2
   At the beginning, the speaker tells us that she *gets in front of the screen*. Which of the social changes could this refer to? Be careful, there are three possibilities. Listen to the rest of the text for confirmation of which one matches exactly.

➤ Question 6
   Listen for why the speaker no longer goes running. How has this affected his health?

➤ Question 7
   The speaker says *it's a lot cheaper than calling them on their mobiles*. Which option does this match?

You will hear **five** short extracts in which various people are talking about current trends in society.

You will hear the recording twice. While you listen you must complete both tasks.

TASK ONE

For questions **1–5**, choose from the list **A–H** the social trend that each speaker is talking about.

A the habit of viewing television while eating
B the growing number of open-plan offices
C the increasing consumption of take-away meals
D the build-up in the volume of traffic
E the expanding use of mobile phones
F the growing popularity of computer games
G the increasing reliance on email
H the tendency for people to make regular use of a gym

Speaker 1 ☐ 1
Speaker 2 ☐ 2
Speaker 3 ☐ 3
Speaker 4 ☐ 4
Speaker 5 ☐ 5

TASK TWO

For questions **6–10**, choose from the list **A–H** how each speaker has been affected by the social trend they are talking about.

A It has created difficulties for me at work.
B It has saved me a certain amount of money.
C It has helped me manage my time better.
D It has enabled me to make new friends.
E It has caused tensions within my family.
F It has had a bad affect on my health.
G It has helped me to be more efficient in my job.
H It has forced me to rethink my finances.

Speaker 1 ☐ 6
Speaker 2 ☐ 7
Speaker 3 ☐ 8
Speaker 4 ☐ 9
Speaker 5 ☐ 10

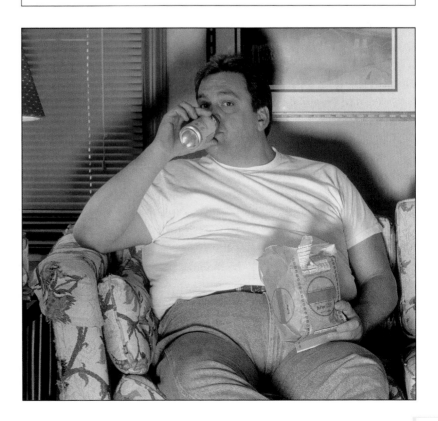

B Law and order

Vocabulary
Law and order
▶ CB pages 127–130

1 Match a word in column A to a word in column B and write the names of the crimes on the lines below. Which are written as one word?

A	B
1 joy	dealing
2 armed	lifting
3 drunk	riding
4 drug	hacking
5 computer	robbery
6 shop	driving

1 ....
2 ....
3 ....
4 ....
5 ....
6 ....

2 Read these definitions and write the names of the crimes. Choose from Exercise 1 and the following list.

arson   burglary   forgery   manslaughter   slander

1 a false spoken statement about someone, intended to damage the good opinion that people have of that person: ....
2 deliberately making something burn, especially a building: ....
3 getting into a building to steal things: ....
4 stealing from a shop: ....
5 killing someone illegally but not deliberately: ....
6 stealing a car and driving it in a fast and dangerous way for fun: ....
7 secretly using or changing the information in other people's computer systems: ....
8 copying official documents, money, etc. illegally: ....

3 Complete the table.

Verb	Noun	Person
mug	1	2
3	*burglary*	4
murder	5	6
–	*arson*	7
steal	8	9
10	*forgery*	11
rob	12	13
14	*joyriding*	15

4 a Complete the text with words from the list. Use each word once only.

acting   catch   commit   detect   fight   liaise   maintain   scene   search

The police policy of 'Stop and (1)...................' is a controversial one. On the one hand, the police see it as a useful technique in the (2)................... against crime and claim that it helps them to (3)................... law and order. They point out that it makes good sense to stop people near the (4)................... of a crime, as they may be involved. The policy also allows them to target people who are (5)................... suspiciously, and look as if they are about to (6)................... a crime. If they stop someone and discover that they are carrying drugs or stolen property, they are able to both (7)................... crime and (8)................... criminals.

On the other hand, the policy results in some sections of the population being stopped much more often than others, with the result that the police are seen as being prejudiced. They therefore have to work hard to (9)................... with local communities, explaining why they stop the people that they do.

b Do the same with the following text.

amnesty   anonymity   arrest   clamp down   come forward   penalty   schemes   tackle

Another controversial subject is the idea of offering the public a weapon (1)................... . At such times, people can take any illegally held weapons to a local police station and no questions will be asked about them. Such (2)................... have resulted in thousands of weapons being removed from the streets, and the police see it as a useful way to (3)................... crime in general, and gang crime in particular.

However, as the (4)................... of the people handing in the weapons is maintained, the police cannot (5)................... anyone for having them. Some people argue that the people who (6)................... and hand in weapons are unlikely to be real criminals. But if this policy is used, and the (7)................... for possessing an illegal weapon is increased at the same time, the police can give a clear message that they mean to (8)................... on people who carry weapons.

Language development
Comparison
▶ CB page 132

Comparatives and superlatives

1 **Identify and correct the mistakes in the following sentences.**
   1 Nirvana are still my most favourite band of all time.
   2 James is slightly taller as his brother.
   3 Life is a great much noisier nowadays.
   4 This is easily the worse murder we have ever had to deal with in this city.
   5 The job now is nothing like dangerous as it was.
   6 Some people think that shoplifting is not such serious crime as burglary.
   7 Murder is by far a most serious crime anyone can commit.
   8 He is one of the most experienced officer in the police force.

so/such

2 **Combine the sentences using *so* or *such* and a *that*-clause. In some cases, both are possible.**
   1 The trial was complex. Therefore it went on for weeks.
   ....
   2 The cost of legal proceedings can be very high. Therefore some people cannot afford it.
   ....
   3 Lawyers tend to earn a lot of money. Many people want to become lawyers.
   ....
   4 Some laws are very outdated. They need to be rewritten.
   ....
   5 The evidence was very strong. The jury reached a decision very quickly.
   ....
   6 After the trial, there were many people outside the court. As a result, we couldn't see anything.
   ....

too/enough

3 **Combine the sentences using either *too* or *enough*. In some cases, it is possible to make sentences with both.**
   1 The police arrived late. They couldn't catch the criminals.
   ....
   2 There were not many officers on duty. They couldn't control the crowd.
   ....
   3 We couldn't ignore the crime. It was very serious.
   ....
   4 There was some evidence against him. Therefore the police could charge him.
   ....
   5 Many crimes are committed. It is impossible for the police to solve all of them.
   ....
   6 The joyrider drove faster than the police cars could go. Therefore they didn't catch him.
   ....

Double comparisons

4 **Match the sentence halves and rewrite them using a form of double comparison (*the -er ... the -er* or *more and more ...*).**
   1 If they change the law soon,
   2 Prisons are becoming
   3 If we have more police officers on the street,
   4 A growing number of police officers
   5 Crimes that are more serious
   6 In some places, criminal gangs

   a generally receive tougher penalties.
   b we will feel much safer.
   c are becoming increasingly violent.
   d it will be better.
   e would like to carry a gun.
   f increasingly overcrowded.
   1 ....
   2 ....
   3 ....
   4 ....
   5 ....
   6 ....

as/like

5 **Complete the sentences with *as* or *like*.**
   1 .... a parent, I feel that more should be done to protect our children.
   2 His parents treat him .... a child, even though he's 16.
   3 The garden looked .... a jungle after being neglected for weeks.
   4 When we went camping, we used a large flat stone .... a table.
   5 Caroline moves and talks exactly .... her mother.
   6 Tom Cruise appeared .... a lawyer in the film.

English in Use
Register transfer (Paper 3 Part 5)

▶ ER page 170

1 Read the notes for new students quickly for general understanding. Then read the information sheet quickly, ignoring the gaps for the moment. Which text is formal and which is informal?

2 a Look at the words and phrases in bold in the notes. Find and mark the same information in the information sheet.

  b Now answer these questions.
    1 Look at question 1. The correct answer is a noun followed by the preposition *at*. Is it:
      a) start?
      b) beginning?
      c) arrival?
    2 Look at question 2. Highlight the verb in the notes, which relates to this gap. Which is the correct answer?
      a) reveal
      b) produce
      c) display

3 Now complete the task using the same techniques.

Language development

Read the texts again. Can you find an example of a comparison and a double comparision?

For questions **1–13**, read the notes. Use the information in it to complete the numbered gaps in the college information sheet. The words you need **do not occur** in the notes. **Use no more than two words for each gap**. The exercise begins with an example **(0)**.

NOTES

> Mark,
>
> Here are the notes to put in the new students' info sheet:
>
> - They should each have been sent a student card before coming here (make it clear they'll have to show it, so we know they are who they say they are).
>
> - All students have an **individual** room key. Remind them to take this whenever they go out (clipping it onto clothes or a belt is one of the most popular ways of carrying it).
>
> - Security in Halls of Residence is getting tighter and tighter. Every Hall of Residence has a six-digit code for the front door. Students should try to remember this, and nobody outside college should be told what it is.
>
> - Students shouldn't leave any valuables (like watches) in their rooms, **where anyone could see them**. They can put any cash in the safe (tell them it's in the Student Office).
>
> - Security guards are always **checking** the college buildings and **the gardens**. Tell students to keep their eyes open and to let these people know if they happen to spot anyone acting in a suspicious way.

COLLEGE INFORMATION SHEET

Student cards: All students should **(0)** ...receive... a student card prior to their **(1)**.................... at college, and should be prepared to **(2)**.................... this at any time as **(3)**.................... of identity.
Room keys: Each student is given their own personal room key. This should be **(4)**.................... them at all times, possibly attached to an **(5)**.................... clothing or a belt.
Security code: The door to each Hall of Residence has a six-digit code, which should be committed **(6)**.................... , if possible. This number should never be **(7)**.................... to anyone outside college.
Personal belongings/Cash: Please do not leave anything **(8)**.................... on display in your room. Cash can be **(9)**.................... in the safe, which is **(10)**.................... in the Student Office.
Security: Security guards patrol the college and grounds on **(11)**.................... basis. Please be **(12)**.................... and inform them if by **(13)**.................... you should see anyone behaving suspiciously.

Writing

Memo (Paper 2 Part 2)

▶ CB page 133

Exam strategy

In the exam, you may be asked to write a memo. A memo gives information, and you should use a neutral style.

1 Read the task below, and decide what two types of information you should include in the memo.

> You are studying at a college in an English-speaking country, and you have joined the Student Union Committee. The committee feels that there is not enough for students to do on the campus in the evenings and at weekends, and has asked you to circulate an email memo to all the students explaining what the problem is and asking them for their suggestions.
>
> Write your **memo** in approximately 250 words.

2 Read a student's answer on the right and underline the correct expression in each pair.

3 To present information clearly and accessibly in a memo, we often use headings and bullet points.

   a Underline the topic sentence of paragraphs A, B and C of the memo. Then match the paragraphs to the headings below. There is one heading you will not need to use.
     Background information
     Initial suggestions
     Your input
     Reasons for suggestions

   b Identify the part of the memo where three bullet points would improve the layout.

4 Find and underline four expressions in the student's answer that are too informal and decide which of the more neutral expressions below can replace each one.
   1 a negative impact on their studies
   2 welcome your input into this
   3 the budget we have to spend
   4 provide feedback

5 Unlike a report or a proposal, a memo often addresses the reader directly. Find and circle five sentences which address the reader in the memo.

6 Imagine that you are a student at the college, and write your own answer to the memo.

To: all students
From: Student Union Committee
Date: May 24th
Subject: Campus life

This is a message from your Student Union **(1)** *as / moreover* we need your help!

Ⓐ **(2)** *As you all know, / It is common knowledge that* the campus is very quiet in the evenings and weekends. We feel that it's time that the college joined the 24-hour society, and **(3)** *doubtless / obviously* we would like to know what you think. Many of you have responded to questionnaires before and told us how much you have appreciated the chance to put forward your ideas **(4)** *such as this / in this way*. So, take this opportunity to influence what happens in your college.

Ⓑ **(5)** *Although / In spite of* the feeling among some students that there could be a bad effect on their work, we feel that there needs to be some fresh approach to activities on campus. **(6)** *As a result / In contrast*, we have come up with the following ideas: a regular disco on Friday evenings, which would not interfere with studies; longer hours for the campus shop – preferably 24-hour opening; and inter-college sports activities on a regular basis.

Ⓒ They are our suggestions – but **(7)** *anyway / now* it's over to you! What you do is send your ideas in to us at the office, and **(8)** *after that / following* we will consider them all together with the amount of money we have. **(9)** *Naturally, / Admittedly,* we want to come up with a clear proposal that can be presented at the next meeting of the Committee with the principal.

Thanks – and we're looking forward to hearing from you all!

Reading
Multiple-choice questions (Paper 1 Part 3)

▶ ER page 168

1 Read the title of the text and the subheading.
  1 What is meant by the phrase *young offender*?
  2 What attitude do you think the young offenders will have towards drama sessions?

2 Read the text quickly to check whether you were right. As you read, make a note of why each of the following people is mentioned in the text.
  1 Nathan   2 Sally Brookes   3 Lou Heywood

3 Read all the questions and underline the key words in each question.

4 a Read question 1 and look at the first word of the options **A–D**. Each of them focuses on Nathan; this tells us that we need to read for what he says or does in relation to Feltham.

  b Read what Nathan says about the place in the text. Now read the options carefully. Which one is closest to your own understanding of what he says?

  c Read the paragraph again carefully to check that your answer is right and that the other options are definitely wrong.

5 Now continue to answer the rest of the questions, following the same procedure.

6 Match the words from the text in column A to a definition in column B.

A		B	
1	loathe	a	not convinced that something is true
2	innovative	b	designed for someone particular
3	detained	c	hate
4	constructive	d	being likely to be hurt
5	sceptical	e	hidden
6	irrational	f	without reason
7	concealed	g	with new ideas
8	vulnerability	h	with a positive outcome
9	tailor-made	i	held as a prisoner

Read the following magazine article and answer questions **1–6**. Mark the letter **A**, **B**, **C** or **D**. Give only one answer to each question.

FACING FACTS

The Geese Theatre Group has a dramatic approach to helping young offenders stay out of custody.

Like many young offenders, 16-year-old Nathan loathes depending on a 'front'. He says: 'It's what landed me in here. I felt I had to be the "tough" guy or the "cool" guy to survive, and the next thing I
5 knew, I was in here for stealing cars.' 'Here' is Feltham young offenders' institution near London where convicted 14–18-year-olds are detained. As Nathan adds, 'Nobody says what they really mean here. It's a frightening place, so you just carry on
10 pretending that you're a particular kind of person because you believe that will keep you the safest. But acting in that way in here just makes you do it all the more when you get out, and so the cycle goes on.'

15 What does make Nathan stand out from other young offenders, however, is his willingness to admit this, and even to change it. It is, he says, the result of an innovative drama course that the Geese Theatre Company – a touring company based at the
20 Midlands Arts Centre in Birmingham – has extended to young offenders to help them examine their reactions to things and develop more constructive ways of handling challenging situations.

25 It works like this. Masks, representing a variety of 'fronts', are worn by the actors who then play out a scene according to the rationale of that behaviour. The mask for Cool ('Listen, you're all making a lot of fuss about nothing – if you want the TV, just
30 steal it') is an ominous, green face with dark glasses; Target (I don't feel in control of this situation – it's everyone else's fault I'm doing this') has an archery target on the forehead. At various points in the performance, the audience of young offenders calls
35 out for the character to lift the mask and explain what he is really feeling –- and how he might find ways to act on that feeling, rather than according to the front. The actor then tests out the consequences of that option.

40 'It's not about truth, but more about what is being withheld – highlighting hidden vulnerabilities and concealed thoughts and feelings,' says Sally Brookes, the theatre company's programmes director. 'That's why we use fragment masks because they display only
45 a fragment of behaviour. Few people are the Joker, the Mouth, the Victim or any other front all the time.' Through workshops lasting one day, and 'residencies', which last several, the company focuses on the young offenders, motivation and ability to change. Brookes
50 says: 'We recognise that wider social and economic factors have a major influence on crime – particularly when it comes to young offenders – but we work from the premise that each person can nonetheless make active choices and has a responsibility for their
55 actions. For us, that's the key point.'

She admits that many of the inmates are sceptical about the idea of drama. 'They feel it's childish and silly,' she says. 'But that's overcome fairly quickly – not only because there is a clear logic to what we're
60 doing, but because they get to explore behaviour patterns one step removed through the medium of an actor. That means they themselves don't end up feeling judged or interrogated. Young offenders are a difficult group to measure in terms of the effects of
65 the course,' she admits, 'but the verbal feedback from prison workers and probation workers, as well as the young people themselves, is certainly positive enough for us to be booked up for months ahead.'

Like all the trainers at Geese, Lou Heywood, the
70 company's touring director, comes from a background of drama training, with a strong interest in issue-based theatre. In addition, all staff receive six months' training in teamwork, the criminal justice system, probation services and aspects of offending behaviour.
75 Lou believes that each workshop must be tailor-made to the needs of a particular group. One, for instance, may focus intensively on aggression, while another may explore a range of knee-jerk reactions and their ramifications. One may focus on behaviour outside
80 prison, while another may include the experience of prison itself. He says: 'The objectives must be clear. One session we recently ran was for young offenders who had been in the institution less than a week. Many seemed confident, but you could tell that
85 almost all of them were frightened, particularly if they didn't understand the system. The first part of the drama involved acting out a scene in which a lad went into his cell for the first time. Using the masks, we explored what he might be thinking. The aim was
90 to let the group talk honestly about the kinds of feelings they might have, rather than letting them out through destructive behaviour.'

1 In the first paragraph, Nathan tells us that at Feltham Young Offenders Institution,
   A he has to hide behind a certain image.
   B he is forced to adopt an unfamiliar role.
   C his behaviour has changed dramatically.
   D he is learning to be a more successful criminal.

2 The drama course he attended has enabled Nathan to
   A consider taking up a career in the theatre.
   B realise why he has been behaving irrationally.
   C stand up to his fellow prisoners more effectively.
   D understand what makes him behave in particular ways.

3 During the sessions, the masks used by the theatre company allow the young offenders to
   A conceal their real identities.
   B appreciate the funny side of their situation.
   C recognise their own failings in certain areas.
   D see that there are different ways of dealing with things.

4 Sally Brookes stresses that the drama workshops aim to give young offenders
   A a chance to take control of their own lives.
   B an opportunity to discuss the causes of crime.
   C an understanding of why a life of crime is wrong.
   D an insight into their reasons for committing crimes.

5 Sally thinks that the main reason for the success of the workshops is that young offenders
   A are unfamiliar with drama techniques.
   B can see what it is that the company is trying to achieve.
   C can recognise their own attitudes in the actors' performance.
   D are young enough to feel uninhibited about taking part in drama.

6 Lou Heywood stresses the importance of sessions which
   A meet the needs of a wide range of participants.
   B reflect the experience of the particular group of offenders.
   C prepare the participants for life outside prison after their release.
   D take account of the behavioural problems of individual offenders.

A Something to say

English in Use
Lexical cloze (Paper 3 Part 1)
► ER page 169

1 Read the title of the text, then read the whole text quickly for general understanding, ignoring the gaps for the moment. What is N'kisi able to do?

2 Read the text again carefully and think about the type of word which will fit in each gap. Then look at the options **A–D** and complete the task. Use the Help clues if necessary.

3 Read through the text again when you've finished to check.

HELP
➤ Question 1
  Only one of the options makes sense if followed by *as*.
➤ Question 2
  Which of these adjectives describes how you feel towards someone you like and spend a lot of time with?
➤ Question 12
  Which of these words collocates with *life* to mean *the average length of time that something lives*?
➤ Question 13
  Is it a consequence or a contrast which is needed here?

Language development

Read the text again and find a sentence beginning with *so*. What happens to the verb?

For questions **1–15**, read the article below and decide which answer **A**, **B**, **C** or **D** best fits each space. The exercise begins with an example **(0)**.

The world's most talkative bird

N'kisi is the name of a grey parrot, bred in captivity, which **(0)** A to the artist Aimee Morgana. Every day, Aimee speaks to her parrot, explaining what she does in simple sentences and encouraging him to develop what she **(1)** as a spontaneous and creative relationship with language. So successful has she been that N'kisi is now the world's most talked-about talking bird.

Parrots and people have been **(2)** companions for centuries, and everybody knows that parrots can be taught to talk. As Aimee explains, however, parrots can do more than just **(3)** back what is said to them. N'Kisi says what he wants, when he wants and, **(4)** most animals trained to perform human-like tasks, he receives no form of reward in **(5)** for his utterances.

N'kisi's vocabulary **(6)** to around 950 words which he uses in **(7)** and with past, present and future verb tenses. What is **(8)** impressive, however, is that N'kisi doesn't speak randomly, but actually **(9)** on what's going on around him, even inventing original expressions, for example calling Aimee's aromatherapy oils 'pretty smell medicine'. He also **(10)** exciting events, like his first ride in a car, and pesters Aimee to take him out again like a **(11)** toddler: 'Wanna go in a car right now!'

The life **(12)** of a parrot is roughly equivalent to that of a human being. Six-year-old N'kisi is **(13)** just beginning his education, and Aimee has **(14)** hopes that his communicative abilities will continue to **(15)** as he matures.

0 A belongs	**B** possesses	**C** retains	**D** shelters
1 A illustrates	**B** describes	**C** demonstrates	**D** emphasises
2 A firm	**B** near	**C** tight	**D** close
3 A respond	**B** reply	**C** repeat	**D** replicate
4 A unlike	**B** dissimilar	**C** different	**D** unrelated
5 A profit	**B** refund	**C** answer	**D** return
6 A climbs	**B** runs	**C** makes	**D** totals
7 A reference	**B** background	**C** context	**D** situation
8 A particularly	**B** largely	**C** chiefly	**D** importantly
9 A mentions	**B** discusses	**C** observes	**D** comments
10 A reminds	**B** recalls	**C** reminisces	**D** reviews
11 A continual	**B** perpetual	**C** persistent	**D** constant
12 A expectancy	**B** assumption	**C** forecast	**D** anticipation
13 A otherwise	**B** therefore	**C** nonetheless	**D** instead
14 A wide	**B** deep	**C** high	**D** strong
15 A gain	**B** enhance	**C** foster	**D** increase

Language development
Reporting structures
▶ CB page 141, GR page 185

Review of reported speech

Tenses in reported speech

1 **Write up the minutes of a meeting held last week, using the reporting verbs given in brackets for each sentence.**
   1 John: 'Sales have increased by 20 per cent.' (*report*)
   2 Dave: 'The new campaign starts in three days' time.' (*announce*)
   3 Adam: 'We're getting a lot of positive feedback from consumers.' (*tell*)
   4 Jenny: 'I met the clients yesterday and I'm sure they don't have any worries.' (*say*)
   5 Adam: 'I haven't seen the new posters yet.' (*confess*)
   6 Dave: 'Unfortunately I don't have them with me, but I'll get everyone a copy tomorrow.' (*admit / promise*)
   7 Jenny: 'Well, guys, keep up the good work. I'll see you all here again this time next week.' (*encourage / remind*)

   1 John reported that ....
   2 ....
   3 ....
   4 ....
   5 ....
   6 ....
   7 ....

Reporting questions

2 **Report the following questions you were asked at a job interview.**
   1 Where have you worked before?
   2 Why do you want to work for this company?
   3 Have you ever worked in marketing before?
   4 What is your favourite advertising slogan?
   5 Are you a good communicator?
   6 Where do you think you will be in ten years' time?
   7 Do you work better on your own or as part of a team?
   8 What did you least like about your old job?
   9 What impression did you have when you came in here this morning?
   10 Can you start next Monday?

   The interviewer asked me:
   1 where ....
   2 ....
   3 ....
   4 ....
   5 ....
   6 ....
   7 ....
   8 ....
   9 ....
   10 ....

Reporting modal verbs

3 **Put the following into reported speech.**
   1 'I might not be here tomorrow,' explained Harvey.
   Harvey explained that ....
   ....
   2 'I shouldn't have said what I did,' said Amanda.
   Amanda said ....
   ....
   3 'We can get it for you by next Tuesday,' promised the shop assistant.
   The shop assistant promised that ....
   ....
   4 'I can help if you need a hand,' said my neighbour.
   My neighbour said ....
   ....
   5 'You don't need to do any more; you've done enough,' I told the class.
   I told the class ....
   ....
   6 'I shan't be here next week. I'll be on holiday,' explained the teacher.
   The teacher explained that ....
   ....
   7 'Shall I put the lights on? It's getting dark,' asked Rachel.
   Rachel asked ....
   ....
   8 'I must admit; it's a great film,' said the critic.
   The critic admitted that ....
   ....

Patterns after reporting verbs

4 Underline the correct option. Only one option is possible.

1 They recommended .... the train.
   A that I took   B to take   C me to take
2 He offered .... a lift home in his car.
   A that he would give me   B to give me
   C giving me
3 They reassured .... home safely.
   A me to get   B me that I would get
   C me in getting
4 They expected .... home before six.
   A me to get   B getting   C that I get
5 She accused me .... dangerously.
   A to drive   B that I drive   C of driving
6 I admitted .... over the speed limit.
   A to go   B going   C it to go
7 The police warned .... it again.
   A me not to do   B me don't do   C that I didn't do
8 I reassured .... go fast again.
   A that I wouldn't   B them not to
   C them that I wouldn't

5 Rewrite the following sentences, using one of the reporting verbs in the list. Report the meaning of the sentence, not the actual words. Think about which of the patterns above to use.

~~advised~~ beg blame deny promise refuse
remind suggest thank (for)

1 My classmate: 'If I were you, I'd ask him to speak more slowly.'
   My classmate _advised me_
2 Dad: 'Don't worry, I will get a film on the way home.'
   ....
3 My colleague: 'There's no way I'm helping you tonight.'
   ....
4 My brother: 'I didn't read your private diary, honest.'
   ....
5 My secretary: 'Don't forget that you've got an appointment at 4 p.m.'
   ....
6 Anne's friend: 'Please, please tell me where you got that shirt.'
   ....

7 The driver: 'It was very kind of you to help me change the wheel.'
   ....
8 Julie: 'It was Gerald's fault that we got lost.'
   ....

Impersonal report structures

6 Rewrite the news story using impersonal report structures. If two forms are possible, write both.

1 Everyone knows that fake CDs are widely available.
   Fake CDs ....
   It is ....
2 A police spokesperson has announced that they have made a major arrest.
   It ....
3 Reports say that 100,000 CDs were confiscated.
   It ....
   100,000 CDs ....
4 The police believe the fake CDs were made abroad.
   It ....
   The fake CDs ....
5 They think that the CDs were smuggled into the country in boats.
   It ....
   The CDs ....
6 They suspect that the man arrested is the ringleader of an international gang.
   The man arrested ....
7 Reputedly, he has made millions of dollars from crime.
   He is ....
   It ....
8 There are rumours that he has homes on five continents.
   He ....
   It ....
9 Some people have suggested that fewer people would buy fake CDs if genuine ones were not so expensive.
   It ....
   ....
10 Some say that the industry is looking at new ways to prevent illegal copying.
   The industry ....
   ....

English in Use
Gapped text (Paper 3 Part 6)

▶ ER page 170

1 a Read the title of the text to identify the topic. In what ways might languages be threatened? Make a list of the reasons why a language might die out.

  b Read the text quickly, ignoring the gaps for the moment, to find out which of the things on your list are mentioned in the article.

2 Now read the text again and do the task, using the Help clues when necessary. Remember to read the sentence before and after the gap for clues in the grammar to choose the correct phrase. There are three phrases that do not fit into the text at all.

3 When you've finished, read through the whole text again to make sure it makes sense.

HELP
➤ Question 1
  The option that fills this gap begins with a verb form.
➤ Question 2
  Think about the use of the article before the gap – what structure are you looking for in the option?

Language development
Read the text again and find three reporting verbs, one of which is a phrasal verb. Look at the tense that is used after all these verbs. Why is this tense used?

For questions **1–6**, read the text and then choose from the list **A–I** given below the best phrase to fill each of the spaces. Each correct phrase may only be used once. **Some of the suggested answers do not fit at all.**

Travels among threatened languages

Mark Abley, an energetic Canadian journalist, went all over the world in search of places where dying or threatened languages were still being spoken. There were certainly plenty to choose from; of the 5,000 or so languages in use at the end of the last century, half of them **(1)**........ . In his book entitled *Spoken Here: Travels among Threatened Languages*, Abley asks how a minority language can compete against the invasion of globalisation and the universal world of pop, available at the turn of a switch. He also points out that where such a language does survive, it is often peppered with scraps of English.

The book contains many examples of the rich diversity **(2)**........ . The Australian Aboriginal language Mati Ke has 30 classes of noun, we are told; another, Murrinh Patha, has 35 distinct classes of verb as well as 31 different pronouns, **(3)**........ . But Abley insists that it is not their complexity that has doomed so many primitive languages; it's just that not enough people think in that particular way any more – or rather that they have been cajoled or bullied into thinking like the people **(4)**........ .

Although a travel writer rather than a linguist by trade, Abley's investigative stamina is tremendous **(5)**........ . He has read the philological experts and gone to immense lengths to meet the speakers and attend their pressure-group meetings; his text is spattered with transcriptions of native words in languages that no one had written down **(6)**........ .

A until the linguists came along
B each with its own particular nuance
C where these were translated for him
D will probably have disappeared by the end of this
E and those who still speak them
F that exists amongst the world's languages
G will find it hard to survive this
H whose culture has overwhelmed them
I whatever lead is being followed up

Listening

Multiple-choice questions (Paper 4 Part 3)

▶ ER pages 170–171

1 Read the instructions for the exam task. Then read the multiple-choice questions and highlight the most important ideas in the question and options. This has been done for you in question 1.

2 ⌒ Listen to the whole recording once, and try to answer the questions. Use the Help clues if necessary. Then listen again to check and complete your answers.

HELP

➤ **Question 1**

Jessica's answer comes after she mentions her mother meeting her from school. What is the multiword verb that means *to embarrass someone*? You will hear this in the part of the text which gives you the answer.

➤ **Question 2**

Listen carefully to how Jessica's mother reacted after she went to university, then you will hear the answer to this question.

➤ **Question 3**

Listen to the whole of Jessica's answer to the interviewer's question. You will hear a phrasal verb that means *to survive on very little money*. This will help you to choose the correct answer.

3 a Complete the sentences with the correct verb from the list in the appropriate form.

attract   catch   make   take

1 I didn't have much money, so was always struggling to .... ends meet.
2 I had a go at modelling, and decided to .... it up professionally.
3 When I was a child, modelling didn't .... my imagination.
4 Her clothes always .... a lot of attention.

b Match the phrases in Exercise 3a to their definitions.

a to make someone feel excited and interested
b to make people take notice
c to have just enough money to buy what you need
d to become interested in an activity and spend time doing it

You will hear an interview with the fashion model Jessica Hanson, who is talking about her upbringing and career. For questions **1–6** choose the best answer **A**, **B**, **C**, or **D**. **You will hear the recording twice.**

1 Jessica says that when she was a child, she
  A found her mother's behaviour embarrassing.
  B was envious of her sister's sense of humour.
  C was fascinated by the glamorous world of fashion.
  D felt most at ease with people of her own age group.

2 Looking back at her schooldays, Jessica feels that her mother
  A expected far too much of her.
  B often caused family arguments.
  C sometimes criticised her unfairly.
  D showed little interest in her achievements.

3 Why did Jessica first take up modelling as a student?
  A It provided her with an additional source of income.
  B She was unable to cope with her university course.
  C It was a result of her mother's contacts in fashion.
  D She wanted to prove something to her parents.

4 In bringing up her own children, Jessica aims to
  A be completely honest with them.
  B teach them to communicate easily.
  C encourage them to be independent.
  D steer them towards worthwhile careers.

5 When asked about her decision to write a novel, Jessica says that she
  A intends to draw inspiration from her own close relationships.
  B suspects the commercial motives of her publisher.
  C is adapting an idea from an earlier short story.
  D is grateful for the support from her friends.

6 How does Jessica feel about her future career?
  A She's determined to make her children her first priority.
  B She's unsure whether she wants to remain in the public eye.
  C She's confident that her writing will bring financial security.
  D She's keen to maintain her contacts with the world of fashion.

B Making a statement

Vocabulary
Clothing and fashion
▶ CB page 143

1 a All of the words below can be used as nouns. Decide whether each word is countable or uncountable, and whether each is formal, neutral or informal. Use a dictionary to help you if necessary.

*cloth   clothes   clothing   dress/attire   garment
kit   outfit   wardrobe   wear*

b Use a suitable word from Exercise 1a in the correct form to complete the sentences.
   1 I'm going to need a complete new summer .... to take on holiday.
   2 The wedding dress was made from the finest silk ....
   3 Only two .... may be taken in the fitting room at any one time.
   4 After getting caught in the rain, their .... were soaked and they had to change.
   5 There was nothing in the suitcase except a few items of ....
   6 I chucked my sports .... into a bag and took it to work so I could go running at lunchtime.
   7 My parents own a shop that specialises in leisure ....
   8 It was an amazing formal party with all the men in evening ....
   9 I spent a fortune on a new .... for the office party.

2 Complete the text with the words in the list. Use a dictionary to check if necessary.

brand   design   label   logo   pattern   style

Marketing clothes and accessories can be a difficult business. Customers want comfort and quality but are also buying a certain **(1)**..................... . An item bearing a designer **(2)**..................... can cost many times the equivalent item from a High Street shop, even if it is a classic **(3)**..................... such as a basic white T-shirt. Some companies, such as jeans manufacturers, generate strong **(4)**..................... loyalty so customers keep coming back to buy more. Some companies like Gap promote their product by producing many items bearing their **(5)**..................... in a prominent position. Other companies use an instantly recognisable **(6)**..................... , such as Burberry's distinctive black and brown check, on a wide range of items.

3 a Use the table to make phrasal verbs connected to clothes and match them to the definitions below. Use a dictionary to help you if necessary.

dress	grow	up	into
take	slip	down	out of
let	wrap	in	on
change	do/zip	out	off

   1 make clothes larger/smaller
   2 make clothes longer/shorter
   3 wear very smart/casual clothes on a particular occasion
   4 replace one set of clothes with another
   5 put on warm clothes
   6 put on/take off clothes quickly and easily
   7 fasten clothes
   8 become too big / big enough for some clothes

b Complete the sentences with the phrasal verbs above.
   1 When I get home, the first thing I do is .... my work clothes and .... something more comfortable.
   2 It's a casual party, so you don't have to ....
   3 When I .... my clothes, I passed them on to my younger brother.
   4 It's very cold, so .... well when you go out.
   5 He .... a pair of shoes and left the house.
   6 Since I've put on weight, I've had to .... my trousers by a couple of centimetres.
   7 If the trousers are too long, you can always .... them ....
   8 .... your coat .... , or you'll get cold.

4 Choose the correct word to complete the underlined phrases.
   1 Whenever a new fashion comes *in / on / over*, you can be sure that Diane will be wearing it.
   2 When I bought these shoes, they were the *peak / top / height* of fashion, but I'd never wear them now.
   3 Long skirts seem to come in and out of *style / mode / trend* every few years.
   4 I never imagined the fashion for tattoos would *take / catch / get* on the way it did.
   5 I'm keeping my old flared trousers until the next time they make a *return / comeback / reprise*.
   6 His i-pod is as much a fashion *statement / comment / announcement* as a music player.
   7 I tend to avoid designer clothes as I don't want to end up looking like a fashion *casualty / victim / sufferer*.

Language development
Word formation
▶ CB page 147

For each word, complete the table. Use a dictionary if necessary. Then choose the correct form of the word to complete the sentences below.

1 desire

noun [C/U]	
verb [T]	
adjective (*describing something worth having*)	
negative adjective	
adverb (from adjective)	
noun [U] (from adjective)	
negative noun [C] (*somebody/something that isn't wanted*)	
adjective (from past participle)	

1 It is highly .... that we keep information about new products a secret.
2 Unfortunately the marketing campaign produced some .... side effects.
3 The shop is very exclusive and has strict security to keep out .... like me!
4 The advertising campaign had the .... effect of increasing sales by 20%.
5 The .... of many products depends as much on fashion as it does on appearance or functionality.

2 origin

noun [C]	
plural noun	
adjective	
negative adjective	
adverb	
verb [I, T]	
noun [C] (thing or person)	
noun [U] (from adjective)	

1 All products should be clearly marked with their country of ....
2 We need people who can come up with .... ideas.
3 A lot of their designs are rather dull and ....
4 I kept a copy of the letter and returned the ....
5 KitKat's slogan was .... used in the 1950s.
6 The company director likes to keep quiet about his humble ....

7 The products are well made, but lack ....
8 The Internet .... from an idea to connect universities.

3 secure

adjective	
negative adjective	
adverb	
negative adverb	
noun [U]	
negative noun [C, U]	
verb [T]	

1 For reasons of .... , we cannot say who is staying in the hotel.
2 With no one to chat to, Jenny felt lonely and .... when she first went off to university.
3 By sending messages in code, companies can communicate .... over the Internet.
4 Make sure you .... all the doors and windows before you leave.
5 Negotiators are still speaking to the kidnappers, trying to .... the release of the hostages.
6 Dan's deepest fears and .... stem from his having been abandoned as a child.
7 It is important to make sure you have a .... connection when shopping on the Internet.
8 The rope was .... fastened, and came loose.

4 popular

adjective	
negative adjective	
noun [U]	
negative noun [U]	
adverb	
verb [T]	
noun [U] (from verb)	

1 The most .... drink in the world is probably tea.
2 The company's .... has declined a great deal in the last ten years.
3 American comedy shows did a lot to .... coffee shops in the 1990s.
4 We stopped making the product because it was so .... with consumers.
5 The tax increases have added to the government's ....
6 In Britain, ball-point pens are .... known as biros, after their inventor.
7 TV programmes have tried to encourage the .... of science and technology.

English in Use
Error correction (spelling and punctuation)
(Paper 3 Part 3) ▶ ER page 169

1 Read the title of the text to identify the topic, then read the whole text quickly for general understanding, ignoring the errors for the moment. Which things most affect comsumers' decisions to buy a particular product?
   a) the price   b) free gifts   c) special offers   d) the packaging

2 Read the text again, sentence by sentence, and complete the task. Use the Help clues if necessary.

3 When you've finished, read the whole text again to check it makes complete sense.

HELP
➤ Question 1
  A punctuation mark is missing in this line.
➤ Question 3
  Check the spelling of the words in this line.
➤ Questions 10–15
  One of these lines is correct. Do you know which one?

In **most** lines of the following text, there is **either** a spelling **or** a punctuation error. For each numbered line (**1–16**), write the correctly spelt word or show the correct punctuation in the box. **Some** lines are correct. Indicate these lines with a tick (✓) in the box. The exercise begins with three examples (**0**), (**00**) and (**000**).

Special offers you can't refuse

The free gifts, competitions and offers on packaged goods at	0	✓
supermarkets are desinged to make the product stand out. On	00	designed
an average family shopping trip in britain, you could come	000	Britain
home with a variety of gifts, such as a free toy, a bestselling	1	
novel or even the chance to win a holiday or a new house.	2	
Clearly it's a marketting strategy that works, or companies	3	
wouldn't do it. Whats more, for a large number of consumers	4	
the decision about which brand to buy is clearly influenced by	5	
the promise of a free gift or the offer on a Product's packaging.	6	
Over 70% of British familys with children visit a supermarket	7	
each week, and over 70% of their buying, decisions are made	8	
on the spur of the moment. 'If you take breakfast cereals targeted	9	
at children as an example, most manufacturers in that secter are	10	
driven by the fact that people won't buy without a premium,	11	
says an expert from the institute of Sales Promotion (ISP). One	12	
couple getting married in London last year took this behavour	13	
to an extreme degre. Heinz, the food manufacturer, was running	14	
a 'win a free house' promotion, so the pair asked all guests at	15	
the wedding for tin's of food instead of conventional presents.	16	

Language development
Read through the text again and find all the nouns ending in -y.
Which ones have a plural in -ies, and which have a plural in -ys?

Reading

Gapped text (Paper 1 Part 2)

▶ ER page 168

1 Read the heading and subheading of the text, to identify the topic. Then read the base text quickly, ignoring the gaps for the moment, and find out who the people (a–c) are, and what the numbers (d–f) refer to.

a) Hamish Pringle
b) David Graham
c) Michael Winner
d) 100
e) 200,000
f) 150

2 Look at question 1 and read the first two paragraphs of the base text again. Use the highlighted words and phrases to help you choose which option **A–G** fits the gap.

3 Read the options **A–G** and underline words and phrases that might help you to match them to the text. Then complete the task.

4 When you have finished the task, read the whole text through to check it makes complete sense.

5 a Match the words in list A to those in list B to form collocations used in the text.

A	B
1 advertising	a broker
2 crunching	b endorsement
3 financial	c order
4 insurance	d campaign
5 pecking	e adviser
6 product	f numbers

b Choose the phrase below which best matches the meaning of each collocation in Exercise 5a.

a a way of ranking people according to importance
b a personal assurance that a product is good
c advertisements and other activities to persuade people to buy something
d doing a lot of calculations
e someone who advises people about how to save and invest money
f someone who sells insurance to people

For questions **1–6**, you must choose which of the paragraphs **A–G** fit into the numbered gaps in the following magazine article. There is one extra paragraph which does not fit in any of the gaps.

In celebrities we trust

Britain's obsession with celebrities means that people there are more likely to trust a soap star endorsing goods in advertisements than a qualified expert. Nick Higham asks why.

Celebrity sells. We all know that: it's one of the oldest clichés in advertising. But why? And why do some celebrities apparently sell more effectively than others? On April 5, the Institute of Practitioners in Advertising (IPA) is holding a
5 half-day seminar on the subject. It'll cost £100 to attend, but delegates will get a free copy of a new book, *Celebrity Sells* by IPA Director General Hamish Pringle. Who says advertising agencies don't understand sales promotion?

1

Of course, the effectiveness or otherwise of an advertising
10 campaign is dictated by more than the shrewdness of the casting. The copywriting, the media planning, the amount spent and the aptness with which the advertisements themselves reflect the existing strategy for a brand are all significant factors. So eliminating all the other variables and
15 isolating the effects of a well-known name and face is not easy.

2

And here another expert thinks he may be on to something. David Graham has been crunching numbers and consulting strategically in the television industry for about 15 years. He's an expert in the analysis of television audience data, on the impact of broadcasting regulation and on the dynamics of the TV business.

3

According to Graham, academic evolutionary psychologists believe we may be genetically programmed to behave in certain ways – a belief they have come to partly by observing that certain parts of the brain are always associated with certain skills or behaviours. There may, for instance, be what Graham calls a 'gossip instinct'. It was a useful thing to have 200,000 years ago, when mankind lived in foraging bands of 150 or so and the modern human brain evolved.

4

This innate ability helps to explain why we pay extra attention to someone we recognise as a star in a TV advertisement or a poster – even though, rationally we would be better off paying attention to an expert. A financial adviser or insurance broker is likely to know more about insurance policies than the film director Michael Winner. But Winner is a celebrity, he draws our attention, and so an insurance company is willing to pay him a lot more than they would a financial expert to feature in its advertising. What intrigues Graham is the possibility of finding practical applications for this kind of theoretical work that go beyond the simple observation that celebrities attract attention.

5

But in due course, the same theoretical framework could obviously be applied to advertising as well. Graham rejects the suggestion that he's just trying to quantify the unquantifiable, or that a possible consequence of this work would be programmes and advertisements that were boringly similar. 'The comforting thing is that people do have an appetite for variety,' he says. 'That speaks against formulaic solutions and repeating oneself.'

6

The analogy here is with our taste for sweet and fattening treats. That developed when we were hunter-gatherers, and fruits and fats were in short supply: we have been programmed to stuff ourselves with sugars and fats whenever we find them. Our circumstances have changed, but our genetic make-up hasn't. Obesity is the result. Perhaps our gossip gene, which also evolved in circumstances rather different from modern society, may be equally damaging.

A But there is one potentially awkward implication in all this. It might strengthen the hand of those who maintain that light entertainment and soap operas are 'fast food for the brain', and that our predilection for them may be harmful.

B Nonetheless, if we all agree that celebrity does sell, one question immediately presents itself. Why? And a second follows. If we can work out why it sells, can we bottle it?

C Yet on television, the gossip about what is happening to the soap-opera families attracts millions more viewers than news documentaries on subjects which actually affect people's lives. And the irony of this is not lost on advertising executives when they're searching for a famous face to endorse a product.

D According to newspaper reports, the author believes the most successful celebrity ever to have appeared in a British advertising campaign is the actress Prunella Scales, whose advertisements for the Tesco supermarket chain have helped generate an additional £2.2bn in sales in the country since 1998.

E He proposes, if he can find partners or clients willing to sponsor a study, to start with soap operas, looking at those moments which produced the highest audiences, and which hold audiences for the longest periods, and seeing what elements they have in common and whether they connect up with the theory of evolutionary psychology.

F To be successful in such a social grouping requires a complex mix of co-operation and competition. It helps to know quite a bit about your fellow group members, especially those of high status in the pecking order. So, successful humans are those who are curious about friends, relatives, colleagues and anyone perceived to have high status – including, in the modern world, 'stars'.

G He thinks a partial answer to the puzzle of why celebrities sell – and also to why some TV programmes work better than others – may lie in the discipline of evolutionary psychology and the associated fields of neuroscience and genetics.

Writing Proposal (Paper 2, Part 1)

▶ CB pages 148–149, WR page 198

Exam strategy

One of the things your written work is assessed on is accuracy. When you check your work, think about the kind of errors you usually make, as you may not see these easily. Always remember to check grammar, spelling, punctuation and formality.

1 a Read the task on page 148 of the Coursebook again. Then read a student's answer on the right.

 b Find and correct four grammatical errors. Check:
 - verb tenses
 - subject/verb agreement
 - reference words
 - articles.

 c Find and correct four spelling mistakes.

 d Find and correct four punctuation errors.

 e The underlined words are either too informal for a proposal, or have been lifted from the input texts. Replace them with suitable words or phrases.

2 Now write your own answer to one of the tasks below. Remember that, in a report, the focus is on an existing situation, but in a proposal there is more emphasis on suggestions for the future. Remember to check your work for errors.

A

You are a member of the Board of Directors of an Adventure Centre. Your Managing Director wants to change the way the Centre organises its publicity, and has asked you to write a proposal suggesting ways in which the publicity could be improved.
Write your **proposal** in approximately 250 words.

B

You are a member of the Board of Directors of an Adventure Centre. You have received complaints from customers unable to find out detailed information about the Centre. You have been asked to write a report explaining why the publicity is not satisfactory and recommending changes.
Write your **report** in approximately 250 words.

Proposal suggesting ways of raising the profile of the Adventure Centre to increase bookings

Introduction

The aim of this proposal are to suggest ways of promoting the Adventure Centre to increase bookings, and make recommendations for action it is based on information gatherd from customer feedback and feedback from colleagues.

Results of feedback

It is clear from customer feedback that the Centre is generaly popular with those who come, but there is a problem with general publicity. Some said that they have not heard of the Centre until a friend told them about them, and others complained that they could not find the website. This last point was backed up by comments from staff.

Suggestions and recommendations

In order to deal with the problems identefied in the feedback and to increase bookings; we recommend the following measures.

1 To address the problem of publicity:

 - journalists should be invited to special Open Days so that features on the Centre can be run in the press.

 - brochures and eye-catching posters should be designed for display in Tourist Information Centres.

 - a specialist should be taken on to redesign the website, to make it faster, user-friendly and more accesible to Internet browsers.

 - the promotional Budget should be increased to pay for these measures.

2 To attract more bookings:

 - introduce a series of special offer's, including offering reduced prices in the low season, and special packages for school parties.

Conclusion

Implementing the measures above should lead to the general increase in awareness of the Centre and a subsequent increase in bookings. If the Centre is to do well, we urge the Directors to put them in place immediately.

A You have to laugh

English in Use
Word formation (Paper 3 Part 4)
▶ CB page 154, ER page 170

1 Read the title of the first text to identify the topic. Then read the first text through quickly, ignoring the gaps for the moment.

2 Read the text again carefully and fill in the gaps, using the Help clues if necessary.

3 Read through the text again when you've finished to check.

4 Repeat the procedure for the second text.

HELP
➤ Question 7
This word requires both a prefix and a suffix – be careful with the spelling.

➤ Question 9
You need to add two suffixes to this noun. The first makes it into an adjective and the second changes that into an adverb.

➤ Questions 10–15
One of these items requires a negative prefix. Read the surrounding text very carefully to be sure.

Language development
How many other words can you form from the word *necessary*? Write them down and check their meanings in a dictionary.

For questions **1–15**, read the texts below. Use the words in the boxes to the right of the texts to form **one** word that fits in the same numbered space in the text. The exercise begins with an example **(0)**.

EXCERPT FROM A MAGAZINE ARTICLE

Being a comedian
In theory, being a stage **(0)** *comedian* shouldn't be a hard occupation. All you need is an **(1)**.................... idea, a funny face, a way with words and enough self **(2)**.................... to stand up in front of an audience and make them laugh. Laughter, we are told, is a tonic that **(3)**.................... can extend your lifespan, so **(4)**.................... is it to the health. The explanation for why we enjoy laughter so much is that it releases things called endorphins in the body, and this gives us a physical high. So it's not just an **(5)**.................... , we really do feel better. Perhaps that explains why almost everyone makes use of laughter as a social lubricant, and why laughter is so **(6)**.................... , spreading from person to person. Indeed, once a group of people is in the mood, even the most awful joke can prompt **(7)**.................... hilarity, as all good comedians know.

(0)	**COMEDY**
(1)	AMUSE
(2)	BELIEVE
(3)	APPEAR
(4)	BENEFIT
(5)	IMPRESS
(6)	INFECT
(7)	CONTROL

REVIEW OF A RADIO PROGRAMME

Laugh out loud (Radio 4: 8.30 p.m.)
When Nicola Green went out with her tape recorder and started laughing in public places, initially people were a little **(8)**.................... . But as she demonstrates rather **(9)**.................... on this short radio **(10)**.................... , once one person starts laughing, it's not long before everybody joins in – it seems to be an **(11)**.................... response. Analysing humour is a **(12)**.................... business, and Green wisely doesn't attempt this, concentrating instead on what makes people laugh, which is not **(13)**.................... the same thing. Children, of course, will laugh at almost anything, just a funny noise will do the trick, and Green's only slightly **(14)**.................... conclusion is that we probably laugh less as we get older. This is probably because we feel **(15)**.................... , vulnerable even, if we really give way to laughter, and this feels less comfortable with increasing age and responsibility.

(8)	SUSPICION
(9)	CHARM
(10)	DOCUMENT
(11)	AVOID
(12)	PAIN
(13)	NECESSARY
(14)	DEPRESS
(15)	HELP

Language development
Participle clauses
▶ CB page 156, GR page 186

-ing clauses

1 Rewrite these sentences using finite clauses and expressions from the list. Make any changes necessary.
and   and as a result   because   just as   when

1 I kept calling the box office, trying to get tickets.

....

2 Having bought my popcorn, I settled down to enjoy the film.

....

3 We stood at the back of the concert hall, trying to see what was happening.

....

4 On arriving at the theatre, I realised that I had left the tickets behind.

....

5 The lights went out, leaving the audience in total darkness.

....

2 Rewrite the following sentences using present participle *-ing* clauses.

1 Because she is growing up in Los Angeles, she dreams of becoming an actress.

....

2 Brad has had a busy year, as he has starred in three films.

....

3 I live in London, so it's easy for me to get to the theatre.

....

4 As I read the review, I realised that I had seen the film before.

....

5 He held a top hat in one hand and a cane in the other and performed an amazing tap-dance routine.

....

6 He couldn't swim, so he had to rely on other actors to do all his swimming stunts for him.

....

3 Rewrite these sentences using either present or perfect participle clauses and a conjunction where necessary.

1 Because she was an art lover, she was very keen to go and see the exhibition.

....

2 After we had packed the car up, we set off.

....

3 Because I had never been to Italy before, I was feeling slightly nervous.

....

4 Although I was pleased to be in New York, I missed my old friends.

....

5 I put the phone down, grabbed my suitcase and ran.

....

6 I hadn't performed on the stage before, so I didn't know what to expect.

....

Past participle clauses

4 Rewrite these sentences using finite clauses and one of the words from the list.
because   if   once

1 The cast chosen, they could start the rehearsals.

....

2 Booked solid for weeks, the show is hard to get into.

....

3 Carefully edited, the chase scenes look spectacular.

....

5 Rewrite these sentences using past participle clauses. Make any changes necessary.

1 I was bored so I fell asleep in the second act.

....

2 If Claudia is given the right coaching, she could be a great soprano one day.

....

3 The show has been rated by the critics as a 'must see' show, so it should be pretty good.

....

4 The set had been poorly constructed and was starting to collapse.

....

5 Had the show been better publicised, it would have been more successful.

....

6 Once the show had been properly advertised, it started to do better.

....

to-infinitive clauses

6 Rewrite these sentences using finite clauses and one of the words or expressions from the list.

and then   and as a result   if   so that

1 I bought a programme to see who else was in the show.

....

2 I sat down and started watching, only to realise I had seen the film before.

....

3 I've seen the Rocky Horror Show enough times to have learnt most of the words.

....

4 To hear her sing, you'd never believe she was totally untrained.

....

7 Rewrite these sentences using *to*-infinitive clauses.

1 We got seats at the front so we would have a better view.

....

2 They sold enough tickets that the production was a financial success.

....

3 If you heard her talk, you'd think she was a great actress herself.

....

4 We arrived at the theatre and discovered that the lead actor was sick.

....

5 I had had plenty of rehearsals and was therefore confident in the role.

....

6 If a new musical is going to be successful, it needs to have at least three great tunes.

....

All participle clauses

8 Correct the mistakes in the following sentences.

1 The plan was for the show transferred to Broadway after a few months in London.

2 The children jumped up, to shout, 'He's behind you!' when the villain appeared.

3 Not to have a ticket, I couldn't get into the concert.

4 Unsuccessfully, I searched the Internet finding the soundtrack.

5 I enjoyed the show, laughed all the way through.

6 Julie was the first person playing the role in the theatre.

7 Walking on stage, the audience greeted the singer with a loud cheer.

8 I'm very disappointed not have seen Elvis perform live.

9 She walked on stage, only realising she had forgotten her words.

10 Rising to their feet, the soloist bowed to the ecstatic audience.

9 Read the text and put the verbs in brackets into the *-ing* or *to*-infinitive form.

The old Theatre Royal had stood empty for many years, **(1)**........................ (*close down*) in the 1980s. But Simon Appleton, **(2)**........................ (*be*) a theatre lover and keen amateur actor, was determined to get it reopened. **(3)**........................ (*persuade*) a bank to lend him money for his scheme, he took on a team of skilled builders **(4)**........................ (*renovate*) the old building and **(5)**........................ (*restore*) it to its former glory. **(6)**........................ (*help*) by a team of willing volunteers, the builders completed the work within a year, and the theatre reopened under Simon's management.

Now, it is a thriving local theatre again, **(7)**........................ (*welcome*) touring theatre and dance companies from all over the world. The theatre also encourages amateur groups, regularly **(8)**........................ (*stage*) performances by local schools and amateur dramatics groups.

English in Use

Register transfer (Paper 3 Part 5)

▶ ER page 170

Complete the task. Remember to:

- use no more than two words in each gap
- think carefully about the words before and after the gap; the correct answer must fit grammatically
- read the text through when you have finished to make sure your answers fit in grammatically and the text makes complete sense.

> **Language development**
>
> Read the texts again. How many participle clauses can you find? Highlight them.

For questions **1–13**, read the magazine article. Use the information to complete the numbered gaps in the informal letter. The words you need **do not occur** in the magazine article. **Use no more than two words for each gap.** The exercise begins with an example (**0**).

MAGAZINE FEATURE

Wildrington Jazz Festival

The annual festival takes place on the 15th–16th July at Wildrington Hall. A wide variety of hands-on musical events are planned, in addition to the excellent Sunday-night concert.

Musical workshops

During the day, participants can enrol on workshops and try their hand at playing instruments like the trombone and saxophone. Workshops are very popular, led by professional musicians who give demonstrations, and encourage participants to create their own music.

Places are limited, so advance reservations are essential. For full details, phone 05667 892455.

Jazz concert

The festival continues for the whole weekend, culminating in the Sunday-night concert, with an opportunity to see Benny Dixon and other top names performing. Held in the park, the outdoor concert goes on well into the night (blankets highly recommended!) and is a very relaxed event. There are no numbered seats, but there's plenty of space on the grass, and picnics are the order of the day.

INFORMAL LETTER

Dear Matthew,

How about going to the Jazz Festival at Wildrington Hall? It's held (**0**) in July , and there's all (**1**)............................ things to do (**2**)............................ as a brilliant concert on Sunday night. Before that, you can sign (**3**)............................ workshops where you get to have a (**4**)............................ playing instruments such as the saxophone or trombone. There are full-time musicians in (**5**)............................ the workshops, who will (**6**)............................ us how the instrument should be played, and then try and get (**7**)............................ music of our own. But we had (**8**)............................ book early to be sure of getting places (there's a number to phone).

The high (**9**)............................ of the weekend is the concert – we can't miss (**10**)............................ to hear Benny Dixon playing live! It's an (**11**)............................ concert that apparently goes on all night (they tell you to take blankets!). It sounds like a very (**12**)............................-back affair – you sit on the grass, and you're (**13**)............................ to take a picnic!

Should be fun

Melanie

Listening
Note completion (Paper 4 Part 2)

▶ ER pages 170–171

1 Read the instructions for the exam task below. Then read the notes and think about the topic. What do you expect to hear? Can you predict the type of information you will be listening for in each item?

2 ⋒Listen to the recording once, and complete the notes. Use the Help clues if necessary.

HELP
➤ Question 1
   Listen for the first number you hear in the recording.
➤ Question 2
   You hear the name of her job twice.

3 Complete the sentences below using a word from the list in the correct form.
character   musical   record
release   screen   soundtrack

1 A .... is a film which contains singing.
2 Actors and actresses have to play many different types of ....
3 The actresses you see on .... are not actually singing the songs that you hear.
4 Asha Bhosle has .... songs in various languages.
5 Asha's new CD has just been ....
6 When you watch a film, you listen to the ....

You will hear a radio talk about a woman called Asha Bhosle, who is a big star in the world of Indian cinema. For questions **1–8**, complete the notes. **Listen very carefully as you will hear the recording ONCE only.**

ASHA BHOSLE

Number of songs she has recorded:

over [_____] **1**

Her job title in the film industry: [_____] **2**

Type of films found in India until 1931: [_____] **3**

Number of languages spoken in India:

approximately [_____] **4**

What made Asha such a big name:

– [_____] **5** *of her voice*

– *the* [_____] **6** *nature of some of her roles*

Asha's latest business venture:

a group of [_____] **7**

Asha's new CD: – *she helped choose the tracks*

– *has* [_____] **8**

and pictures to help European listeners

Vocabulary Music ▶ CB pages 160–161

Answer the following questions by choosing **A**, **B**, **C** or **D**. Look up any words that you do not know in a dictionary.

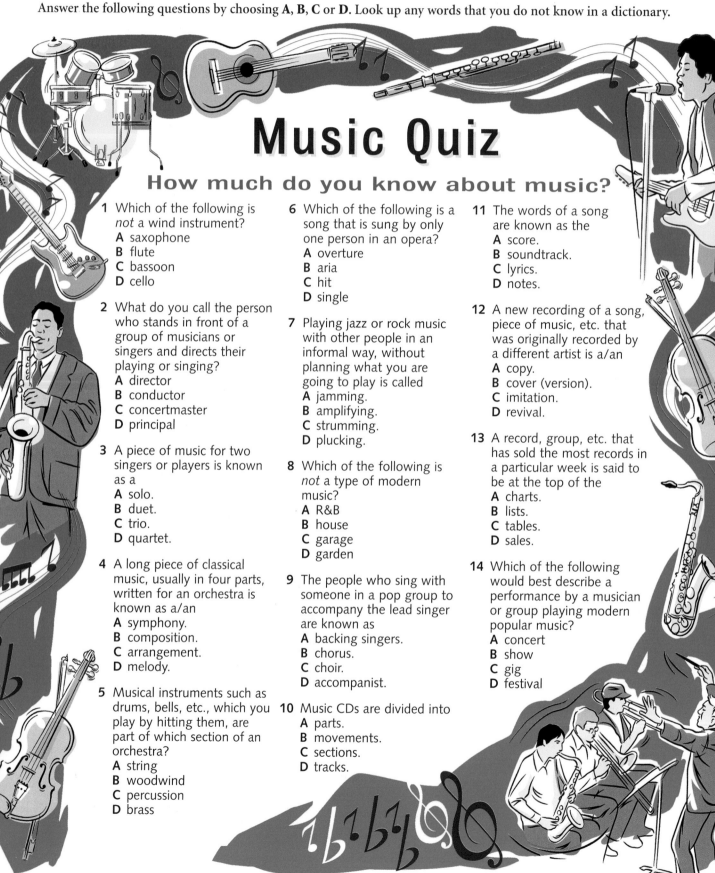

Music Quiz

How much do you know about music?

1 Which of the following is *not* a wind instrument?
A saxophone
B flute
C bassoon
D cello

2 What do you call the person who stands in front of a group of musicians or singers and directs their playing or singing?
A director
B conductor
C concertmaster
D principal

3 A piece of music for two singers or players is known as a
A solo.
B duet.
C trio.
D quartet.

4 A long piece of classical music, usually in four parts, written for an orchestra is known as a/an
A symphony.
B composition.
C arrangement.
D melody.

5 Musical instruments such as drums, bells, etc., which you play by hitting them, are part of which section of an orchestra?
A string
B woodwind
C percussion
D brass

6 Which of the following is a song that is sung by only one person in an opera?
A overture
B aria
C hit
D single

7 Playing jazz or rock music with other people in an informal way, without planning what you are going to play is called
A jamming.
B amplifying.
C strumming.
D plucking.

8 Which of the following is *not* a type of modern music?
A R&B
B house
C garage
D garden

9 The people who sing with someone in a pop group to accompany the lead singer are known as
A backing singers.
B chorus.
C choir.
D accompanist.

10 Music CDs are divided into
A parts.
B movements.
C sections.
D tracks.

11 The words of a song are known as the
A score.
B soundtrack.
C lyrics.
D notes.

12 A new recording of a song, piece of music, etc. that was originally recorded by a different artist is a/an
A copy.
B cover (version).
C imitation.
D revival.

13 A record, group, etc. that has sold the most records in a particular week is said to be at the top of the
A charts.
B lists.
C tables.
D sales.

14 Which of the following would best describe a performance by a musician or group playing modern popular music?
A concert
B show
C gig
D festival

Language development 3
Dependent prepositions

▶ CB page 163

Form

1 Choose the correct option. One or two options may be correct.

1 Jenny has always been interested in ....
   A acting.   B becoming an actress.
   C to act.

2 I .... to her joining a theatre company.
   A don't oppose   B have no objection
   C don't object

3 There is something strange about .... to play villains.
   A he wants   B him wanting
   C his wanting

4 Many people discourage their children .... actors
   A to become   B from becoming
   C become

5 Be nice to the critics. Our success depends on ....
   A them.   B their reviews.
   C get a good review.

6 When I started acting, I dreamt of .... an Oscar.
   A win   B me for winning   C winning

7 I'd like to discuss ....
   A the plot with you.
   B about the plot with you.
   C you with the plot.

8 He's accustomed to .... in rehearsals.
   A spend hours   B spending hours
   C the hours he spends

Prepositions after verbs and adjectives with related meanings

2 Words with related or opposite meanings often take the same preposition.

a **Complete each sentence with a preposition that can be used with all three verbs.**

1 My children both *hope / long / yearn* .... a part in the school play.

2 Mike and Jeff are bound to *fall out / quarrel / squabble* .... who gets the best part.

3 If I know Nicole, she'll *boast / brag / rave* .... getting the leading role.

4 The preparations and rehearsals *culminate / end / result* .... a huge show for the public.

5 William was *suspected / accused / convicted* .... stealing instruments from the theatre.

6 We are planning to *campaign / demonstrate / protest* .... the closing of the old theatre.

b **Complete each sentence with an alternative adjective that fits the preposition.**

annoyed   deficient   pleased   perfect   rude   scared

1 As a director, he was always very *polite* / .... *to* his actors.

2 I was most *upset* / .... *at* missing the first part of the performance.

3 Looking at his height and appearance, you'll soon realise he's *wrong* / .... *for* the part.

4 The show was totally *lacking* / .... *in* drama and suspense.

5 The director must be pretty *disappointed* / .... *with* the reviews he received.

6 I could never be an actor, as I'm *terrified* / .... *of* going on stage.

Confusing pairs

3 Read the text and underline the correct preposition in each pair.

Years ago, I secretly dreamt **(1)** *of / about* becoming an actor. When I heard **(2)** *of / from* friends about a local drama group that was putting on a play, I went along for an audition. When I arrived at the theatre, I asked **(3)** *for / after* the show's director and was introduced to a young man called Gavin, who was known locally **(4)** *for / by* his modern interpretations of Shakespeare.

The audition seemed to go well and I was pleased **(5)** *with / at* my performance. A couple of days later, I heard **(6)** *about / from* Gavin and he told me that I would be just right **(7)** *about / for* the part of a fairy. I didn't really care **(8)** *about / for* the role, but had to accept it gratefully.

Gavin was anxious **(9)** *for / about* us all to learn our lines as quickly as possible so we could get started with the rehearsals. I was slightly disappointed **(10)** *in / at* the news that I had only one line to learn. I was, however, most impressed with my costume, which was made **(11)** *of / from* some old silk curtains, as wearing it really helped me to get into the character.

Unfortunately, every time I tried to say my line, Gavin got annoyed **(12)** *about / with* me and shouted **(13)** *at / to* me to speak with more emotion. Some of the cast gave me some tips, and I was glad **(14)** *for / of* the help, but I never got much better.

Two days before the opening night, I was so afraid **(15)** *for / of* going on that I decided to quit. I felt sorry **(16)** *about / for* Gavin, but what else could I do? I felt quite bad **(17)** *at / about* it at the time, but later I could laugh **(18)** *about / at* it.

English in Use
Open cloze (Paper 3 Part 2)

▶ ER page 169

1 Read the title and the text on the right quickly for general understanding, ignoring the gaps for the moment. Why do some people not approve of singers like Hayley Westenra?

2 Now read through the text again carefully and do the task. Use the Help clues if necessary.

3 Read through the text again when you've finished and check that the words you've chosen fit in with the overall meaning of the text.

HELP
➤ Question 1
Is the missng word going to be positive or negative? Read on in the text to see how popular Hayley's albums are.
➤ Question 13
Think about the sequence of tenses in the sentence.

For questions **1–15**, complete the following article by writing each missing word in the space. **Use only one word for each space.** The exercise begins with an example **(0)**.

The voice of tomorrow causes a storm

Hayley Westenra, a pretty teenage soprano from New Zealand, has found **(0)** _herself_ at the centre of an unseemly row in the classical music world. Her latest album is about to be released, and there is **(1)**.................... sign that it will make her into an even bigger star. This, however, will only serve to annoy further some purists in the world of classical music. These critics of **(2)**.................... is known as 'crossover' classical music, **(3)**.................... basically means classical hits marketed as easy listening, regard the popularity of artists **(4)**.................... as Westenra, Charlotte Church and Russell Watson **(5)**.................... a symptom of an inexorable cultural decline; a 'dumbing down' of a serious art form.

Hayley is dismissive **(6)**.................... such people. 'I don't really understand their position,' she says, adding **(7)**.................... anything which increases the appeal of classical music amongst the young must be a good thing. She has heard from many young fans who have **(8)**.................... up the violin or piano as a result of enjoying her albums. They **(9)**...................., she argues, certainly never have **(10)**.................... interested in classical music **(11)**.................... it hadn't been made accessible to them.

She **(12)**.................... well have a point there, of course. Until the recent spate of crossover releases, interest in classical music amongst young people **(13)**.................... been in steep decline **(14)**.................... decades. It's hard to believe this revival of interest can be sustained **(15)**.................... there are young stars like Hayley Westenra to be its role models.

Language development

Read the text again and find one adjective which is followed by the preposition *of*, and one which is followed by the preposition *in*.

Writing

Review (Paper 2, Part 2)

▶ CB pages 164–165, WR page 199

Exam strategy

Try to use a range of sentence structures in your writing, to make it interesting. Don't always begin sentences in the same way, but do make sure that you express your ideas clearly. This is very important when you are writing a review, because you want to involve the reader in the topic and influence their opinion.

1 Read and analyse the task below.

You have been asked to review two computer games for an international student magazine, and recommend one of them. Describe and evaluate each game and make your recommendation.

Write your **review** in approximately 250 words.

2 Read sections A and B of a student's answer on the right. The sentences always follow the same structure, so the text is not very interesting to read. Rewrite the underlined sentences, beginning with the words given below.

1 Having ....

....

2 Although ....

....

3 In my ....

....

4 In spite ....

....

3 Read section C of the answer. The student has used sentences that are too simple. Combine the groups of sentences so that they are more complex.

4 Which of these conclusions do you think is the best way to finish the review?

1 All in all, if you're looking for fast fun, challenge and value for money, then *Demons on the Loose* fits the bill.

2 All things considered, you should buy *Demons on the Loose*.

3 Quite simply, I would advise you to add *Demons on the Loose* to your collection of games if you come across it, although I wouldn't go out of my way to find it.

5 Read the complete review again. It is too short, so write it out again, adding some details of your own from the points below to make the correct number of words.
   - how to play the game
   - the graphics
   - who would enjoy the game
   - why you recommend it

Ⓐ I appreciate it when new games come on the market, but unfortunately, not all of them are equally good. I have recently tried out two games, and had mixed reactions to them.

Ⓑ The first game is called *Castle Raider*, and is a 'search and rescue' game. I enjoy playing computer games, but I want to be challenged by them. I did not feel that this game was challenging enough. There are 16 levels. Each level is more complex than the last, but I found they were easy to get through and took very little time. I like the graphics but they did not make up for the rather boring game.

Ⓒ (1) The second game is considerably more interesting. The game is called *Demons on the Loose*. (2) The game involved attacking villains and demons. The villains and demons are hidden among the graphics. The graphics are very realistic. (3) This game is better than *Castle Raider* because it is much more difficult to find the demons. The levels are difficult to get through. Imagine a game which takes four hours to complete a level! The game gives you value for money.

6 Do the following task.

You have been asked to review two videos from your school library for the school magazine, and recommend one of them. Describe and evaluate each video and make your recommendation.

Write your **review** in approximately 250 words.

Reading
Multiple matching (Paper 1 Part 4)

▶ ER page 168

Mourad Mazoud

1 Read the title and the subtitle of the text.
- Where does the music being reviewed originate from?
- Which countries do you think will be mentioned?

2 Read the text quickly for general understanding. Were your predictions correct?

3 Read the instructions for the exam task. Then read all the questions and underline the key words in each question.

4 Now complete the task. Remember that:
- you should always read the relevant piece of text carefully, to check it has exactly the same meaning as the question
- many of the questions contain two points. The relevant piece of text must match both points in the question exactly, not just part of it
- when you have found a match for the question in the text, write the question number in the margin next to the relevant piece of text – you will need to go back and check it later.

5 Match the adjectives from the text in column A with their definitions in column B.

A	B
1 innovative	a of very good quality
2 cross-cultural	b difficult to explain or define
3 top-notch	c very different from each other
4 groundbreaking	d involving aspects from different cultures
5 disparate	e new and exciting
6 indefinable	f very beautiful
7 sublime	g trying something new that no one has tried before.

Answer questions **1–17** by choosing from the seven music reviews (**A–F**). Some of the choices may be required more than once.

Which CD album

has an impressive sound despite some slight technical defects?	1 ....
includes music that has been written by the artist or artists?	2 .... 3 .... 4 ....
is produced by someone with diverse business interests?	5 ....
features artists who are rarely heard outside their own culture?	6 ....
is better organised than other albums of its type?	7 ....
is influenced by the artist's multicultural upbringing?	8 ....
has packaging which provides useful information?	9 ....
was well received by critics when it was first released?	10 ....
demonstrates a talent for performing in front of an audience?	11 ....
includes outstanding performances from previously unknown artists?	12 ....

Which artist or group

did not initially plan a career in the music world?	13 ....
is praised for a consistently dynamic performance?	14 ....
makes good use of instruments not normally associated with the type of music?	15 ....
has had little recognition in their home country?	16 ....
is said to show great musical potential?	17 ....

World music

The best new CD releases from round the world are reviewed by Daniel Connolly.

A Jali Roll (revisited + 1)

In 1989, two West African masters of the kora sound teamed up with a group of English musicians to record an album that was praised in the British music press and was a big hit in their home
5 country. Now is certainly the right time for its rediscovery, with the renewed interest in kora music following releases by the likes of Toumani Diabate. What a hidden treasure this album is; Dembo Konte and Kausu Kuyuteh sing and play a
10 mixture of traditional songs and their own compositions, supported by a fine musical backing. The sound is primarily West African, with the unlikely but successful addition of accordion, trumpet and slide guitar. This is an early experiment
15 in cross-cultural music that deserves a second hearing.

B The Music of Mali

A fine collection of top-notch tracks by the stars of this musical nation. Putamayo is a US label with a forte for innovative compilations, backed up by
20 intelligent sleeve notes (the latest crop includes *Jamaica*, *Gypsy Caravan* and *Cajun*). My favourite tracks are those which showcase top-flight artists who have made this music so popular across Europe. As well as established stars such as
25 Khaled and Natacha Atlas, there are some excellent tracks from singers less well-known outside the Arab-speaking world. Highly recommended.

C Salsa Afro Cubana

Cuban born Osvaldo Chacon trained as a teacher in
30 Havana, but found music to be his true vocation. Rather unusually, he moved to London in 1997, formed a group and dedicated himself to salsa timba – a heavier and more varied style of salsa with an irresistible dance beat. With these eight
35 self-composed tracks, the young Cuban proves himself to possess a fast-developing talent; someone to keep a close eye on.

D Band of Gypsies

This exciting group has a formidable reputation as a live act, and this album of tracks recorded over
40 three concerts in their native Bucharest goes some way to showing why. It's a non-stop musical maelstrom, punctuated by odd moments of gentle recovery, before setting off again on the merry-go-round of gypsy reels and rhythms. Ironically, after a
45 decade of international success, these concerts were the first in the city, but judging from these performances, they should soon be making as much of a mark there as they have elsewhere. Some live albums suffer from inferior recording, but
50 the raw intensity of the music here makes up for the lack of studio polish.

E Próxima Estación: Esperanza

Following up the four-million-selling *Clandestino*, this magazine's record of the year, is no mean feat. The former front man of the indefinable anarchic
55 French rock band Mano Negra, Manu Chao has now created an individual style, reflecting his mixed ethnic background and the sounds he has collected on his travels in Latin America. *Next Station: Hope*, as the album title translates, is
60 very much a continuation of *Clandestino* in terms of music style and themes, with the songs gently flowing into each other, accompanied by a stream of everyday sounds. At the heart are Manu's melodic tunes sung in a mixture of French, Spanish
65 and English, though the music has more of a Caribbean feel to it this time, with reggae rhythms abounding. Not as groundbreaking as *Clandestino*, but a satisfying part two for Manu Chao fans.

F Arabesque 2

This is the second wonderfully crafted collection of
70 Arabic-influenced music put together by Algerian Mourad Mazouz, aka Momo (not to be confused with the band of the same name; he is in fact owner of, and inspiration behind, popular restaurants in London and Paris). While most
75 compilations sound like a disparate collection of tracks, *Arabesque 2* is an entity in its own right, with a groove that flows throughout, uniting the songs and instrumentals as if they were recorded as one. Songs from fairly well-known artists, such
80 as Khaled and Rachid Taha, are combined with sublime offerings from unfamiliar names. This is a must-have title.

Practice exam

Reading

Paper 1 Part 1

Answer questions **1–18** by referring to the review of photography books on page **117**. Indicate your answers **on the separate answer sheet**.*

For questions **1–18**, answer by choosing from the books (**A–F**).
Some of the choices may be required more than once.

A Walker Evans   **D** The Art of Seeing
B The Century of the Body   **E** Portraits
C Missing Link   **F** Around the World in Eighty Years

According to the article, which book

can be criticised for a lack of honesty in both text and photography?   **1** ....

celebrates the life of a photographer from another age?   **2** ....

shows images by a photographer who is renowned in a different genre?   **3** ....

sets out to be an historical record by portraying people over a period of time?   **4** ....

reflects one photographer's fascination with a particular group of artists?   **5** ....

features photos from a number of sources with a clever technical design?   **6** ....

records the variety of a photographer's work, compiled by several writers?   **7** ....

has a title which is more impressive than the photos it contains?   **8** ....

is a visual record of the photographer's personal life?   **9** ....

depicts a lively period of history using traditional photographic techniques?   **10** ....

includes an informative narrative which links the work with broader themes?   **11** ....

presents pictures from photographers who are seen as leaders in their field?   **12** ....

contains intricate photos of mostly household situations?   **13** ....

is suitable for the less-experienced photographer?   **14** ....

has a generic theme that is not reflected in its titles?   **15** ....

shows that one photographer's best work was produced while he was in journalism?   **16** ....

features professional photographs from a well-respected organisation?   **17** ....

shows one photographer's ability to improve the appearance of ordinary locations?   **18** ....

*Your teacher will supply you with an answer sheet.

PHOTOGRAPHY BOOKS
Nigel Stanton reviews the best of today's books on photography.

This year's collection of photography books is led by the multi-authored study of photographer **Walker Evans.** Many people will be familiar with his best-known work
5 which recorded the lives of poor Alabama sharecroppers in the early 20th-century. He did much more in his lifetime, however, so this retrospective tribute is well deserved. Evan's dates were 1903–1975, and he was a
10 photographer from 1928 until his death. Some of his last photos, which are in colour and have still-life subjects, look rather like the work of contemporary urban pop artists. Seen as a whole – there are 200 plates in this
15 magnificent volume – Walker Evans' career impresses by virtue of its diversity and simple love of mundane, man-made things. As is clearly illustrated here, his camera lens transformed the humdrum billboards,
20 shacks, garages and subways of American cities by delicate use of light and quietly monumental composition. Evans was also a subtle portraitist of working men and women, though his interest in faces seems to
25 have declined in the latter part of his life.

Two large survey books are useful introductions aimed at novices and students of photography. William Ewing's **The Century of the Body** is chronological. There
30 are 100 photographs, one for each year of the 20th century. Each of them is concerned with the human form, while the book's commentary makes a connection between the examination of the body and wider
35 cultural issues. An excellent present for any concerned young person. **Missing Link** is subtitled *The Image of Man in Contemporary Photography.* There are plenty of pictures of women, so one can't help but find this
40 somewhat misleading. Almost all the photos, by 60 artists from American and European countries, are manipulated. They are posed, hi-tech and ingeniously constructed. Yet no portrait in **Missing Link** is candid, and none
45 of its documentary aims to reveal the truth.

Many of today's photographers have rejected the traditions of humanist photography. Even news camerawork has been affected. Ulli Michel's mistitled **The Art of Seeing**
50 displays favourite shots by two dozen staff photographers from Reuter's, the long-established international news agency. Although the name is venerable, this photography business was founded as
55 recently as 1985. The book is rich, powerful and particularly contemporary. More sedentary journalists correctly regard photographers who record events in war situations as the heroes of the profession. Yet
60 something is wrong with these pictures. Even the most dramatic of them look staged, or resemble stills from a movie, and there's no essential difference in style between these pictures and photos of international sports
65 events.

The use of black and white, sometimes in stark contrasts and with hard silhouettes, gave a particular manner to 1960s photography, especially in London. A
70 handful of new books turn their backs on the colour technology to remind us of swinging days. John Hedgecoe's **Portraits**, records four decades of work. But surely he was at the peak of his professional career during his 14-
75 year association with *Queen* magazine. His portraits are full of detail and are often of domestic contexts. The most effective of them show a real curiosity about classical musicians and writers, especially the
80 scruffier ones, whereas he's over-respectful of painters and sculptors.

Photography also provides us with souvenirs of precious moments and sights. Eric Newby's **Around the World in Eighty Years**
85 is an excellent photographic autobiography. We all know that he's been one of the best of our travel writers, and it is very good to find how his skills with a camera lens complement his personal journeys and
90 precise reminiscences.

Paper 1 Part 2

For questions **19–24**, you must choose which of the paragraphs **A–G** on page **119** fit into the numbered gaps in the following magazine article. There is one extra paragraph which does not fit in any of the gaps. Indicate your answers **on the separate answer sheet**.

FISHING FOR THE BIGGEST PRIZE

Boosted by television, tournament angling is rapidly becoming a thriving international business. Tony Harris reports.

If you were to consider which sports are the favourites of the media, fishing would not necessarily be the first one to spring to mind. Yet, in some countries today, angling is one of the most popular participant sports, following closely behind swimming and walking. Indeed, particularly in the USA, fishing is now one of the top favourites as a televised sport. On a Saturday morning, you can watch men, and the very occasional woman, catching fish on four different channels.

19

The willingness of anglers in the USA to watch fishing on screen, however, has brought a massive infusion of money from advertisers. In the frequent commercial breaks, every item of fishing equipment imaginable is promoted, from fluorescent plastic worms to electronic fish-finders. In addition, a whole range of products from the mainstream corporate world is marketed with the same level of enthusiasm, everything from biscuits to financial services.

20

At the centre of this rapidly growing business is a modestly sized fish called the freshwater bass, which can weigh four to five kilos when fully grown. A fiercely aggressive fish, in recent years it has become the most popular game fish in the country, mainly due to its tendency to fly out of the water when offered the bait at the end of a fishing line.

21

Nevertheless, for the television cameramen, this newcomer to the world of media sport is presenting a challenge. Fishing is not a pastime that easily holds the attention of today's television audiences. With a 20-kilo camera on his shoulder, the cameraman has to keep the tape rolling for eight hours

continuously, just in case he misses his assigned angler catching a fish. When it arrives, the moment lasts about ten seconds. With huge prize money at stake, the anglers will not risk losing the fish, they swing them into the boat with as little ado as possible.

22

On a cold February day in Alabama, USA, I have come to view just such a well-orchestrated spectacle. During the previous five-day tournament, the anglers have been using their skill and experience to compete against each other. I've watched them hurtling across the waters of the lake at insane speeds in their top-class speed boats, trying to be the first to reach the best fishing spots.

23

Despite all this, it is surprisingly difficult to catch the daily quota of fish needed to qualify for the weigh-in. In fact, many of the competitors may go all day without catching a single one. It is, therefore, inevitable that the less successful anglers are quickly eliminated from the competition. Today, the 175 initial entrants have been gradually whittled down to just ten finalists.

24

More recently, an angler called Darren Nixon, is said to have caught an even larger fish. This claim is still the subject of angry debate, but mainly, I feel, because Nixon used a cheap, unobtrusive plastic boat and maintained that stealth is the most important thing: because the biggest fish are the oldest and consequently the most suspicious. What if Nixon is right? Could it be that the $45,000, 125kph, seven metre-long modern bass boat is actually an impediment to catching the biggest fish?

A As a result, a peaceful rural pastime has been transformed into a marketing phenomenon; in chain stores and shopping malls you can buy leaping-fish T-shirts, and virtual fishing computer games. There are several bass-fishing websites. As a market for consumer products, bass fishing is rapidly becoming bigger than golf and tennis combined.

B Due to the growing commercialisation of the sport, once established in their position the fishermen use the very latest technology to assist them to catch the fish, the five largest of which they bring to the final weigh-in. They can employ electronic sonar depth finders and high-resolution display screens, which map out the topography of the lake bed and reveal any fish around the boat.

C This is in stark contrast to the image of fishing in other parts of the world. Although it has long been a much-loved hobby, there are few anglers who would attempt to support their families through the income they receive from fishing alone. In the USA, however, anglers are fishing a circuit of big-money tournaments, where not only can you be a professional, you can also acquire celebrity status through frequent appearances on the back of cereal packets.

D I watch the anglers standing apprehensively on the central stage, waiting to discover who will receive the winner's $110,000 cheque. It is worth reflecting in these days of electronic sonar fish-finders, that the world-record bass, weighing over ten kilos, was caught in 1932, by a keen amateur fisherman, from a home-made rowing boat using a $1.33 rod. He had the fish weighed and verified at a local fishing shop, then later cooked and ate it.

E The anglers have benefited from yet another technical evolution in the sport during the last ten years. They each have GPS navigation systems built into the consoles of their boats, and before the race, the professionals spend several days scouting the lake and logging co-ordinates of likely fishing areas.

F On each of these, it is possible to see tournament anglers catching endless fish from a lake, one after another. They do this for five minutes, followed by a series of adverts. In real life, what you see is the anglers standing on their boats with their lines in the water. After spending two hours standing doggedly not catching fish in one part of the lake, they then set off, in their high-speed boats, to spend a further two unproductive hours in a different area.

G To compensate for these visual shortcomings, the organisers of the bass-fishing tournaments make the ceremony of the final weigh-in, when the overall winner is discovered, the highlight of the whole broadcast. When constructing their programme, this showdown between the two leading anglers has the style of a TV quiz show, in an effort to liven up the sight of two fishermen totally absorbed in weighing plastic bags of fish.

Paper 1 Part 3

Read the following magazine article and answer questions **25–29** on page **121**. On your answer sheet, indicate the letter **A**, **B**, **C** or **D** against the number of each question. Give only one answer to each question. Indicate your answers **on the separate answer sheet**.

What makes a good leader?

*Middle manager **India Gary-Jenkins** went on a course in leadership skills and got a few surprises.*

The tutor came into the room, coffee in hand, ready to teach. With a glum look on his face, he said: 'Leaders are born, not made. Who would want to be led by you?' This was what I experienced when, in pursuit of personal growth, I recently completed a course on leadership and organisational development. I wasn't sure if the tutor meant that the group of people sitting before him seemed a pathetic group to be leaders, or if he really wanted to know the answer. I hadn't thought about who would want to be led by me, but it was a perplexing and humbling question.

I've learned that any time a course begins with a rhetorical question, one should be prepared for self-reflection at dizzying heights. I was quite nervous: the course was going to force me to ask questions of myself that I wasn't sure I wanted the answers to. Sweat broke out on my forehead and panic crept across my face. I knew I was an effective manager, but I wasn't sure that I was a leader at all. I hoped that my fear of exploring my own weaknesses wasn't burrowing through the surface and betraying the confident stance that I usually project.

The road to discovering leadership can be challenging. Some people really are born leaders. We all know them: the captain of the football team; the top manager who turns the company round and the professor who stands in front of hundreds of students. There are, however, others, myself included, who have to dig deep to find the leader within. While born leaders naturally demonstrate their prowess by larking about and being the life of the party, the quiet leaders are often overlooked and underdeveloped. On my course, I learned that the most competent leaders are not always the ones that are obvious to us. They are people who have the exceptional skill of making decisions that others want to follow, often without even knowing they are being led.

The tutor challenged us to observe people who demonstrate unconventional leadership skills. I thought about the older brother whose younger brother follows his every move, the mother who leads her children by nature and the builder who is leading a team to complete a project. Leadership is all around us. There are born leaders in every race, gender, community and industrial sector. Before I changed my frame of reference, I'd always thought of leaders as people standing on podiums rallying the masses for change. I had been ignoring the beauty of change around me – including the benefit that the leaders all around us contribute to our everyday lives. Suddenly, my future as a leader didn't seem so bleak. I realised that my tutor had been trying to get me to recognise that I was born a leader. He'd known it before I or anyone else had come into his room. In reality, there was no skill he could teach me that I didn't innately know. He'd only facilitated my being able to recognise it. For years I'd been ignoring my own contribution to leadership.

I tell you this story, not to give you anecdotes about my coming into leadership, but in an effort to change your frame of reference about your own. You were born a leader with infinite possibilities. If your company is looking for leaders, let them know they've got one. Evaluate the leadership skills that you demonstrate and concentrate on building them. The extent to which you demonstrate your leadership is up to you. So, now that you have the data you need, I will pose the question to you. Who would want to be led by you?

> **6Leaders are born, not made. Who would want to be led by you?9**

25 What first impression did the writer gain of the course she attended?

    A   She was surprised by the tutor's casual appearance.
    B   She found the tutor's opening remarks rather offensive.
    C   She was intrigued to find out about the other participants.
    D   She realised that she was going to be made to think quite deeply.

26 In the second paragraph, we learn that the writer

    A   felt threatened by the issues raised on the course.
    B   doubted whether the course would be useful for her.
    C   lacked confidence in her ability to do her current job.
    D   realised that her feelings had been perceived by others.

27 In the third paragraph, the writer makes the point that the best leaders

    A   are those who take the trouble to learn the skills of leadership.
    B   may not actually be the people in the most prominent positions.
    C   are those who make us aware of their natural leadership abilities.
    D   may never be in a position to use the natural abilities they possess.

28 As a result of following the course, the writer came to appreciate that

    A   we all have the potential to be good leaders.
    B   she had nothing to learn from her course tutor.
    C   her course tutor had underestimated her abilities.
    D   leadership skills are very different to other skills in life.

29 In the final paragraph, the writer encourages us to

    A   support the leaders in the places where we work.
    B   demand that our leadership potential is recognised.
    C   develop the leadership qualities that we already possess.
    D   rethink our ideas about why it is necessary to have leaders.

Paper 1 Part 4

Answer questions **30–48** by referring to the newspaper article about marketing methods on page **123**. Indicate your answers **on the separate answer sheet**.

> For questions **30–48**, answer by choosing from the six sections of the article **A–F**.
> You may choose any of the sections more than once.

In which section(s) are the following mentioned?

music reflecting the intricate design of the product being advertised	**30** ....
an unexpected transformation in the style of advertising for one product	**31** ....
a link between the type of product being advertised and the title of the chosen music	**32** ....
a lack of musical knowledge within advertising companies	**33** ....
music creating an impression of sophistication	**34** .... **35** ....
the music used in adverts becoming stereotyped	**36** ....
people reacting to music in adverts intuitively	**37** ....
the possibility of music discouraging people from buying a product	**38** ....
music being inspired by the advert itself	**39** ....
music for adverts relating particularly to the gender of the target market	**40** .... **41** ....
music in adverts broadening people's musical tastes	**42** ....
familiar music in an advert encouraging people to buy a product	**43** .... **44** ....
music creating a cosmopolitan atmosphere	**45** ....
music gaining popularity through being used in advertising	**46** ....
a certain piece of music appealing to a diverse range of consumers	**47** ....
a contrast between the style of music and the visual effect of the advert	**48** ....

MARKETING MELODIES

Music is proving to be a powerful advertising tool. Kate Hinxton goes in search of the key to successful sales.

A How often have you heard a piece of music and immediately conjured up the image of a well-known television advert? Music has the power to evoke deep emotion, but it is now widely accepted in the marketing world that it also acts as a useful tool in coaxing people into opening their wallets. But why do TV advertisers think classical music in particular will sell their products? Advertising psychologists believe it works in two ways. Firstly, when a well-known piece of music is chosen, it creates a mental link for the listener with something that they have previously heard. Consequently, particular pieces are chosen either for their well-established popularity, or because they have gained favour through being an integral part of a certain advert. The second theory is backed up by research into the electrical activity of the brain, showing that the right side tends to recognise enjoyable music. By stimulating the part of the brain associated with pleasure, advertisers are preparing the bed in which the emerging flower of extravagance will bloom happily.

B The process of choosing a particular composer to represent a product or brand is often haphazard, as advertising teams are rarely made up of musical connoisseurs. Julie Moor, from a leading London ad agency confirms that it often comes down to gut instinct. 'Creative teams can often spend months listening, it can be quite tricky finding the right track. It's so subjective – everyone's opinion, whether creative director or client, is clouded by their emotional attachment to a piece of music.' Sometimes the juxtaposition of images that convey one emotion, with music that conveys a very different one, can have great success. Take, for instance, a recent ad for Levi jeans, showing denim clad youths crashing through walls in what seems a desperate bid for freedom; the sublime phrases of Handel's *Sarabande* work against the aggressive images to give the ad a haunting, almost spiritual quality. Music is invaluable in helping to build a strong brand identity – one of the major concerns of contemporary advertising.

C When writing the music for ads, it is not essential for the composer to have a deep understanding of the product itself, but more an appreciation of the underlying message. Rather than searching through the archives for well-known music, advertising companies often employ composers to create the music to complement a specific ad in production. Indeed, certain composers seem to lend themselves to specific products, and a quick survey of ads over the years throws up some intriguing trends. When it comes to promoting food – in ads mainly targeted at women – Tchaikovsky is the industry's clear favourite, being used to sell products from mayonnaise to chocolate. The editor of a prominent food magazine explains: 'The music is hypnotic, and this taps into the documented psychological effect you get when you eat chocolate. It takes your mind off things, in the same way that Tchaikovsky does.' But it may also be significant that the music from Tchaikovsky's *The Nutcracker* is full of food references, *The Dance of the Sugar Plum Fairy*, for example, is suggestive of confectionary.

D The style of composer used for the car industry is all about power and austerity in ads which are aimed at male consumers. Mahler and Beethoven are both front-runners, as classical music seems a winner for marketing luxury cars, whereas jaunty pop tracks fit with zippy, little run-about models for use around town. Audi has been represented by Beethoven's *Moonlight Sonata*, and Mahler's *Symphony No. 5* was the driving force behind Hyundai's recent ads. Adverts for cars often tend to use classical music in a very clichéd way, and some brands will use it as a means of reaching the 'intelligent' consumer, where it puts across a performance message of superior engineering. James Salton, author of a book on music and meaning, has some ingenious explanations. 'There's probably a parallel to be drawn between the complexity of Mahler's orchestration and the technical wizardry of the modern car. I'd also like to suggest that, unconsciously perhaps, Mahler's music suits the tense, neurotic experience of modern driving, whereas Beethoven is an appropriate choice when the associations of the word "classic" is desired.' For marketing the travel industry, there has been an eclectic choice of music, with one of the most successful being *Lakme*, a 19th-century Orientalist opera which is an ideal representation of both the East and West, dreaming up visions of far-flung, exotic places.

E Puccini, it seems, has the power to make the excesses of fast living and fast food respectable: he scored a surprise hit in Playstation 2's campaign for one of their new computer games, with *O mio babbino caro*. Then *Nessun Dorma* made the perfect choice for a Burger King commercial, giving a decidedly budget product an improved marketing image, whilst bringing in customers thanks to the footballing associations of the piece which was used as the theme for the 1990 World Cup. Handel is a popular choice for big-name retailers, too, and there have been several delicious coincidences, when the same music has been selected by polar opposites in the retail world. Why is it that a high-class department store feels that the strains of Handel's *Water Music* will appeal to their clientele, in the same way as it appeals to the customers crowding the aisles of a budget supermarket?

F In a recent development, classical music is beginning to be used in ads that target young people. Julie Moor says 'The brand of Levi jeans was reinvented in the eighties with ads featuring fifties pop songs. Now they've turned to classical music, but they haven't changed their market.' But why should young people suddenly relate to classical music? 'It's a trend,' says Moor. 'Who knows what it'll be next year?' But advertisers can use classical music in a creative way. Pop music is becoming so fragmented and there are many small tribes of pop music fans. You've got to be conscious of not alienating people. The surprising solution is a classical piece – it's more neutral, and people can react honestly to what they hear, rather than being conscious of what has current media approval. So classical music is good for your wealth – as an advertiser. However, there are those who will be horrified by its use to encourage consumerism. The optimists amongst us will rejoice at the fact that millions of people are hearing classical music on primetime television. Who knows what it may have done for the sales figures of Puccini and Handel?

Writing

Paper 2 Part 1

1 You are the secretary of your local international student club, which organises a trip abroad every year. Last year, you were one of a group of students who went on a two-week visit to the UK. The president of the club has asked you to write a report about the trip.

Read the extract from the president's memo below, and the extract from the brochure describing the trip, together with your comments. Then, **using the information carefully**, write your report for the president with any recommendations you may have.

MEMO

I understand there were mixed responses to last year's trip to the UK. Could you write a report for the committee so we can plan the programme for the trip for next year? We would appreciate the details of any feedback you received from the other students, including both the positive and negative aspects of the tour. We are particularly interested in the general opinion about the accommodation which was provided. In view of the fact that the main focus of the trip is for language learning, do you feel the accommodation was suitable?

We are considering changing the format of the trip next year, so you could make any recommendations you may have about the way in which the trip could be improved.

Thanks

Tim Belman

Visit UK

Enjoy learning English and discovering the culture, with one of our two-week trips to the UK. You will attend classes with a qualified teacher and also have the chance to see both the capital city and explore the countryside of Britain. This is a two-centre holiday, and you will have the opportunity to stay in London during the first week, then in the second week you travel north to Scotland. This is a wonderful language-learning experience.

This year's programme:

Week 1:

Monday	Travel overnight to UK
Tuesday	Stay in central London hotel
	Open-air bus tour of London, with commentary in own language
Wednesday to Friday	a.m.: Language classes
	p.m.: Sightseeing visits in London
Saturday	Train journey to Edinburgh, Scotland
	Stay with families

Week 2:

Sunday	Tour of Edinburgh, the city and castle
	Evening: display of traditional dancing and music
Monday to Friday	Stay in country hotel
	Hill-walking in the Highlands.
Saturday	Fly back to London from Edinburgh
Sunday	Travel home

Annotations:
- exhausted
- staff unfriendly
- 9 a.m. start too early
- some younger students found museums boring. The older students wanted to go out in London in the evening. This was a problem, as nothing had been organised. The younger students would not be allowed to go.
- too long
- good for language
- enjoyable
- beautiful, but weather cold. Not enough warm clothes.

Now write your **report** for the president (approximately 250 words). You should use your own words as far as possible.

Paper 2 Part 2

Choose **one** of the following writing tasks. Your answer should follow exactly the instructions given.
Write approximately 250 words.

2   You see this announcement in an international student magazine.

> **LANGUAGE LEARNING**
> We would like you to write an article about language learning in
> your country.
>   Describe how learning a language 20 years ago was different
> to learning one now. Explain why these changes have occurred
> and say how you think language learning might change in the
> future. The best article will be published in a special edition of the
> magazine.

Write your **article**.

3   The director of an international sports centre has asked you to provide a reference for a friend of yours who has
applied for work as a sports instructor with the teenagers who attend the centre. The reference should include
relevant information about your friend's:
- character
- previous experience
- skills and interests
- suitability for working with teenagers

Write your **reference**.

4   You see this advertisement in an international student magazine.

> We are a travel organisation and we are planning to hold an
> International Cultural Exhibition in London. This exhibition will
> give visitors information about the culture and customs of
> different countries. Tell us what your country should include.
> Write us a proposal, suggesting what should be included in your
> country's display and explaining why your choice for the display
> best represents your country.

Write your **proposal**.

5   Your company regularly uses a local hotel for its overseas guests and for important business meetings. You have
received several complaints from your guests about the service at the hotel, and you feel the facilities are
inadequate. Write a letter to the manager of the hotel explaining the problems that you and your guests have had.

Write your **letter**.

English in Use

Paper 3 Part 1

For questions **1–15**, read the article below and then decide which answer **A**, **B**, **C** or **D** best fits each space. Indicate your answer **on the separate answer sheet**. The exercise begins with an example **(0)**.

Example:

Learning at a distance

The idea of distance learning has been in **(0)** B for a long time. In recent years, due to the rapid **(1)**........ in computer technology, an extremely adaptable method of study has evolved around this idea. Distance learning is becoming increasingly popular with students, and the **(2)**........ of today's university population is changing as a result. For students whose chosen university is beyond daily travelling distance, studying online using what is known as e-learning is an attractive **(3)**........ because it enables them to complete a degree without the expense of paying for accommodation in the **(4)**........ of their place of study. Similarly, parents at home bringing up young children can **(5)**........ advantage of this flexible method of study because web-based support materials can **(6)**........ with any individual time schedule.

Initially, as e-learning **(7)**........ in popularity, there was a certain amount of **(8)**........ amongst university tutors, who feared that students studying in the isolation of their own home might be **(9)**........ of daily contact with their fellow students, something they regarded as an important **(10)**........ of a university education. It soon became **(11)**........ , however, that e-learning can actually improve communication, through the creation of so-called 'discussion boards', where the students submit their questions online, making them readily **(12)**........ to all. This system encourages a **(13)**........ exchange of opinions between students, and it also means that the tutor's response to each query is immediately available to a wide **(14)**........ . Nevertheless, it is recognised that human support is still a key factor in the learning experience, and on most distance-learning courses, students are **(15)**........ with face-to-face contact at some point.

0	**A** actually	**(B)** existence	**C** continuity	**D** duration
1	**A** alterations	**B** movements	**C** openings	**D** advances
2	**A** proportion	**B** composition	**C** arrangement	**D** alignment
3	**A** option	**B** selection	**C** preference	**D** favorite
4	**A** whereabouts	**B** situation	**C** vicinity	**D** precincts
5	**A** have	**B** get	**C** gain	**D** take
6	**A** stay in	**B** put in	**C** fit in	**D** go in
7	**A** grew	**B** emerged	**C** leapt	**D** enlarged
8	**A** attention	**B** trouble	**C** worry	**D** concern
9	**A** deducted	**B** deprived	**C** denied	**D** deleted
10	**A** issue	**B** aspect	**C** item	**D** point
11	**A** evident	**B** conspicuous	**C** distinct	**D** straightforward
12	**A** allowable	**B** accessible	**C** achievable	**D** applicable
13	**A** busy	**B** restless	**C** lively	**D** bustling
14	**A** following	**B** assembly	**C** reception	**D** audience
15	**A** offered	**B** provided	**C** delivered	**D** permitted

Paper 3 Part 2

For questions **16–30**, complete the following article by writing each missing word in the correct box on your answer sheet. **Use one word only for each space**. The exercise begins with an example **(0)**.

Example: | **0** | *in* | **0** |
| --- | --- | --- |

The first lady of space

In June 1963, a 26-year-old Russian woman took a giant step for womankind **(0)** in the male-dominated world of space exploration. Valentina Tereshkova **(16)**........ 71 hours to complete 48 orbits of the earth in her spacecraft. Not **(17)**........ was she the first woman to travel in space, but she stayed up there longer than any of the men who had gone before her. It required a very special woman to complete **(18)**........ a task successfully, yet Valentina came from a small town on the Volga river, where she **(19)**........ up in a harsh farming environment. What's more, **(20)**........ her mother was a widow, Valentina was ten years old before she first went to school.

Eventually, the family moved to the city, and Valentina **(21)**........ herself working alongside her mother in a textile factory. She also joined a local aviation club where she took **(22)**........ parachuting as a hobby, making **(23)**........ total of 126 jumps. In 1961, when news of Yuri Gagarin's first manned space flight reached the factory, everyone was filled **(24)**........ excitement and national pride. Valentina's mother said that the next person in space **(25)**........ to be a woman. Inspired by her mother's words, Valentina found out that actually anyone **(26)**........ volunteer for the space programme if they wanted to, so that is **(27)**........ Valentina did. Much **(28)**........ her astonishment, she was chosen. One explanation for her selection was the **(29)**........ that cosmonauts were required to jump from their spacecraft after re-entry to the earth's atmosphere and parachute to safety – a task at **(30)**........ Valentina had excelled in trials.

Paper 3 Part 3

In **most** lines of the following text, there is one unnecessary word. It is **either** grammatically incorrect **or** does not fit in with the sense of the text. For each numbered line **31–46**, write the unnecessary word. The exercise begins with two examples **(0)** and **(00)**.

Examples:

0	✔
00	*have*

0	

00	

So you want to be a travel writer?

0   If you've done a bit of travelling, I expect you kept what you

00 reckon is a pretty fascinating travel journal. You might have

31 even think this deserves a wider audience and is so good enough

32 to be published. Well, I'm afraid that when sending an unsolicited

33 manuscript to your average travel editor is unlikely to get you

34 anywhere, because for the simple reason that they receive them

35 by the sackload each month. So if you're serious what about getting

36 into travel writing such as a career, you've got to find

37 some way of making your work stand out from the crowd. That is

38 where our seminars on travel writing come in to. We have brought

39 together with a whole bunch of experts in the field, and they're ready

40 to pass on and the secrets of their success. They'll be giving you the

41 lowdown on guidebook writing, telling you what makes it a good

42 travel article and showing you how to turn your ideas into good

43 stories. The day also includes an individual appraisal session,

44 where you get also the chance to talk to top writers about your own

45 work and ideas. All in all, you should not come out of these seminars

46 with the skills to make sure of your travel-writing dreams come to life.

Paper 3 Part 4

For questions **47–61**, read the two texts below. Use the words in the boxes to the right of the texts to form **one** word that fits in the same numbered space in the text. Write the new word in the correct box on your answer sheet. The exercise begins with an example **(0)**.

Example:	0	*completely*	0

PIECE OF DESCRIPTIVE WRITING

Water of life

After a three-week trek through the rainforest, we had become so used to the sound of cicadas that it took me a few moments to realise that it had stopped **(0)**........ and the **(47)** .... trees and foliage had become eerily silent. This short silence was followed by a stiff breeze, which increased rapidly in **(48)**........ , swiftly followed by a heavy **(49)**........ that drenched us in seconds. Desperate to protect my camera **(50)**........ from the huge **(51)**........ raindrops, I found an enormous tree root and managed to bury my bag underneath, just before losing my footing and sliding 20 metres down the steep **(52)**........ slopes of the mountain. Having recovered both my **(53)**........ and my gear, we continued our climb, and a perfect rainbow formed over the water vapour lifting off the forest canopy.

(0) COMPLETE
(47) ROUND
(48) STRONG
(49) POUR
(50) EQUIP
(51) TROPIC
(52) MUD
(53) COMPOSE

ARTICLE IN A DESIGN MAGAZINE

Handset blues

In the average living room, you'll find at least three remote-control handsets, each controlling one element of the audio-visual **(54)**........ system. The one for my video has 39 buttons, only six of which I use on a **(55)**........ basis. Meanwhile, my mobile phone seems to have an almost **(56)**........ number of complex **(57)**........ in its menu structure, most of which appear totally **(58)**........ to the business of making or receiving phone calls. I know I should try harder to understand the full **(59)**........ of these gadgets, but as long as they perform their primary functions, I can't be bothered. But isn't it time manufacturers put a bit more thought into the **(60)**........ of the buttons? The design is hardly user-friendly to say the least, and I can't be the only one to find them **(61)**........ .

(54) ENTERTAIN
(55) DAY
(56) LIMIT
(57) OPERATE
(58) RELEVANT
(59) POTENT
(60) LAY
(61) IRRITATE

Paper 3 Part 5

For questions **62–74**, read the following informal email giving advice about how to give a presentation at a job interview. Use the information in it to complete the numbered gaps in the formal book extract. The words you need **do not occur** in the informal email. **Use no more than two words for each gap**. The exercise begins with an example **(0)**.

Example:

0	*bear in*	0

EMAIL

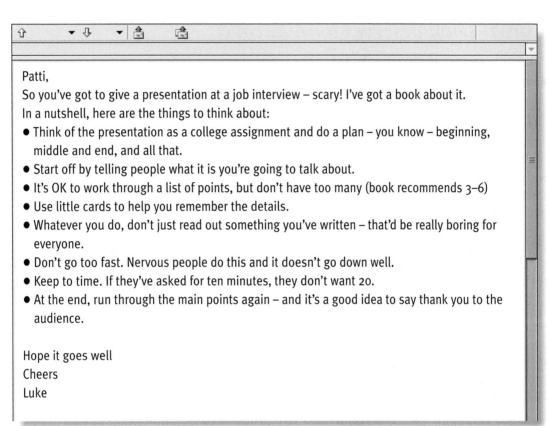

Patti,

So you've got to give a presentation at a job interview – scary! I've got a book about it.

In a nutshell, here are the things to think about:

● Think of the presentation as a college assignment and do a plan – you know – beginning, middle and end, and all that.

● Start off by telling people what it is you're going to talk about.

● It's OK to work through a list of points, but don't have too many (book recommends 3–6)

● Use little cards to help you remember the details.

● Whatever you do, don't just read out something you've written – that'd be really boring for everyone.

● Don't go too fast. Nervous people do this and it doesn't go down well.

● Keep to time. If they've asked for ten minutes, they don't want 20.

● At the end, run through the main points again – and it's a good idea to say thank you to the audience.

Hope it goes well

Cheers

Luke

EXTRACT FROM A SELF-HELP BOOK

GIVING A PRESENTATION

Here are some suggestions to **(0)**............................. mind if you are asked to give a presentation as part of a job interview.

Approach the structuring of a presentation as **(62)**............................. were a college assignment, with an introduction, conclusion, etc. At the outset, you should **(63)**............................. your listeners of the topic you **(64)**............................. to address. **(65)**............................. means refer to a short list of points as you speak – **(66)**............................. three, but no more than six is a good rule of thumb – and make use of prompt cards as a **(67)**............................. of the details or examples you wish to mention. You should, however, avoid **(68)**............................. costs the temptation to read from a script, as this will make the presentation **(69)**............................. to listen to. **(70)**............................. time. Anxious speakers often rush through points; this creates **(71)**............................. impression, as does **(72)**............................. the given time limit. Finally, summarise your key points as you **(73)**............................. the presentation to a close. And, of course, **(74)**............................. of thanks to the audience never goes amiss.

Paper 3 Part 6

For questions **75–80**, read the following text and then choose from the list **A–I** given below the best phrase to fill each of the spaces. Write one letter (**A–I**) in the correct box on your answer sheet. Each correct phrase may only be used once. **Some of the suggested answers do not fit at all**.

A great book deserves a great cover

Over the years, designing book jackets has attracted some of the world's top graphic designers, and it's easy to see why. Creating images to partner great literature is an exciting proposition. Of course, there's more money to be made designing the packaging for frozen food, but book-cover design is more dignified **(75)**........ .

Today, of course, the marketing wizardry that goes into frozen-food packaging is also applied to novels and biographies. The marketing folk have moved into the once genteel world of publishing, **(76)**........ . Even so, it's hard to find truly awful designs in a bookshop, even if you look on the shelves devoted to airport blockbusters **(77)**........ . Odd, therefore, that when many well-designed books are published in translation, their jackets are redesigned.

You expect covers to be altered to accommodate language changes, but you'd have thought that, in this age of global branding, there would be one jacket for all editions. It works for perfume, **(78)**........ . It would seem to make economic sense to use an original cover design because it already exists as artwork **(79)**........ . So why does this not happen?

The answer seems to be that books, and especially novels, are culturally sensitive things: a visual image might have a subtle resonance in one country, **(80)**........ . So the one-size-fits-all approach, common in global design, just doesn't seem to wash when it comes to book covers.

A   and this means rethinking the cover

B   and the confessions of celebrities

C   and yet appear meaningless elsewhere

D   and so it appeals to them too

E   and so a worthwhile activity for designers

F   and presumably the author has approved it

G   and other examples of the genre

H   and you would expect the same to apply to books

I   and dragged it into the modern era

Listening

Paper 4 Part 1

You will hear part of a radio programme in which the presenter, Hilary Barrington, is talking about the experience of swimming with dolphins. For questions **1–9**, complete the sentences.

You will hear the recording twice.

Dolphin quest

Dolphin Quest is located in the **1** [　　　　　　　] once used by the navy in Bermuda.

All visitors to Dolphin Quest are required to wear a **2** [　　　　　　　]

Non-swimmers sit on a **3** [　　　　　　　] just below the surface of the water.

Before approaching the dolphins, visitors make a signal with their **4** [　　　　　　　]

The dolphins' skin is described as **5** [　　　　　　　] to the touch.

Visitors are told that **6** [　　　and　　　] are regarded as a sign of appreciation by the dolphins.

Hilary says that, for the dolphins, meeting humans seemed to be an **7** [　　　　　　　] experience.

Hilary says that experts regard contact with dolphins as a good way of relieving **8** [　　　　　　　]

At Dolphin Quest, visitors pay **9** [　　　　　　　] for half an hour with the dolphins.

Paper 4 Part 2

You will hear a radio report about an unusual orchestra that plays musical instruments made out of vegetables. For questions **10–17**, complete the notes.

Listen very carefully as you will hear the recording ONCE only.

Vienna Vegetable Orchestra

Dates of the music festival: [| 10]

Pieces the orchestra will play: – traditional folk

                – [| 11] by Gershwin

The orchestra's inspiration: instruments made from recycled materials

                       in [| 12] and other places

Examples of vegetables used: – pumpkin (for the drums)

                – [| 13] (for the flute)

                – leeks (for the violin)

Making the instruments: – use only [| 14] fresh vegetables

                – in Britain, [| 15] vegetables are the best size

                – avoid storing vegetables in [| 16] conditions

After the concert: vegetables made into [| 17] for the audience

Paper 4 Part 3

You will hear an interview with the artist Jocelyn Burton, who makes jewellery and other objects out of precious metal. For questions **18–24**, choose the correct answer **A**, **B**, **C** or **D**.

You will hear the recording twice.

18   Why did Jocelyn first start making things out of silver at art college?

    A   She failed to make the grade as a painter.
    B   She was advised to learn a practical skill.
    C   She had to do it as part of her course.
    D   She realised it would allow her to develop artistically.

19   How did Jocelyn feel during her fine art classes?

    A   aware that she wasn't wholly committed
    B   intimidated by her classmates
    C   unappreciated by her tutors
    D   lacking in original ideas

20   In her first job, Jocelyn felt

    A   proud that her work was sold in fashionable shops.
    B   frustrated to be working only with jewellery.
    C   determined to become recognised as an artist.
    D   unsure of the value of the experience she gained.

21   How did the work of Jocelyn's own studio contrast with that of other silversmiths?

    A   It was more affordable for ordinary people.
    B   It was aimed at a totally different market.
    C   It was slightly heavier in weight.
    D   It was designed to be amusing.

22   When describing her current work, Jocelyn says that

    A   she remains open to new ideas.
    B   she has established a recognisable style.
    C   she prefers to work with one particular metal.
    D   she now aims to make more functional objects.

23   Jocelyn gives the example of the teapot to illustrate her point that some objects

    A   are only intended to be decorative.
    B   reveal the real ambitions of their designers.
    C   are only valuable because they are made of silver.
    D   reflect the style of the period in which they were made.

24   From what she says about meeting her clients' requirements, we understand that Jocelyn

    A   is still not confident about her drawing ability.
    B   is unwilling to alter her designs once work has started.
    C   is impatient with people whose instructions are unclear.
    D   is keen to get the details of a design right from the outset.

Paper 4 Part 4

You will hear five short extracts in which various people are talking about a school teacher who influenced them.

You will hear the recording twice. While you listen you must complete both tasks.

TASK ONE

For questions **25–29**, choose from the list **A–H** what each speaker remembers about their teacher.

A   He put pressure on me to achieve high academic standards.

B   He encouraged me to take risks.   **Speaker 1**   [ ] 25

C   He punished me in a way that was unfair.   **Speaker 2**   [ ] 26

D   He showed me that I had become self-centred.

E   He made me take responsibility for my own actions.   **Speaker 3**   [ ] 27

F   He taught me the importance of being honest.   **Speaker 4**   [ ] 28

G   He inspired me through his enthusiasm for his subject.   **Speaker 5**   [ ] 29

H   He believed in me when others didn't.

TASK TWO

For questions **30–34**, choose from the list **A–H** what has happened to each speaker as a result of their teacher's influence.

A   I've been able to motivate my colleagues.

B   I've acquired friends with a shared interest.   **Speaker 1**   [ ] 30

C   I've decided to follow a career in education.   **Speaker 2**   [ ] 31

D   I've got qualifications which will help my career.

E   I've realised a long-held ambition.   **Speaker 3**   [ ] 32

F   I've been able to get on better with my family.   **Speaker 4**   [ ] 33

G   I've had the opportunity to go self-employed.   **Speaker 5**   [ ] 34

H   I've started to earn a high salary.

Speaking (15 minutes)

Paper 5 Part 1 (3 minutes)

The examiner will ask you a few questions about yourself and then ask you to talk to your partner.

Interlocutor   Good morning (afternoon/evening).

My name is .... and this is my colleague ....

And your names are?

Can I have your mark sheets, please?

Thank you.

First of all, we'd like to know a little about you.

- Where do you come from?
- How long have you been studying English?
- What other languages do you speak?

Now I'd like you to ask **each other** something about:

- your favourite leisure activities
- something you'd like to learn to do in the future

(Ask candidates further questions in turn.)

- How do you think you will use English in your future life?
- What has been the hardest thing for you in learning English? Why?
- Do you hope to travel in the future? Where would you like to go?
- How do you think travel is going to change in the future?

Thank you.

Paper 5 Part 2 (4 minutes)

People and pictures (Compare, contrast and speculate)

Interlocutor   In this part of the test, I'm going to give each of you the chance to talk for about a minute and to comment briefly after your partner has spoken.

First, you will each have the same set of photos to look at. They show people and pictures.

(*Candidate A*), it's your turn first. I'd like you to compare and contrast two or three of these situations, saying what feelings the people might have towards the pictures. Don't forget, you have about one minute for this.

Now (*Candidate B*), which person do you think feels most attached to their picture?

Crowds (Compare, contrast and speculate)

Interlocutor   Now I'm going to give each of you another set of pictures to look at. They show people in crowds.

Now (*Candidate B*), it's your turn. I'd like you to compare and contrast two or three of these situations, saying why the people are in the crowd and how they might feel about it.

Now (*Candidate A*), which crowd do you think it would be most exciting to be in?

Paper 5 Part 3 (4 minutes)

Interlocutor   Now I'd like you to discuss something between yourselves, but please speak so that we can hear you. Look at these pictures. A secondary school is organising a work-experience programme for its 16-year-old students. Each student will spend a week doing a job to find out about working life.

Talk about what the school students would learn by doing each of these jobs and say what problems they might face in doing them. Then decide which three jobs would be the most suitable for inclusion in the scheme.

You have about four minutes for this.

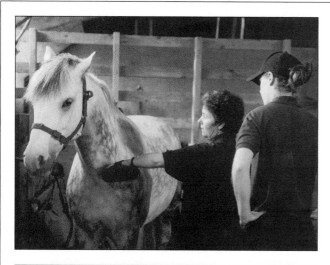 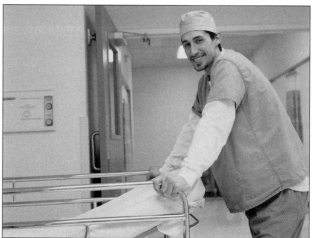

Paper 5 Part 4 (4 minutes)

Discuss these questions.

- How useful do you think a scheme like this would be for the students?

- Is it important to try a range of jobs before finally choosing a career?

- In what other ways can young people find out about the range of jobs available to them?

- When young people have to choose which subjects to study, should they be thinking of a future career or following their interests?

- Do you think the education system should prepare young people for the world of work, or does it have another purpose?

KEY

Module 1

English in Use p.6

2b
1. C (*a lasting impression* = collocation)
2. D (to provide a contrast, not a reason or time marker)
3. D (*to put something on record*)
4. B (*deeply affected* = collocation)
5. A (*leaves* + *-ing*)
6. C (*outlook on* (approach to, attitude to, feeling about))
7. A (non-financial context)
8. A (*a clear idea* = collocation)
9. C (*to accept an offer*)
10. B (= to remember)
11. D (*a worldwide scale* = collocation)
12. C (*with* not part of phrasal verb)
13. B (*by chance* = collocation)
14. C (*to tire of something/somebody*)
15. A (= *see by chance*, link back to gap 13)

Language development pp.7–8

1

	a		b	
1	a	have told	b	has been telling
2	a	has been wearing	b	has worn
3	a	have eaten	b	have been eating
4	a	have been taking	b	have taken
5	a	have (always) lived	b	have (only) been living
6	a	have been hearing	b	have heard
7	a	have cooked	b	have been cooking
8	a	has stolen	b	has been stealing

2a 1 was   2 moved   3 started   4 was   5 has been playing
6 studied   7 graduated   8 have influenced   9 has learnt
10 moved   11 has been living / has lived   12 became
13 released   14 has sold   15 has released

3
1. I **was living** at home when I passed my driving test, but after that I moved out.
2. When the accident happened, John **was driving,** but it wasn't his fault.
3. He said he was feeling sick and he **apologised** for not coming.
4. My tooth was hurting again, so I **decided** to visit the dentist that afternoon.
5. I had already **heard** the news when the director told me.
6. When I arrived, I saw that 20 people **were waiting**; some **had already been waiting** for over three hours.
7. When my exam results **came**, I got exactly the grades that I **had been hoping / had hoped** for.
8. I think my boss **had slept** badly the night before, as he was being very critical that day.

4 1 were   2 had given up   3 worked   4 (had) agreed   5 had been working / had worked   6 felt   7 wanted   8 had been planning / had planned   9 ended up   10 celebrated   11 was working   12 was / used to be   13 (had) quit   14 had bought   15 gave in   16 had never travelled   17 was

5 1 we'll have been living   2 we're moving   3 We're buying   4 we plan   5 is going to take   6 have finished   7 is   8 I'll be starting   9 will take

6 1 about   2 unlikely   3 verge   4 expect   5 are   6 not   7 bound   8 due

7 1 was going to / was about to   2 were due to be   3 were going to be   4 was due to have   5 was due to   6 about to

8 1 will have finished   2 am going to spend   3 will probably stay   4 are starting   5 due to open   6 will be serving   7 will be   8 were going to work   9 was/is planning   10 'll need   11 starts

English in Use p.9

2
1. He finds it strange that people should want to visit it.
2. Fewer people are doing/seeing carpentry these days.

3 1 out   2 from   3 been   4 same   5 ✔   6 of   7 ✔   8 were   9 ✔   10 become   11 ✔   12 seeing   13 get   14 and   15 as   16 nor

Listening p.10

1a 1   a radio programme
2   a course to help young people run their own business

1c 1 the name of an organisation   2 questions 6 and 7
3 question 2

2 1 Commercial Institute   2 accountant   3 toolkit   4 resources
5 finance   6 Leadership   7 Realising your Dream
8 thinking ahead   9 work experience   10 November 8th

4 1   The student has written some information (*City's*) that is already in the notes, but has missed out the name.
2   This is the type of company Vimmi ran, not what she's qualified in.
5   The student has paraphrased the answer – but *money* is too vague and general to be correct here. Always use the word you hear in the recording.
6   The student has written words from the recording (*says it all*) that are not part of the name of the session.
8   The student has heard the wrong verb – *being* instead of *thinking* – which changes the meaning, and has written *a head* instead of *ahead* – which means something different!
10   The student has written the simple number *eight* instead of the ordinal number (*eighth*). It would have been better to write *8th*, as numbers don't need to be written as words. He/She has also spelled *November* incorrectly.

Tapescript

And next up on the programme, we have news of a series of seminars to be held in the city later in the year. The course title *Dawn of Opportunity* has been given to the series of five day-long events which are being organised by the city's <u>Commercial Institute</u> in collaboration with the local development agency, which is providing the funding.

The aim is to give young people under the age of 25 affordably priced help in setting up their own business ventures, under the guidance of some of the city's leading strategists. Vimmi Singh, a trained <u>accountant</u> who ran her own highly successful Internet sales company before joining the Institute, will be leading the workshops. She is confident that the seminars will provide enterprising young people with what it takes to get a business off the ground.

I've got the programme for the five sessions here in front of me, and each has a suitably inspiring title. For example, the first one is called 'Envisioning your Business'. This first session will help course participants in the important task of defining the basic idea on which their business will be based. They'll come away with what's known as a '<u>toolkit</u>' – in other words, the basic skills and information needed to start thinking about setting up in business.

Session 2 is entitled 'Dynamics', and this one will help those taking part to translate their vision into reality. They'll be encouraged to think about the key <u>resources</u> that will be needed for their business to run smoothly – because their success is going to depend on their ability to make use of these in the future.

Session 3 goes by the name 'Fuelling the Business'. This session recognises that getting the most appropriate form of <u>finance</u> →

for a business can be daunting for young entrepreneurs who are not experts. This session shows what is available, so that participants can see what might be most suitable for them.

The title of Session 4, 'Leadership', says it all. This one's designed to introduce the key concepts in managing a business and focuses on providing insights into team-building skills, motivating staff and getting the best out of people.

Session 5 is called 'Realising your Dream'. In this session, those taking part will be shown how to develop what's called a 'route plan'. It is an exercise in setting personal objectives, based on one's unique skills and style. It sets the business agenda for the first 12 months, and covers the process of getting started, thinking ahead and dealing with unexpected setbacks.

So, if you're under 25 and thinking of starting your own business, this could be the course for you. The price is £200, but in order to enrol, you'll need to have had at least three years' work experience. You don't need to have been to university or anything like that, but you must have a business idea you want to develop. The five sessions are on October the 4th, 18th and 25th and November the 1st and 8th at the Nelson Hotel in West Street. To book a place, call Vimmi Singh on …

Language development pp.11–12

1a 1 A new training manager is required (by the company).
2 The post has been advertised in all national newspapers (by the Human Resources Department).
3 A highly motivated individual is being sought (by the company).
4 Someone was being trained for the role, but she left.
5 Forty-five applications have been received so far (by the company).
6 Unsuccessful candidates will not be contacted.
7 Only the five best candidates are going to be interviewed.
8 The interviews will have been completed (by the Director) by the end of next week.

1b 1 An aptitude test must be completed by each candidate.
2 I should have been warned that the interview room was unavailable.
3 The interviews will have to be rearranged.
4 I must be told about any changes to the schedule.
5 Something has to be done about the lack of space.
6 The company's interview procedure could have been improved.

2 1 The police officer was told a lie (by Jenny).
2 Louis hates being told what to do.
3 ✗ – intransitive verb
4 I don't like being checked up on.
5 Our customers are encouraged to give us their opinions.
6 ✗ – intransitive verb
7 I think his arm is / has been broken.
8 The cause of the accident is being looked into (by the police).

3 1 being 2 being 3 to be 4 to be 5 being 6 to be
7 being 8 to be

4 1 I wanted to be offered the opportunity to travel.
2 She could remember being carried out of the burning building.
3 He didn't expect to be made redundant.
4 She is hoping to be elected as mayor.
5 My father insisted on being called 'Sir'.
6 I hate being let down at the last minute.

5 1 to have/get; altered 2 having/getting; cut
3 to have/get; laundered 4 had/got; enlarged
5 have/get; redecorated 6 have/get; checked
6 1 had 2 get 3 have/get 4 having/getting 5 needs
6 having/getting 7 to 8 had 9 was 10 to 11 get 12 need

English in Use pp.12–13

1a 1 c 2 relatively formal
1b 1 To give information about the writing course.
2 It is more informal.
2b 1 b 2 c 3 b 4 are requested
3 1 get/travel 2 lot / variety / large number 3 small
4 private lesson/session 5 must / have to / need to
6 ask you 7 choose/pick one 8 hand in / give in / send in
9 before 10 free 11 end of 12 dinner / evening meal / supper 13 let them 14 discount on

Reading pp. 14–15

3b 1 *a huge number of people are involved … it's important that we're all pulling in the same direction* (line 27)
2 *My age does count against me at times … I've learned to be diplomatic* (line 24)
3c B (*the most satisfying part of the job is helping my clients to relax* (line 42))
4 1 A (*a huge number of people are involved … it's important that we're all pulling in the same direction* (line 27))
2 D (*You have to show yourself to be a bit ahead of the rest, so you stand out from the crowd.* (line 86))
3 C (*he refuses to be told what to say and likes to do his own research* (line 63))
4 A (*My age does count against me at times* (line 24))
5 D (*she has 'the perfect job' … it has so many different elements* (line 95))
6 B (*I enjoy … helping my team to develop skills that will help them when it comes to thinking about promotion* (line 46))
7 D (*The editorial team thought I was crazy … but … I stuck to my guns* (line 91))
8 C (*There was no explanation for what the programme was* (line 55))
9 B (*the most satisfying part of the job is helping my clients to relax* (line 42))
10 C (*I've had fantastic opportunities to go places I've always wanted to see* (line 73))
11 B (*My parents would've liked me to stay close to home where they could keep an eye on me* (line 35))
12 A (*'I plucked up the courage to ask him for a job' … Kieran's cheek paid off, and he began working amongst some of the best production teams* (line 13))
13 C (*'It was a totally new environment for me' … viewers perceived his chatty presentation as a fresh, irreverant style of journalism* (line 58))
14 A (*I'd always wanted to act, but … I realised I'd never make the big time* (line 9))
15 B (*you have to concentrate totally on your personal objectives* (line 38))

Writing p.16

1 1 international student readers
2 b
3 *why you are nominating your friend, how your friend would benefit from the holiday*

MATHEMATICS TUTOR
BE THE FIRST

Qualified experience teacher.
All levels Ks1,Ks2,Ks3,GCSE,AS and A2

Exam preparation.
I WILL HELP YOU TO BE VERY
CONFIDENT AT MATHS
Mob:07747622565 (Malik)
We speak English, Arabic

2a Reason for nomination: paragraph 2
Final recommendation: paragraph 5
Name of nominee: paragraph 1
Benefits of winning: paragraph 4
Specific example: paragraph 3

3 1 rely on   2 a little depressed   3 He is always willing to help.
4 Allow me to   5 with an excellent mark   6 a valuable benefit
7 Moreover   8 benefit greatly from

4 *Complete model answer with corrected mistakes underlined*
My best friend
The moment I saw the advert for the 'Best friend' award, I knew who I wanted to nominate – my oldest and best friend, Julio. I <u>have known</u> Julio since we were four years old, when we started school together. The teacher put us next to each other in class, and we've been inseparable ever since. I can always turn to him in a crisis, or when I'm feeling a bit down. Nothing is ever too much trouble for him.
Let me give you an example. Last summer I was working for an important exam, but it was very difficult. Julio gave up all his evenings to help me study, and never <u>complained about</u> the time he could have been spending on something else. I managed to pass with flying colours – and it was <u>entirely</u> due to him. Having his help was a real plus.
This holiday would be perfect for Julio for two reasons. First, he has given up so much time for me, I wish I could find a way to repay him. Second, <u>he has never</u> been abroad, but he would love to see new things and <u>experience</u> different cultures at the same time. The Caribbean would be the perfect destination for him to do this. Plus, he is a fantastic photographer, so we could send in some pictures from our trip to the magazine.
So, for being the best friend anyone could ask for and a person who would get so much out of this holiday, I nominate Julio.

Module 2

English in Use p.17

1b c)
2b 1 C (= *found by chance*)
2 D (*to run a course*)
3 B (*signed up for* (*enlisted on, enrolled on, joined*))
4 A (= *soon*)
5 A (*to illustrate a point* = collocation)
6 C (following *below*)
7 B (*rose + from*)
8 A (contrast to what was expected)
9 D (*dared + to*)
10 D (*in the event* is a fixed expression)
11 C (it is *deep breathing* that helps you relax)
12 B (*to overcome an obstacle*)
13 A (*a wave of optimism* = collocation)
14 B (*reminding + me*)
15 C (*credit-card limit* = collocation)

Language development p.18

1a 1 which   2 who   3 where   4 whose   5 when   6 whom
7 that   8 why
1b sentence 7
2 1 those   2 which   3 both   4 whom   5 which   6 why   7 at   8 on
3 1 A, C, D   2 B, C   3 C, D   4 A, C   5 A, D   6 A, B   7 A, B
8 B, C

4 1 a locket containing a lucky charm
2 People wishing to learn
3 Jeremy is the person to talk to
4 People asked to choose

English in Use p.19

1b 1 It was fake.
2 They were fascinated because their own culture lacked a sense of wonder.
2 1 I   2 H   3 G   4 A   5 E   6 D

Vocabulary p.20

1a 1 epic   2 scene   3 location   4 plot   5 score   6 soundtrack
7 screenplay   8 adaptation   9 background   10 close-up
1b 1 epic   2 plot   3 background   4 location   5 screenplay
6 adaptation   7 soundtrack   8 scenes   9 close-up
2 1 on a shoestring   2 was a runaway success   3 cult classic
4 on the edge of your seat   5 a dramatic finale   6 lavish production   7 sequel to   8 blockbuster / box-office hit/smash
9 remake

Listening p. 21

1a 1 five   2 superstitions that they have   3 two   4 twice
2 1 C (*don't have the hassle of getting valuable gear to the venue … Once I'm in the water … my breathing and rhythm … competitors in the other lanes*)
2 H (*training on the roads … at the track … I've no equipment to blame*)
3 G (*road races … going downhill at speed … get a puncture*)
4 B (*the actual sport involves a lot of sitting in one position … before I get behind the wheel … first past that flag*)
5 D (*weeks on end alone … on deck … on shore*)
6 G (*my father gave me a lucky coin … My brother's got one, too*)
7 E (*I can't think what makes me do it, actually*)
8 D (*I get so wound up at the top races, I need all the help I can get!*)
9 B (*it gives me the time and space to empty my head of other rubbish*)
10 H (*he's a comfort to me … he's there to keep my spirits up in the darker moments*)

Tapescript

Speaker 1
I have to travel a lot to international competitions, which I don't much enjoy, but at least I <u>don't have the hassle of getting valuable gear to the venue</u>. A few years ago, <u>my father gave me a lucky coin</u> – he was a sailor and said it'd always brought him good fortune when travelling. <u>My brother's got one, too</u>. I always get really excited before a race. I know it's silly, but in the changing rooms I touch the coin before going out, just for luck. <u>Once I'm in the water</u>, though, I think of nothing but <u>my breathing and rhythm</u>. I never look at the <u>competitors in the other lanes</u> – that'd just put me off.

Speaker 2
It was when I started winning races that the sport really took over my life. I'm fortunate that, where I live, <u>training on the roads</u> is no problem, and I go out in all weathers. But it's all about preparation, not luck. I never shave before an important event, though – that's my only superstition – <u>I can't think what makes me do it, actually</u>, because there are much more important things to focus on – it's just become a tradition. My mum says it →

saves your strength, not shaving – but she's only joking! She knows that <u>at the track</u>, it's all down to me. <u>I've no equipment to blame</u> if I fail, so I concentrate on giving my best.

Speaker 3

My parents have always supported me and come to all my <u>road races</u>. It was at my first big event that my boyfriend gave me this silver necklace to wear. I won that time, so I've worn it ever since. I suppose that's a superstition, although it can't really make a difference, can it? But if I took it off now, it'd seem like tempting fate. I have to admit, though, that when I'm waiting at the start, I touch it. <u>I get so wound up at the top races, I need all the help I can get!</u> Especially when I'm <u>going downhill at speed</u>! I just hope I don't <u>get a puncture</u> – that'd be a disaster!

Speaker 4

I don't like the monotony of gym work, so I do things like going to the pool, or out on my bike to keep fit, because <u>the actual sport involves a lot of sitting in one position</u>. The nearest I get to a superstition is always getting up early and going for a run on the day of a big race. Apart from the physical benefits, <u>it gives me the time and space to empty my head of other rubbish</u> before I <u>get behind the wheel</u>. I don't actively think about the dangers when I'm racing, otherwise I'd be on edge all the time, but I need to have 100% concentration if I want to be <u>first past that flag</u>.

Speaker 5

I couldn't imagine not having a mascot – I've had my teddy bear since I was little. Of course, I don't believe that he helps me win, but <u>he's a comfort to me</u>. I spend <u>weeks on end alone</u>, away from my family, so <u>he's there to keep my spirits up in the darker moments</u>. I like the idea of upholding traditions, but I don't take these things too seriously. You know, like, for the celebrations at the end of my last race when I dressed him up in a pirate costume and paraded him up and down <u>on deck</u>. I don't carry him round everywhere <u>on shore</u>, though – that would be taking it a bit far!

Language development p.22

1 1 C (A is too short, B turn the student into the questioner)
 2 A (neither B nor C talks about the student's family)
 3 B (A doesn't say what the student likes, C answers a slightly different question, about the student being happy)
2 1 B   2 C   3 B   4 A
3a 1 suppose (or: *think, guess, reckon*)   2 believe   3 see
 4 interesting   5 saying   6 think (or: *see*)   7 matter   8 have

Tapescript

Examiner: I'd like you to ask each other about places of interest you have visited in this country.

Candidate 1: Where have you most enjoyed visiting here?

Candidate 2: Well, I <u>suppose</u> that one of my favourite places is the Museum of Modern Art. Have you been?

Candidate 1: Not yet, but <u>believe</u> it or not, I was planning to go next week. What do you like about it?

Candidate 2: Well, you <u>see</u>, I didn't know much about art before I started going there, but I learn more each time I visit.

Candidate 1: That's <u>interesting</u>. So what you're <u>saying</u> is that it's worth visiting a few times?

Candidate 2: Definitely. So, what's your favourite place?

Candidate 1: Let me <u>think</u>. It's probably the old town with its ancient buildings. As a <u>matter</u> of fact, I've been working in a shop there.

Candidate 2: Oh, <u>have</u> you? What has that been like?

Candidate 1: Hard work, but great for my English!

Language development p.23

1 1 a; the; the; the   2 the; the; ø   3 an; a; ø; the
 4 ø; the; the; ø; a   5 the; ø; the; the   6 ø; ø; the   7 a; ø; ø
2 1 Some of the girl's clothing **was** torn.
 2 He gave us some very useful **advice**.
 3 None of the information he gave me **was** correct.
 4 A number of students **have** complained …
 5 A lot of people **enjoy** watching sport.
 6 The number of people interested in the job **has** surprised us.
3 1 little   2 some   3 much   4 many   5 any   6 a lot of
 7 less   8 enough
4 1 both   2 both   3 Neither   4 both   5 both   6 neither
 7 each   8 either   9 Neither   10 both
5 1 shred   2 pinch   3 drop   4 piece   5 slice   6 bit   7 hint
 8 heap

English in Use p. 24

1b 1 Because he seems to be an unusually lucky person.
 2 three
2b 1 not   2 a   3 into   4 it   5 from   6 with   7 which   8 before
 9 time   10 as   11 either   12 the   13 looking   14 would   15 his
4 articles in Q2 and Q12
 pronouns in Q4 and Q15
 Q9 completes the fixed phrase *just in time*
 Q13 completes the phrasal verb *looking forward to*
 prepositions in   Q3 *plunged into*
                   Q5 *suffering from*
                   Q6 *escaped with*

Writing p.25

1 1 to promote the leisure complex
 2 give <u>a brief description of the complex</u>, outlining <u>why it is important to the town</u>, <u>describe its main facilities</u> and <u>plans for the future</u>
 3 informal
2 a 4   b 2   c 1   d –   e 3   f –
3 1 C   2 A   3 D   4 B
4/5 *Complete model answer*
 THE NEW METRO COMPLEX
 It's here at last! Are you bored? Are your evenings dull and uninteresting? Help is at hand!
 Whether you are 14, 40 or 80, the New Metro Complex has something for you.
 When will the New Metro Complex open?
 Opening Day is September 15th, and for the first week there's a spectacular offer of BUY ONE GET ONE FREE on all available facilities. Don't miss out! Come to the old converted Cattle Market on September 15th!
 Why is the New Metro Complex important for this town?
 The Complex offers a ONE-STOP SHOP for everyone in the town, a place where you can meet friends, relax and socialise, get fit or go shopping – all under one roof! As well as this, it will attract more people from the outlying towns and villages. This can only be good for local businesses!

What can you expect to find in the New Metro Complex?
In the welcoming atmosphere of the complex, you will find:
- three restaurants catering for a wide variety of tastes
- five cafés for a quick bite to eat
- an indoor sports arena which will host tournaments and provide facilities for local clubs
- a five-screen cinema showing the latest films
- specialist boutiques
- a multi-storey car park ensuring easy access to the complex

There's more to come
Doesn't that sound excellent? Well, that's not all! No leisure complex would be complete without a bowling alley, and there are plans to add this within two years, with a small theatre being completed a year after that.

Come along!
Why not come along on September 15ᵗʰ and give it a try? There will be special competitions and offers on the day, and even a special appearance by a mystery celebrity. Don't miss it!

Reading p.26

1 creating or doing something false in order to mislead people
2   1   He wants to find out why people react in particular ways in buildings that are believed to be haunted.
    2   They recorded people's reactions in old buildings that are believed to be haunted.
    3   People often felt the most scared in the exact places that are believed to be haunted.
    4   He thinks that changes in the temperature and magnetic field in the atmosphere cause the experiences.
    5   He plans to build a fake haunted house where he can make these changes to temperature and magnetic fields artificially.
3   1 E   (*such an unusal idea* links to *evidence to support this explanation* (line 14))
    2 G   (*the precise spots reputed to be haunted* (line 23) links to *One was Hampton Court ... Another was the South Bridge*)
    3 C   (*This provided Wiseman ...* links to *As a result ...* (line 27))
    4 H   (*to prepare people psychologically* (line 31) links to *Wiseman insists that he should be able to tell the volunteers*)
    5 F   (*people found the special effects less believable as they became more obvious* (line 40) links to *It's the same in everyday life, we are sensitive to very slight alterations*)
    6 A   (*historic venues already full of ghostly folklore* links to *So, at present, he is searching for disued buildings ...* (line 56))
    7 D   (*attracted a record number of visitors* (line 62) links to *Indeed, his experimental haunted house could prove to be a bargain*)

Module 3

English in Use p.28

1b They usually choose other famous people as their friends.
2   1 attractions   2 supposedly   3 tension   4 outward   5 rivalry
    6 tactical   7 admiration   8 personal   9 highly   10 strength
    11 rejection   12 appointment   13 creative   14 responsibility
    15 unacceptable

Language development p.29

1   1   The planet **V**enus is warmer than **M**ars because it is closer to the sun/**S**un.

2   This winter, I'll be working every **S**aturday in **D**ecember in the run up to **C**hristmas and **N**ew **Y**ear.
3   **M**y friend **F**abio's father has a house near **L**ake **C**omo in the north of **I**taly.
4   **I**'d like to study **S**panish in **S**outh **A**merica in either **A**rgentina or **C**hile.
5   **S**he's the new doctor; she's taken over from **D**octor **D**igby.
6   **F**or more information, please contact **B**arclays **B**ank at 42 **H**igh **S**treet, **B**iggleswade.
7   **T**he sacred **R**iver **G**anges starts high in the **H**imalayan mountains and eventually flows through **B**angladesh into the **B**ay of **B**engal.
8   **A**re you fascinated by fame? **D**o you seek out celebrities? **I**f so, read *Stalkers Weekly*, the new magazine for star spotters.

2   1   If **you're** going out for coffee, **I'd** love a cappuccino!
    2   Please ask the maintenance man if **he's** fixed the tap in the kitchen. Apparently **there's** been a leak in there.
    3   I need a laptop. **Mine's** broken so **I'm** using yours. OK?
    4   **How's** the report coming on? **I'll** need it in the morning.
    5   **Who'll** be locking up tonight? I **won't** be here.
    6   Janine says you **can't** call her at home because **she's not / she isn't** going to be there tonight.
    7   Daniel called to say he **won't** be coming in today as **he's** got a headache.
    8   Melanie says **she's** booked the Victoria Hotel. She says **it's** a great place and has its own pool.
    9   Melissa says if **she'd** known there was going to be a strike, **she'd have / she would've** set off earlier.
    10 Dave and Mike said **they're not / they aren't** going to be more than ten minutes late.

3   1   It was the American journalist Henry Louis Mencken who said, 'A celebrity is one who is known to many persons he is glad he does not know.'
    2   'Fame and tranquility can never be bedfellows,' said Michel de Montaigne, the 16ᵗʰ-century French writer.
    3   'I may be a living legend,' said singer Roy Orbison, 'but that doesn't help when I've got to change a flat tyre.'
    4   The actor Alan Alda once joked, 'It isn't necessary to be rich and famous to be happy. It's only necessary to be rich.'
    5   It was the actor and film director Woody Allen who remarked, 'I don't want to achieve immortality through my work. I want to achieve it through not dying.'

4   Robert Garside is nothing if not dedicated. For the last six years, the 36-year-old Briton has had just one goal: to be the first person to run around the world. Since starting out in New Delhi in October 1997, Robert has dodged bullets in Russia, outrun thieves in Mexico and found true love in Venezuela. Garside, who often feels homesick, says, 'I miss a really good pot of tea!' In June 2004, he plans to set off on his next venture: to become the first person to swim around the world, covering a distance of approximately 25,000 miles. He says that, as with the run, the greatest problems will be, 'isolation, politics and the weather.'

English in Use p.30

2   1   the newsreaders' appearance
    2   that she is rich
3   1 thousands of   2 it's   3 judgements   4 you? It   5 guarantee
    6 ✔   7 ✔   8 comment   9 ✔   10 asked if   11 Luckily
    12 said, 'Be   13 While   14 private   15 ✔   16 especially

Writing p.31

1 1 <u>It is hard to say why the marriages of well-known actors seldom last.</u> <u>Some</u> have said it is because of the pressure of being in the public eye. <u>Others</u> have suggested it is because actors spend a lot of time away from their partners as they are touring or filming. ~~Many films take months to shoot and there are often delays.~~ <u>Another possible reason</u> is that the opportunities for being unfaithful are so much greater, especially if you are in constant contact with adoring fans. ~~Some actors are gorgeous and have huge fan clubs.~~ <u>The final reason</u> could be that actors are people who crave constant attention and need to be loved, and it is hard to maintain that level of devotion in a long-term relationship.

2 I'm not that interested in fame. ~~Some famous people have far more money than they need.~~ <u>For me, the most important thing in life is to know that I have used my time and energy well.</u> <u>So</u> I'd rather have a lower paid job where I was helping others than earn a fortune making money from those around me. <u>Some people</u> judge their success by how much they have gained for themselves, <u>whereas</u> I'd like to be judged on what I have given back, not on what I have taken from life. ~~My mum has always gone out of her way to help people.~~ The more people give, the more everyone has. When I'm old, I'd like to be able to look back on my life with a clear conscience.

2 1 A – too specific, not just about magazines
B – correct
C – too vague

2 A – correct
B – too specific – not just about young people
C – too specific – not about TV

3a Paragraph 1: 3
Paragraph 2: 1
Paragraph 3: 4
Paragraph 4: 2

3b *Suggested answer*
A paparazzo's days are often long and boring. A typical day would start early in the morning and not finish until late at night, and a large part of that time would be spent standing around, waiting for something to happen. The job can be depressing at times, as we know that if we can't produce a picture worth selling, we won't get paid. So why do we do it? Because we are all waiting for that one piece of luck that will bring us the picture worth a million.

Other paparazzi are friends as well as rivals. After all, we're all in the same boat. So while we're waiting, we chat and compare the stories we're working on, sharing ideas and experiences. This comradeship makes the job more bearable and a lot less lonely.

The paparazzo is nothing without his camera. It goes everywhere with you, as you never know when that big story is going to happen right in front of your eyes. Regular practice is important, as being able to use your camera quickly and accurately is one of the paparazzo's most important skills. It is also vital to keep it in good working order and update it regularly to keep up with new technology. You really can't afford to be let down by your equipment.

To be successful, the paparazzo needs a network of contacts. We rely on these contacts to give us information and tip-offs, so we have to get on well with all kinds of people, from hotel porters and barmen to taxi drivers and even hairdressers. These people are all in contact with the rich and famous, and they could all one day phone with the one big story that all paparazzi are waiting for.

Listening p.32

1a 1 Anita Roddick, a well-known businesswoman
2 a TV programme in which she pretended to be an old woman

1c 1 Q2   2 Q3   3 Q5 and Q7

2 1 undercover research   2 make-up artist   3 invisible
4 tinned food / tins of food   5 anger; impatience
6 senior citizen   7 wisdom   8 employment

4 2 This student has got the wrong person – it was the make-up that made Anita look older than her mother – their clothes were very similar.

5 This student has only written part of the answer – the word *and* in the box indicates that two words are needed.

6 This student has included information (*such as*) which is already in the sentence stem (*like*) and only included part of the answer. With these words in the gap, the sentence doesn't make sense.

8 This student has got the right answer – but hasn't spelled it correctly.

Tapescript

Hello, I'm Anita Roddick. Many of you will recognise me as the founder of The Body Shop. Well, I'm now 62 and have no plans to retire from my business, having become a non-executive director and consultant to The Body Shop. I've also set up a new venture, Anita Roddick Publications Ltd. But it suddenly occurred to me that I still have no idea what being old is going to be like, how people will perceive me, so I decided to do a bit of what I call '<u>undercover research</u>'.

So Discovery Europe, a TV company, arranged a <u>make-up artist</u> and costume designer, and for four days I was transformed into an old lady. Actually, the make-up artist went a bit overboard and gave me so many wrinkles that when my mother – who's now 87 – appeared on the programme with me, she looked ten years my junior! We were dressed similarly, however, and that certainly was a first for us!

Anyway, the idea was that I'd go out onto the streets to find out how the elderly are treated. Predictably, I suppose, in modern Britain, the answer is often 'badly' – although there are some notable exceptions. What struck me most was how I seemed to become <u>invisible</u>. I guess I'm used to being recognised in the street, but when I was dressed as an old person, people seemed to look through me as if I wasn't there.

For example, I was carrying two shopping bags, and not just little ones with a loaf of bread in – big ones bulging with <u>tinned food</u>, which anyone could see I was struggling with – but no one offered to help me. And when it came to crossing a busy road, I deliberately acted as if I were confused by the traffic and the noise. Now you'd think people would be sympathetic, or at least understanding in that situation, but all I could sense was people's <u>anger</u> and <u>impatience</u>. Drivers were banging their hands on their steering wheels because they had to wait until I got out of the way. In our modern world of fast communications and busy urban lifestyles, I concluded, we seem to have lost the art of kindness. There is a debate about what to call older people in Britain. Terms such as 'old-age pensioner' and '<u>senior citizen</u>' now sound patronising, whereas trendy terms like 'silver surfer' just seem silly. I personally favour 'elder'. Native Americans call their old people 'elders', and it denotes <u>wisdom</u>. It illustrates their approach, which is much more one of respect.

In modern society, people seem to be judged on the basis of their economic productivity – and perhaps that's why in countries with the highest participation rates of older people in <u>employment</u>, such as Sweden, older people are treated with more respect. There are more than ten million people in Britain over the age of retirement, and I really think it's time they made their voice heard.

Language development pp.33–34

1 1 must / have (got) to / need to   2 needs to / has to
3 must not   4 will have to / (will) need to   5 needn't / doesn't have to   6 must have   7 needn't / don't have to   8 needn't have

2 1 must / should / ought to   2 Should/Must   3 shouldn't
4 should have   5 should / ought to / must   6 should / ought to

3 1 couldn't / wasn't able to   2 were able to   3 could have
4 will be able to   5 haven't been able to / can't
6 won't be able to / can't   7 could / was able to   8 can

4 1 could   2 might   3 might have   4 can   5 should
6 shouldn't

5 1 This can't be the building we're looking for.
2 I suppose that he might/could have phoned while I was out.
3 Someone must have broken into the house while we were out.
4 Michael was in New York all last week, so it can't have been him that you saw.
5 He can't/couldn't have crashed the car.

6 1 could   2 would   3 will   4 shall

7 1 A   2 C   3 B   4 C   5 A   6 B   7 A   8 B   9 A   10 B   11 C
12 A   13 B   14 C   15 C   16 A   17 B   18 B

English in Use p.35

1b 1 Because computers are expensive
2 By providing cheap computers for schools

2 1 B   2 H   3 D   4 I   5 A   6 F

Language development

might feel justified … , **can** step in … , the charity **had to** work hard …

Reading pp.36–37

1 *Suggested answers*
1 An 'ethical employer' is one that is socially aware and formulates its policies to put environmental and social principles before profit.
2 It is aimed at students and new graduates looking for a job.

2 **Rachel Hare** is a student at **London University** whose views are reported.
Lauren Steadman works for *Ethical Consumer Magazine*, which advises people on this issue.
Helen Wallis works for *People and Planet*, which is an ethical careers service.
Tom Chance is a student at **Reading University** whose views are reported.
The Industrial Society is an organisation which does research in this area.
Axiom Software is a graduate careers publisher. It carried out a survey.

6 1 A   (*we should be slightly sceptical when … companies say they are committed to 'socially responsible behaviour'* (line 1))
2 C   (*more than half of UK graduates said they would choose a job … rather than one with a more lucrative salary* (line 25))
3 A   (*companies have sophisticated PR … without much substance to try to look good* (line 44))

4 B   (*workshops … on how to … the chance to talk through the issues … arrive at their own particular priorities* (line 51))
5 C   (*Helen helps them investigate whether the company … is living up to those standards* (line 65))
6 D   (This is a global question. You get the answer by understanding the writer's attitude throughout the text.)

Writing p.38

2 Introduction: c   Overview: a   Evaluation of events: b

3 1 In addition   2 On the other hand   3 This was in spite of the fact that   4 Finally   5 Apparently

4 More money was raised than on the same day last year.
The event was organised by about 50 people.
People felt obliged to give money when they were approached directly by collectors.
The jumble sale was enjoyed by everyone attending it.

5 *Complete model answer*
Introduction
The purpose of this report is to describe the fundraising day held on June 16th. It was an extremely enjoyable day. I will evaluate its success and make recommendations for future events.
Overview
On the whole, the day was a great success. Events organised included house-to-house collection and street collection, a jumble sale, an appeal for money in the local paper. More money was raised than on the same day last year, and more people attended. The event was organised by about 50 people, mostly students from the university.
Evaluation of events
Some events were more successful than others. It was clear that one event raised a lot more money than the others, and this was the house-to-house collection. This raised 40% of the overall total. This may be because people felt obliged to give money when they were approached directly by collectors. In addition, the street collection was successful financially, probably for the same reason (it accounted for 30% of the total). On the other hand, the jumble sale was enjoyed by everyone attending it, but it only raised 20% of the money. This was in spite of the fact that the sale was the only interactive event of the day. Finally, the last 10% came from various activities including an appeal in the local newspaper. Apparently, these were less successful because they lacked the personal touch of the house-to-house and street collections.
Recommendations
There are several recommendations that can be made. Firstly, in view of the success of events with the personal touch, I would suggest that a greater range of interactive activities should be provided, so that everyone can get involved. These should include a sponsored run, street parties (organised through local schools) and a sponsored walk for older people.
In addition, all officials should be given a badge when they are collecting money so that they can prove that they are genuine collectors. Finally, the event should be advertised in advance so that more people can plan to attend.
Conclusion
To sum up, this year's event was extremely successful, and with some careful thought and planning, even more money could be raised next year.

Module 4

English in Use p.39

1 1 architect
   2 the Nobel Peace Centre in Oslo
   3 She is the managing director of his business.
2 1 C (*cast* = film/play, *side/team* = sport, *team + of, crew* = boat/film)
   2 A (*responsible + for*)
   3 D (*to single out* a special person)
   4 B (a *figure* is a person)
   5 C (*late thirties* = collocation)
   6 A (*in addition to* is a fixed expression)
   7 D (*to house* is a transitive verb)
   8 B (*to gain recognition*)
   9 A (*to be in great demand* = collocation)
   10 D (*public appearances* = collocation)
   11 B (*to take the load off* someone's *shoulders*)
   12 C (*dealing + with*)
   13 B (organisations have a *base*)
   14 A (*practised at, skilful in, experienced at*)
   15 C (= *not common*)

Language development p.40

1 1 difference 2 persistence 3 confidence 4 appearance
   5 performance 6 correspondence 7 dependence
   8 assistance 9 existence 10 preference
2 1 responsible 2 believable 3 collapsible 4 defensible
   5 adaptable 6 suitable 7 reversible 8 breakable 9 flexible
   10 adjustable
3 1 insecure (unsafe, unpredictable, unwell)
   2 unable (incapable, informal, inadequate)
   3 unrealistic (irresponsible, irrelevant, irrational)
   4 unpleasant (impatient, improbable, immature)
   5 unlucky (illegal, illogical, illiterate)
4 1 a generalise b generalisations c generally d generalities
   2 a intended b intentions c unintentional d intentionally
   3 a dependable b independent c dependence d independence
   4 a powerful b powerless c empower d powerfully
   5 a original b origin(s) c originality d originally
      e unoriginal
   6 a pleasure b pleasant c displeased d pleasing
      e pleasurable
   7 a various b varied c variable d variance e varying
      f variety g variously

English in Use p.41

1 1 Job-sharing is when two people share a job, dividing the
      hours and work between them.
   2 Yes
2 1 existing 2 entitled 3 specialises 4 proposals 5 adaptable
   6 responsibility 7 favourably
4 8 relationship 9 fashionable 10 residential 11 strengths
   12 adventurous 13 creative 14 hidden 15 beneficial

Listening p.42

1a 1 five 2 difficult decisions they have made 3 two
1c 1 b 2 c
2 1 A (*I was made redundant … I'd hardly got any savings … I
          was desperate*)

2 C (*I can't believe I ever had the nerve to take such a risk*)
3 A (*the higher you go in architecture, the less actual designing
        you do … I was so frustrated!*)
4 B (*it's anything but nine-to-five*)
5 C (*realised it was time to do my own thing*)
6 C (*If something goes wrong, I just think 'so what? I'll just do
        something else instead'*)
7 C (*it sucks the energy out of you!*)
8 B (*Male friends say they'd change places with me any day*)
9 A (*I've started teaching local children … I've discovered that I
        have a real affinity with the young*)
10 B (*I do find the 150-kilometre round-trip to do our shopping a
         bit much … Our nearest neighbours are six kilometres
         away*)

Tapescript

Speaker 1
<u>I was made redundant</u>. It happened overnight, and even though
I'd been in a well-paid post, <u>I'd got hardly any savings</u>. Jobs in my
line of work are few and far between, so <u>I was desperate</u>. When a
friend said he was selling his health-food shop, I just said I'd buy
it – the words just popped out of my mouth. I had to take out a
huge loan to do it, and initially it was really touch and go, because
I'd never set up a business before. I'm sure my friends thought I'd
go under, and looking back, <u>I can't believe I ever had the nerve to
take such a risk</u>. But I turned the corner eventually.

Speaker 2
I started working as an architect in London, building new
cinemas. That's where I first encountered visual impairment
issues – planting a seed for the future! Later, I realised <u>the higher
you go in architecture, the less actual designing you do</u>; soon I
was taking a managerial role, with three people under me. <u>I was
so frustrated</u>! I'd been working voluntarily with blind people and
decided to give up my job and train as a rehabilitation worker.
After a year training to get the qualifications I needed, I've got
used to the drop in salary, but my social life has suffered a bit,
because <u>it's anything but nine-to-five</u>. Helping people rebuild
their lives, though, is a real inspiration.

Speaker 3
I was feeling lonely after my children left home. Then one day I
thought, 'You're in a rut – be brave, do something different.' The
first step was buying a motorbike – I'd always wanted one. The
family all teased me at first. But I soon loved the freedom it gave
me, and <u>realised it was time to do my own thing</u>. I'd been saving
up for a new kitchen, but instead I sold the house and went to
India to do teaching. I've had to get on with so many new people
and I've learned to trust my own instincts. <u>If something goes
wrong, I just think 'so what? I'll just do something else instead'</u>.

Speaker 4
When our second child was born, Anna didn't want to be a full-
time mum. She's a lawyer, and her work brought in more money
than mine, so it made sense for me to stay at home to look after
the children. Some men would feel awkward in my position, but I
appreciate being around to see my kids grow up. <u>Male friends say
they'd change places with me any day</u> given half the chance – they
think it's an easy option – but they haven't a clue what I actually
do. The children just never stop – <u>it sucks the energy out of you</u>!
The house gets pretty chaotic at times – I don't care about that
particularly, but it's all go!

Speaker 5
When Pete took early retirement, we took the chance to change
our lives dramatically. We decided to go to Africa. We knew it was
right for us, having seen the freedom of the African bush, and

experienced the wonderful climate on previous holidays. The brilliant thing is <u>I've started teaching local children</u>. Although I was really nervous at first, <u>I've discovered that I have a real affinity with the young</u>. Pete has surprised himself, too – he's started doing DIY, which he hated in England. <u>I do find the150-kilometre round-trip to do our shopping a bit much</u>, so once a month's enough. <u>Our nearest neighbours are six kilometres away</u>. It's a good thing Pete and I don't fall out!

Vocabulary p. 43

1 1 c get on with   5 a look up to
   2 f fell for   6 d relies on
   3 g takes after   7 e let down
   4 b fell out over

2 1 the black sheep of the family   2 seen eye to eye
   3 get their own way   4 hit it off   5 run in the family
   6 've lost touch

3 1 close family   2 siblings   3 extended family
   4 confidant/mate   5 circle of friends   6 acquaintances
   7 friend of a friend   8 colleagues   9 partners   10 companion
   11 flatmate   12 associate   13 ex

Language development pp. 44–45

1 1 It came as no surprise to me that my brother passed his exam with flying colours.
   2 I'm horrified that you could accuse me of such a thing.
   3 It is likely that the deal will be finalised tomorrow.
   4 I'm delighted that I can bring you this good news.
   5 It is ridiculous that funding for the project has been cut.
   6 There is no proof that he is/was involved in this fraud.
   7 I really regret that I didn't go to university when I was young.
   8 It was obvious to the jury that she was guilty.

2 1 G 2 C 3 A 4 F 5 I 6 E 7 B 8 H

3 1 how 2 when 3 why 4 where 5 which 6 what 7 who

4 1 What 2 Why 3 Who 4 How 5 Who; What (*either order*)

5 1 Whether 2 if/whether 3 if/whether 4 whether
   5 if/whether 6 whether 7 if/whether 8 whether

6 1 Growing up 2 keeping 3 to assert 4 to criticise / criticising 5 to say 6 Going 7 to be 8 having

7 1 It can be helpful to discuss problems with a friend.
   2 His aim is to become a top chef by the age of 30.
   3 Tom's really keen for us to meet Mary.
   4 The only way the company can survive is to cut costs.
   5 The ability of human beings to solve problems is one of the definitions of intelligence.
   6 The tendency is for the oldest child in a family to be the most ambitious.
   7 The main priority of younger siblings is to establish their own identity.
   8 The most valuable contribution therapists can make is to help people recognise patterns of behaviour they need to change.

8 1 a It would be a great honour to meet the Dalai Lama.
      b Meeting the Dalai Lama would be a great honour.
   2 a It is very important to spend time on your own.
      b Spending time on your own is very important.
   3 a It would be very hard to find out his true identity.
      b Finding out his true identity would be very hard.
   4 a It is ridiculous to say that the company is not interested in making money.
      b Saying that the company is not interested in making money is ridiculous.

English in Use p.46

1 1 They do special physical exercises to help them concentrate and learn better.
   2 The children settle down more quickly and concentrate better.

2 1 do 2 is 3 other 4 are 5 what 6 which 7 same 8 and
   9 as 10 sure 11 one 12 into 13 through 14 addition 15 go

Writing p.47

1 1 an article
   2 why you think the family is still the most influential part of a young person's life
   3 c

2 Plan B

3 1 Blood is thicker than water.   2 incredible demands
   3 bombarded on all sides   4 a vast array   5 the going gets tough   6 play a part   7 through thick and thin   8 bedrock

4a 1 c 2 d 3 b 4 a

4b 1 c 2 d 3 b 4 a

4c … probably have problems of their own!
   … no one is a better friend than a parent!
   Where do young people get their role models from?
   Is it the exotic media stars admired by so many?

5 Title a) is the most suitable.

Reading pp.48–49

1 1 They are all twins.
   2 high-achieving, well-respected in their particular field
   3 competition between brothers and sisters

2 1 Bryony and Kathryn: athletics/sport
      Neil and Adrian: acting
      Louise and Jane: art
      Anita and Carole: music
   2 They are all very close, although they don't always agree on everything.

3b 1 *feel left out* means that someone felt excluded.
   2 *they do row about … petty things* means that they fall out over unimportant matters.

3c *people's indifference to our distinct personalities* suggests that people assume they are identical
   we … forced to accept / we tolerate it suggests that they resent this

4 1 B (*there's this unexplained synchronicity … the producers appreciate it* (line 51))
   2 A (*their brother … did feel left out* (line 17))
   3 A (*what they do row about … invariable over petty things* (line 20))
   4 D (*We feel we take more risks precisely because there's two of us. We spur each other on* (line 110))
   5 C (*they wanted to give us just one fee for our exhibitions!' 'That's taking sisterly love a bit far!'* (line 85))
   6 B (*These two films represent the … twins' big break … they have been avid film fanatics for years* (line 34))
   7 C (*The former found the separation 'a bit traumatic'; the latter viewed it as 'a terrific challenge'* (line 61))
   8 B (*he doesn't see them following the same path … I'm sure we'll head in different directions* (line 40))
   9 D (*we take after our mother, who's very musical* (line 94))
   10 A (*they don't seem to be competitive … It's not something we get worked up about* (line 10))
   11 B (*people's indifference to our distinct personalities … We tolerate it* (line 56))

12 C (*They ended up producing all but identical photographic displays … They are not identical; in fact, you might not even think they were sisters* (line 64))

13 D (*there's a danger of living up to that label after a while* (line 113))

14 C (*they … never had any irreconcilable differences … there's an enormous element of trust … there's no need to define who's responsible for what* (line 79))

15 A (*have to face up to building separate lives … but neither relishes the prospect … it's scary* (line 25))

16 D (*advantageous to both of them intellectually and socially … they have the best of both worlds* (line 99))

Module 5

English in Use p.50

2 1 celebration   2 growth   3 movement   4 innovative
5 prominently   6 supporters   7 assortment

4 8 response   9 undeniable   10 options   11 analysts
12 wisdom   13 products   14 perception   15 indulgence

Language development pp.51–52

1a 1 angry–irate   2 bad–disastrous   3 pleased–delighted
4 interesting–fascinating   5 large–huge   6 hungry–ravenous
7 similar– identical   8 small–minute   9 valuable–priceless
10 rare–unique

1b *Suggested answers*
1 slightly –   2 fairly –   3 quite +   4 absolutely +
5 completely +   6 rather –   7 utterly +   8 a bit –

2 1 most   2 dead   3 somewhat   4 a bit   5 incredibly   6 rather

3a 1 sensitive   2 ashamed   3 useless   4 unacceptable
5 useless   6 educated   7 disturbed   8 healthy

3b 1 highly sensitive   2 highly critical   3 utterly useless
4 totally unacceptable   5 utterly useless   6 highly educated
7 deeply disturbed   8 perfectly healthy

3c 1 heavily armed   2 perfectly understandable   3 highly critical
4 heavily dependent   5 bitterly cold   6 totally unacceptable
7 painfully aware   8 deeply moving   9 highly respected
10 totally incompetent

4 1 tight/tightly   2 right   3 mostly   4 late   5 hard   6 hardly
7 hard   8 cheap (*informal*)/cheaply   9 deadly   10 dead
11 wide   12 widely   13 free   14 freely

English in Use pp.52–53

1a 1 a hotel manager   2 in the leaflet for guests   3 informal
1b 1 hotel guests   2 formal
2b 1 c   2 a   3 highly   4 b
3 1 request   2 notice   3 as possible   4 highly/strongly
5 majority   6 to sample/taste   7 bases on   8 the interests
9 prohibited/forbidden   10 be accompanied   11 at all
12 ensure / make sure / take care   13 deposited/placed

Listening p.54

2 1 C (*I reckoned that the idea of organised walking tours could easily catch on with people of all ages*)
2 B (*I really want to think carefully about what we do with the money we make*)

3 D (*they soon find something in common with each other*)
4 C (*judging by our clients' response, I believe the sentiment is appreciated*)
5 A (*All those recruited need to embrace the company's objectives … reinforced through ongoing training*)
6 A (*there's even a danger that certain travel journalists are getting bored with it, portraying it as wishy-washy idealism*)

Tapescript

Int. = Interviewer, CW = Christopher Winney

Int.: Welcome to the Holiday programme. Today I'm talking to Christopher Winney, who runs a holiday company with a difference. He organises walking tours for holiday makers all over the world, but says his main aim is to support the environment. Christopher, you've just won an award for actively promoting responsible tourism via your company, ATG Oxford. Tell me, what inspired you to set up the company?

CW: I used to be a not-terribly-successful travel writer and when I was asked to do a book on long-distance walking, I jumped at the chance in the knowledge that it might lead to other commissions. So, I walked from London to Rome, and it was the most enjoyable thing I've ever done. I thought, 'Why isn't everybody walking across Europe?' Well, of course, people have been doing it for centuries! But nobody seemed to be tapping into the business potential. I reckoned that the idea of organised walking tours could easily catch on with people of all ages, especially if it was linked to the principles of conservation and sustainable tourism, because people who like walking generally like to give something back.

Int.: So, how exactly does ATG give something back? Is it financial?

CW: We give away ten per cent of our pre-tax profits to environmental charities. We also try to source only locally produced food and support local industries on our walking tours. You can't get away from the fact that there's an additional cost involved, but it's easily justified. I'm not a do-gooder with a mad gleam in my eye, but if the objective of my business was just for me to enjoy a better lifestyle, it'd be a very limiting exercise. I really want to think carefully about what we do with the money we make, and if the choice is paying off my bank loan or restoring a unique piece of landscape, then there's no contest.

Int.: So, what sort of people do your holidays appeal to?

CW: Nice ones. Walking is a great leveller. We have all sorts, from the rich and famous, to people who have really saved hard to afford one of our holidays. But people who are attracted to what we offer tend to be like-minded. We cater for all levels of walkers – you don't have to be superbly fit! There are some clients who hardly get any exercise normally, but they still end the holiday smiling! Our clients come from all backgrounds, but they soon find something in common with each other; people who go walking tend not to be elitist.

Int.: Running a business without advertising is quite a risk. What made you decide to stop?

CW: If what we're offering isn't good enough to make people come back year after year, and recommend our products to their friends, then we're failing in our task. I had no argument with the advertising we did, we just realised we could do without it. Deciding to cut it out, and to put revenue into conservation projects instead, was a nervous moment, but we've survived. For a company founded on principles of conservation, it wasn't a hard choice to make, and <u>judging by our clients' response, I believe the sentiment is appreciated</u>.

Int.: And what's the key to ensuring that what you offer really represents responsible tourism?

CW: Travel and tourism is a tough industry, but good environmental practice is just a question of awareness. Of course, it's about maintaining high standards in terms of providing the right kind of activities, and also making sure that the accommodation available meets the needs and expectations of clients. But above all, it's down to the people you employ. <u>All those recruited need to embrace the company's objectives</u>, and this has to be <u>reinforced through ongoing training</u>. For instance, we like to use exclusively organic produce on our trips, which requires someone on the ground locally to keep a close watch on participating hotels and restaurants. It's important to have confidence in all aspects of the service you provide. It's a question of going the extra mile.

Int.: How do you see the future of environmentally friendly tourism?

CW: When we started, many people were ignorant of the whole concept. Now, though, it's something everyone's at least heard of – <u>and there's even a danger that certain travel journalists are getting bored with it, portraying it as wishy-washy idealism</u>, which couldn't be further from the truth. Personally, I'd like to see more of the large companies becoming voluntarily involved in conservation, and playing their part in convincing the tourists. If this doesn't happen, tourism will have an increasingly destructive effect in many areas of the world; careful investment in local communities, on the other hand, creates a wealth of common understanding and goodwill, which is of immense long-term value.

Int.: Thank you, Christopher. We'll have to leave it there. I wish you every success.

Vocabulary p.55

1 1 d   2 c   3 a   4 f   5 h   6 g   7 b   8 e
2 1 renewable energy   2 sustainable   3 biosphere
    4 hydroelectric   5 Solar   6 Tidal   7 environmentally friendly
    8 biodiversity
3 1 increased/risen   2 rise/increase   3 inefficient   4 consumes
    5 exhaust   6 destruction   7 contribute   8 tackled   9 means
    10 fuels   11 renewable

Language development p.56

1 1 were walking; was; would you know
     or are walking; is; do you know
    2 can see; are
    3 (will) have; crouch
    4 hadn't been standing; would have survived
    5 would not have been injured; had not been carrying
2 1 If I knew how to light a fire, I would have lit one.
    2 If I hadn't studied economics at university, I wouldn't understand how the economy works.
    3 If she had told us where she was going, we would know where to look for her.

4 If we had taken sensible safety precautions, we would not be in danger now.
5 If I didn't work in a zoo, I wouldn't have been bitten by a snake.
6 If I hadn't handed my essay in this morning, I would be able to show it to you.
7 If it had snowed last night, it would be freezing on the mountain today.
8 If he had (got) his phone with him, he would have called me to say he was going to be late.

3 1 A   2 B   3 C   4 A   5 B   6 A   7 D
4 1 …you **should** eat organic food.
    2 If the company **hadn't dumped** / didn't dump chemical waste in the river, the fish **wouldn't** have been killed off.
    3 Unless we ~~don't~~ stop burning oil, we'll destroy the ozone layer.
    4 ✔
    5 If the government **changes** the law, companies **will** have to stop dumping waste. / If the government **changed** the law, companies would have to stop dumping waste.
    6 If it **makes** you happy, I'll recycle all these magazines. / ✔
    7 I'd be grateful if you **could/would** investigate the issue of water quality soon.

English in Use p.57

1 1 He doesn't like them very much.
    2 No good in windy weather / people are always losing them
    3 humorous
2 1 it's   2 ✔   3 look as   4 their   5 struggling   6 ✔   7 frame
    8 umbrellas   9 ✔   10 'You   11 employee   12 reporter, 'but
    13 convenient   14 can't   15 ✔   16 thought

Language development

if we can invent ingenious things like the mobile phone, someone should've thought up a gadget to replace the umbrella by now

Reading pp.58–59

1 1 a society where things that are unwanted or unused are just thrown away
    2 He doesn't like the fact that things are just thrown away.
    3 c
5 1 C   (*devising new ways to use art and humour to get us thinking about the environment … what our attitudes to rubbish … say about society* (line 5))
    2 D   (*to get them thinking about the value of things … the material you throw away … paid for and consumed!'* (line 23))
    3 B   (*they were … wary that I might give people the impression that our National Parks are filthy* (line 31))
    4 C   (*it's really rather creative behaviour* (line 49))
    5 A   (*Steve's in his element as his adopts the role of lively, gesticulating artiste* (line 60))
    6 D   (*until now I've always kept my dislike of detritus quiet … he'd summed up the essence of ecology; that everything matters* (line 81))

Writing p.60

1 1 Chiara   2 the President of the Student Union
2 *Points to include*
    ● What happened at Chiara's college: litter-picking day, free meal for volunteers, introduction of fines for dropping litter, no-smoking policy

- Why it would be a good thing: raise awareness among students
- What it would involve: organising publicity (leaflets and posters), providing cleaning materials and rubber gloves, providing a reward for helpers

3 *Missing parts*
- introduction of a no-smoking policy
- explain why it would be a good thing – to raise awareness among students at this college
- provision of cleaning materials and rubber gloves

4 *Complete model answer (missing information in bold)*

Hi Cris

I am writing to tell you about a special event that was organised at East College and was extremely successful.

It was a clean-up day, aimed at solving problems of litter in the college. The day started with volunteers meeting up outside the Union building – they picked up litter around the grounds and gave out leaflets to other students, encouraging them to be tidier. They all had a free meal afterwards, and what was so good about the day was the impact it seems to have had on the college afterwards. Students have become a lot more aware of the importance of keeping the campus clean. They also tried imposing fines for dropping litter, which was not very successful, **and introduced a no-smoking policy on campus, which, on the other hand, has been extremely popular and successful.**

I think we should do the same thing here, **to raise awareness of this important issue among our students.** We would need to organise some publicity (posters and leaflets) and some sort of reward for volunteers. At East College, they provided a free meal, but I think that would be really difficult to organise. We could give volunteers a free ticket to the next disco instead. **We would also need to provide cleaning materials and rubber gloves for the volunteers. The rubber gloves, it seems, were especially popular!**

Can we meet to talk about it? What about next Saturday?

Best wishes

Sam

5 *Suggested answer*

Hi Jon – hope you're well. Just wondered if you'd be interested in getting involved in organising a 'clean-up' day at college. I thought you could design a poster and some leaflets that we can distribute round campus. I know you're busy, but it should only take you a day.

Let me know what you think.

Sam

Module 6

English in Use p.61

2 1 ageing   2 unpleasant   3 conference   4 passionate
5 pressures   6 lengths   7 frightening

4 8 extraordinary   9 Lawyers   10 disqualify   11 competitors
12 hypothetical   13 horizontally   14 treatment
15 modification(s)

Language development p.62

1 1 The person who   2 What / The thing that   3 The reason
4 What   5 The place where

2 1 The place where all the teenagers usually hang out is the park.

2 The reason I was so angry with her was that she had promised to be home by nine o'clock.

3 The thing that is so impressive is his ability to score goals from outside the penalty area.

4 What drives me mad is her habit of leaving her things all over the house.

5 The time they're due to arrive is six o'clock.

6 The person you need to talk to about this is your tutor.

3 1 The reason she dialled 999 is that she panicked.

2 The place where we usually meet is the café on the High Street.

3 The people the aid agencies are trying to help are the refugees.

4 The country that has the best health service in Europe is France.

5 What / The thing that I would really like to do is train as a doctor.

6 The month when our sales are highest is August.

4 1 No, it was Louis Pasteur who discovered the process of fermentation.

2 No, it was the science of microbiology that Pasteur founded.

3 No, it is pasteurisation that is now routinely used to treat milk for domestic consumption.

4 No, it was the germ theory of disease which/that was Pasteur's most important medical discovery.

5 No, it was in 1885 that he created a vaccine for rabies.

5 1 It was last Wednesday when/that I developed a bad allergic reaction.

2 It was on the way home that I first felt ill.

3 It was because I felt so lousy that I went back to bed the following morning.

4 The cough was bad, but it was the headache that was the real problem.

5 It was only when I saw the doctor that I discovered the cause.

6 It was on Monday that I felt well enough to go back to work.

7 It was someone at work who suggested what might have caused the problem.

8 It was breathing in paint fumes that caused the problem.

English in Use p.63

1b 1 It would help people to look younger for longer.
2 It would mean that people would not need plastic surgery.

2 1 E   2 C   3 G   4 A   5 H   6 F

Language development

What scientists hope is that …

It is for this reason that …

Writing pp.64–65

1 1 These   2 or   3 Instead   4 and   5 rather than   6 Whereas
7 others   8 too   9 although

2 1 B   2 A   3 A   4 C   5 B   6 A   7 C   8 B   9 B   10 B   11 A
12 B

3 1 one   2 to   3 that   4 does   5 did   6 so   7 both   8 yours
9 there/then   10 such

4 *Suggested answer*

Aromatherapy uses fragrant oils, which are rubbed into the body. It is good for both physical and emotional disorders, as it works on both a physical and an emotional level. You can have a whole course of treatments, but you don't have to. Just one is enough to feel some benefit. If relaxation is the aim try aromatherapy, if not try something else.

5 1 A, C   2 B, D   3 B, C   4 A, C   5 A, B   6 C, D   7 B, D
8 C, D

6 1 d   2 f   3 h   4 a   5 e   6 b   7 c   8 g

Listening p.66

1 1 b)   2 a word or expression   3 c
4 a bank/friend/family member, etc.

2 1 stones   2 (a) couch potato   3 cycling   4 parents
5 personal trainer   6 handbags   7 clinic   8 *Fun and Fitness*

4 1   Judy does say she uses oils, but not at varying temperatures.
The words *heated and chilled* are the cue for the correct
answer, which is *stones*.

2   The student has written the words *health fanatic*, but this is a
distractor. Judy says she hated exercise in her 20s. The correct
answer is introduced by the cue *what people call*.

7   The student has written *perfume*, but this is a distractor. You
have to listen carefully to the verb tenses. She says that last
year, she set up a website selling handbags (the correct
answer) and next time she is going to try selling pefume.

8   The student has written *The Easy Way to Health*. These words
occur immediately after the word *book*, but you have to wait
until the next sentence for the actual title of the book,
introduced by the cue *it's called*.

5a 1 c   2 d   3 b   4 a

5b 1 redundancy payout   2 health fanatic   3 energy levels
4 lifestyle

Tapescript

Hello, my name's Judy Simpson, and I work as a complementary
therapist – helping people to feel better by using a range of
holistic body treatments. I've been a therapist for five years now,
doing a range of treatments including aromatherapy, using
essential oils, and acupuncture – but the newest is a healing
therapy which uses heated and chilled <u>stones</u>, which everybody
seems to love.

Funnily enough, I haven't always been a health fanatic, in my 20s
I'd never heard of complementary therapy – I was what people
call a '<u>couch potato</u>' because I actually hated exercise in any form.
I had a good job in catering, but I was working long, irregular
hours, eating badly and not getting enough exercise. It wasn't
until I went on holiday with some friends that I realised just how
unfit I was – it was a <u>cycling</u> trip, and I just couldn't keep up with
the others. I decided there and then to take control of my life, I'd
always wanted to be self-employed and run my own business – it
was just a matter of deciding what to do.

That's when I saw a training course for complementary therapists
advertised in a magazine. The idea of doing this sort of work on a
freelance basis appealed to me. But, the course was fairly
expensive – beyond my means, anyway. It was at that point that I
was unexpectedly made redundant, so I had to do something. I'd
only been in the job a couple of years, so there wasn't a big
redundancy payout, but fortunately my <u>parents</u> stepped in with a
timely loan, which allowed me to sign up for the course.

And it really changed my life, making me think about my own
diet and lifestyle. I learned being totally obsessive about these
things isn't a good idea, but we all need to find the right balance
in our lives. Much to the amazement of my friends, I even got
myself a <u>personal trainer</u> – mainly because I couldn't stand the
thought of spending hours at the gym. As a result, my energy
levels increased tremendously and I realised that complementary
health has an effect on every area of your life.

My new lifestyle has given me confidence to try lots of new things.
For instance, I love <u>handbags</u>, and last year I set up my own
website selling them. It was a disaster – I hardly sold any – but at
least I'd tried it and I've no regrets – I'm going to try selling
perfume next time. At the moment, though, I'm very involved in
the designs for my own <u>clinic</u>, which is due to open in about six
months – so I don't have a second to spare.

If you think a healthy lifestyle is for you, but you're confused by
all the stuff you read in the media, I've just written a book about
finding the easy way to health, it's called *Fun and Fitness* – and
I've got a copy here if anybody would like to look at it. Believe me
if I can do it – anyone can!

Now if anyone's got any questions, I'll be …

Language development p.67

1 1 working   2 to be   3 (to) clear   4 digging / to dig
5 to remove   6 scratching   7 using   8 saying   9 to think
10 dig   11 to be   12 to be

2 1   The teacher asked me to wait outside.
2   My friends warned me not to trust her.
3   I arranged for some friends to help me move house.
4   My parents refused to let me stay out late.
5   We all had to wait for Jane to finish her meal.
6   He wanted her to go with him.

3 1   a   eating   b   to take
2   a   swimming   b   to swim
3   a   to start   b   travelling
4   a   him buying   b   to buy him
5   a   to say   b   getting

4 1 reading   2 to iron   3 to inform   4 studying   5 to tell
6 giving up   7 to pick up   8 to ask   9 arriving   10 showing

English in Use p.68

1 1   Trainee museum guides
2   To tell her about the training sessions
3   The guide is formal (uses the passive, etc.); the email is
informal

2b 1 c   2 a

3 1 got to   2 get paid   3 top of   4 show/display   5 the moment
6 an idea / a picture   7 the/a chance   8 before   9 meant to /
supposed to   10 brush   11 no more / no longer   12 as long
13 to do

Language development

Additional payment is made for this, <u>however,</u> over and above
the agreed salary.

You do get paid for these, <u>though,</u> on top of the normal salary.

You <u>also</u> get a brochure so that you can get an idea of how the
museum is organised.

<u>Then,</u> in the afternoons, you get the chance to watch an
experienced guide working with visitors.

You're <u>also</u> given an info sheet, two weeks before the training
sessions.

Writing p.69

1 1   a A   b B
2   a both   b both   c A   d A   e B   f both
3   a B   b A

2/4 *Complete model answer for Text A*

Come to sunny Compton!

There are many reasons why Compton should feature on your list of places to visit in this region, and not the least of **these** is its family orientation. ~~It's a great place for families to spend time together.~~ Families will have a good time here, and there are some really interesting places for **them** to visit.

Known locally as the jewel of the coast, its golden sandy beaches are delightful and are also extremely safe for small children. ~~The beaches are beautiful and not dangerous.~~ Compton also has a lifeguard station within easy reach.

The town has something for everyone. For the best view of the picturesque old buildings, it's a good idea to take the sightseeing bus tour – **this** takes two hours and is well worth it.

Places to visit include the museum, with its fascinating exhibition showing the history of Compton, and the zoo, which boasts many rare and beautiful species of animal. The castle is also well worth a visit, and has beautiful gardens and a specially designed play area for children.

A range of accommodation is available, with plenty of small friendly hotels that are ideal for families.

If you want to visit somewhere all the family will love, look no further than Compton!

3/4 *Complete model answer for Text B*

Compton is a ~~nice~~ **lively** place to have fun with friends – it's a ~~nice~~ **thriving** town with lots going on.

What's the town like? The town itself is interesting, with good shops – these include not only extremely ~~nice~~ **exclusive** boutiques selling expensive designer clothes, but also cheaper chain stores. You won't have any trouble finding what you want in Compton, and you can be sure of finding the most up-to-date merchandise there.

So what is there to do in the evenings? Compton has a good nightlife, too, including ~~nice~~ **trendy** clubs and a cinema complex which shows the latest films.

There are dozens of cafés and restaurants serving delicious food at very reasonable prices, and loads of friendly pubs and nightclubs where you can meet people and have fun. There are also plenty of buses, which continue running late into the night, so getting home won't be a problem. Come to Compton for the time of your life!

Reading pp.70–71

1 1 a

2 Because he argues that the Tyrannosaurus Rex was a scavenger, contrary to popular belief.

3 Tyrannosaurus Rex had blunt teeth, not the sharp teeth needed for tearing meat; it had legs designed for walking, not running; the numbers of Tyrannosaurus Rex were in similar to proportion to scavengers of today, such as vultures.

3 1 D (*you come up with a supposition … You can't just overturn a hypothesis …* links to *the controversial theory he's been working on* (line 9))

2 F (*It has now reached the point where … inviting people to make up their minds* links to *an idea … met with … scepticism … but … recently been gathering momentum* (line 13))

3 B (*… so left without a degree* (line 26) links to *Ironically, Horner has now become one of the world's foremost dinosaur experts*)

4 G (*By calculating this biomass … it's possible to work out how many of each type existed* links to *If you look at how many meat eaters there were … compared with the scarcity of the herbivorous dinosaurs* (line 45))

5 A (*where the flocks of vultures wait to feed on animals killed by hyenas* (line 52) links to *Horner frequently likens Tyrannosaurus Rex to these scavenging birds*)

6 E (*somebody else could study this and find out that there's something weird going on. But nobody has done it yet* (line 56) links to *it could be more rigorous, but in the absence of a more wide-reaching study, it's going to stand*)

Module 7

English in Use p.72

1 1 The family sailed to Australia.

2 Jonathan continued to work.

2 1 B (*described + as*)

2 D (*to get something out of your system*)

3 A (*at all costs* is a fixed expression)

4 C (*in no sense* is a fixed expression)

5 B (= *enthusiastic*)

6 A (*leave* is *granted* by an employer)

7 C (*omission* and *default* refer to things; *truancy* implies lack of permission)

8 D (= *provided that*)

9 B (*up to speed* is a fixed expression)

10 A (= *thing about*)

11 C (*to fulfil* a *duty*)

12 B (*to set foot* in a place)

13 D (*entirely dependent* = collocation)

14 C (*fit + out*)

15 A (*to enable someone to do something*)

Language development p.73

1 1 enquiries   2 satisfying   3 likeable   4 volcanoes   5 shelves
6 hesitation   7 occurrence   8 advise   9 dying
10 preferred; preference

2 1 impossible   2 remarkable   3 embarrassed   4 exceed
5 acceptance   6 unbelievable   7 incredible   8 volunteered

3 1 receipt   2 guarantee of success   3 occupation
4 achievement   5 immediate   6 separated   7 approximately
8 decision   9 necessarily   10 leisurely

4 Dear (1) Sir/Mad~~d~~am
I am (2) ~~writting~~ **writing** to (3) complain~~e~~ about the service I
(4) ~~recieved~~ **received** in your restaurant last night. (5) Generall~~y~~
the food was poor and the service was (6) awful~~l~~.
The (7) potato~~e~~s were nearly raw, and the (8) ~~source~~ **sauce** that
the chicken was cooked in was much (9) ~~saltyier~~ **saltier** than
was (10) nec~~e~~essary.
The (11) ~~waitor~~ **waiter** kept (12) dropping (13) ~~thinks~~ **things,**
including two (14) ~~knifes~~ **knives**, which he then put back on the
table for us to use.
In (15) ~~addittion~~ **addition** we were forced to wait nearly an
hour between the main course and the (16) ~~desert~~ **dessert**.
When we pointed this out to your staff, they became rude and
(17) ~~aggresive~~ **aggressive.**
I don't think you realise how much (18) distress this causes to a
person like myself who (19) a~~l~~lways (20) ~~trys~~ **tries** to maintain
the highest (21) ~~standads~~ **standards** in all aspects of my (22)
~~live~~ **life**.
I look forward to hearing your (23) ~~explainations~~ **explanations**
and how you propose to compensate us.
Yours (24) ~~sincerly~~ **sincerely**

English in Use p.74

2 1 excitement 2 risky 3 flight 4 frightening 5 safety
6 effective 7 concentration

4 8 overcome 9 physically 10 Participants 11 enthusiast
12 jokingly 13 governing 14 motivation 15 satisfaction

Language development

balloon, appearance, thrill, middle-aged, travelling (UK English),
*Sitting, all, getting, call, bungee, still, challenging, cross-country,
mountaineering, spoof, outdoor, well-pressed*

Writing 1 p.75

1 1 D 2 B 3 C 4 A 5 C 6 B 7 A 8 C 9 A 10 C
11 B 12 C 13 D 14 A 15 B

2 1 cost 2 prepared 3 accept 4 made 5 happy/content
6 secret 7 laughing 8 surprise

3 1 surprise 2 sale 3 apologies 4 suit 5 generosity
6 assistance 7 trustworthy 8 insistent

Listening p.76

1 1 a 2 b 6 b

2 1 240 kilometres 2 wildlife 3 climbers; doctors / medical
experts; mountaineering experts 4 1980 5 starvation
6 sleep(ing) 7 fittest 8 31

3 2 Although elephants are mentioned as an example, he went to
study wildlife in general.
3 This student has heard the right information, but has not
written it down correctly. *Medicine* does not have the same
meaning as *doctor/medical expert*, and *mountaineer* has been
incorrectly spelled. Remember, always write the words you
hear and check your spelling.
4 There are two years mentioned; this student has written the
wrong one.

4 1 b 2 d 3 e 4 c 5 a

Tapescript

In a new four-part television series called *Feats of Endurance,*
which begins on Channel Three next Tuesday, we'll be looking at
some famous examples of people who've pushed themselves to
the limits of human endurance and beyond.

In the first programme, we go back 2,500 years and look at the
case of the world's first marathon runner, Pheidippides. No one
has yet equalled the exploits of this Greek soldier, sent to get help
during the battle of Marathon. Experts have calculated that he
must have run 240 kilometres in two days, before returning to
help win the battle, then running a further 40 kilometres to carry
the news of victory to Athens. The modern marathon race of 42
kilometres commemorates his feat.

The second programme features J. Michael Fay, who, in 1999,
walked an incredible 3,200 kilometres across Africa as part of an
in-depth study of the continent's wildlife. After 456 days, he
reached his destination having survived close encounters with
elephants, gorillas and many smaller examples of the wildlife he'd
gone to study.

Programme 3 looks at mountains and oceans. The air on top of
the world's highest mountains is so thin that most climbers and
doctors had always believed it would be impossible to climb them
without oxygen. But both the medical and mountaineering
experts were proved wrong in 1978, when Reinhold Messner and

Peter Haebler made it to the top of Mount Everest without
oxygen. To prove the point once and for all, Messner repeated the
climb in 1980, but this time on his own.

The fourth programme looks at two cases of deprivation – people
who went without things for long periods. Steven Callahan spent
76 days alone at sea in a life raft after his yacht sank in the
Atlantic. By the time he was rescued, he'd survived starvation,
dehydration and the constant leaking of the raft, not to mention
frequent visits from inquisitive sharks. With no food supplies,
Steven survived on the few fish he was able to catch and water he
purified himself. Although Steven ended up in the record books,
that wasn't his intention, unlike Randy Gardner, who, in 1964,
went an amazing 265 hours without sleep – that's over 11 days
wide awake – in an attempt to set a new world record. With
friends and cold showers to prevent him dropping off, Randy
ended up having hallucinations before clinching the record. When
it was all over, he dozed off for an uninterrupted 14 hours.

In the last programme in the series, we meet Paddy Doyle. Paddy
is an endurance athlete, who not only runs marathons, but does
so with a 20-kilo pack on his back. He's widely regarded as the
world's fittest man, and it's difficult to imagine anyone fitter,
except perhaps Pheidippides. Paddy, who's 38, has had 31 separate
entries in the Guinness Book of Records and has broken a
staggering 124 world records in his lifetime, ten of which are still
standing.

The series begins at 8 p.m. next Tuesday, here on Channel Three.

Vocabulary p.77

1a 1 d 2 g 3 a 4 c 5 f 6 b 7 h 8 e

1b 1 I used to buy shoes in the sales for the sake of it.
2 The exhibition was excellent, so I couldn't tear myself away
and get the train home.
3 I keep telling myself there was nothing I could have done to
help.
4 You can never get served, even though the shop is not short
of staff.
5 Although Alice was pregnant, she concealed it from her
friends.
6 She pretended that she was in control of the situation, but
she was fooling herself.
7 I'd feel nervous without my address book.
8 I spent so much time playing and thinking about chess that it
took over my life.

2 1 bug 2 hooked 3 freak 4 mood 5 break 6 collapse
7 choice 8 throwing 9 leads 10 sucked

3 1 got 2 tear 3 in 4 another 5 given 6 sake 7 short
8 told 9 myself 10 over

Language development p.78

1 1 didn't 2 could 3 would 4 would 5 hadn't

2 1 I wish that chocolate **didn't** bring me out in a rash.
2 I wish I **could** remember where I've put my keys.
3 He talks as though he **earned/earns** a huge salary, but I know
he doesn't.
4 I'd sooner **spend** my money on clothes than food.
5 If only travel ~~would~~ cost less, I'd travel a lot more.
6 It's time we **stopped** messing around and **started** work.
7 I'd rather you **spoke** to James because you know him better
than I do.
8 I wish I **hadn't spent** all my money yesterday, then I would
still have some in my bank account.√

3 1 I wish I was fitter.
　2 If only I had my phone with me.
　3 I wish I could find a job that I really enjoyed.
　4 If only I had studied French at school.
　5 If only my daughter told me where she was going.
　6 I wish I hadn't left my sunglasses on the beach.
　7 If only someone would invent decent clothes that didn't need ironing.
　8 I wish I hadn't called the shop assistant dishonest.
　9 I wish these aeroplane seats were wider.
　10 If only my parents could have come to the wedding.

4 1 He talks to his dog as though he was talking to a human being.
　2 I'd rather you didn't wear your shoes in the house.
　3 Suppose/Supposing you moved house, where would you go?
　4 He'd sooner stay where he is than move house.
　5 It's time I settled down and got a place of my own.
　6 I've lived here six months, but it feels as if it's longer.
　7 It's high time we had this room redecorated.
　8 Supposing/Suppose the rent went up, could you afford to stay?

5 1 She talks to me as though she was my mother.
　2 I'd sooner you drove, if that's OK.
　3 It's time we went to bed.
　4 I'd rather you didn't tell me how the film ends.
　5 Supposing the information turns out to be wrong, what will you do?
　6 She looked as if she had been crying.
　7 Suppose she had drowned? How would you have felt?
　8 It's high time you got a job and became independent.

English in Use p.79

1 1 a　2 She got a headache.　3 Yes
2 1 in　2 ✔　3 have　4 me　5 ✔　6 if　7 same　8 ✔　9 up　10 of　11 them　12 those　13 the　14 fully　15 ✔　16 and

---

Language development

… unless I had another mid-morning, my energy level would slump …

If I was looking for evidence of the latter, it wasn't hard to find.

… providing you can break the habit completely, you'll really feel the benefits.

Reading pp.80–81

3b *professionally I had bitten off far more than I could chew*
3c *we hit it off with the locals*
4 1 B　(*from the moment we set foot on the island … we hit it off with the locals in no time* (line 35))
　2/3 B　(*We wasted no time in abandoning … much to the horror of my parents* (line 37))
　　D　(*If we'd listened to the pessimistic predictions of our relations, we'd never have carried on* (line 78))
　4 E　(*I didn't want all my eggs in one basket* (line 99))
　5 B　(*I used to think I wasn't cut out to be a full-time mother. But here I can combine work and childcare …* (line 48))
　6 A　(*had to draw on the experience of people I knew from the world of art and design* (line 14))
　7 D　(*Even though the odds were stacked against us – given our cottage-sized budget … crumbling ruin … neither of us ever questioned what we'd taken on* (line 74))

8/9 D　(*I can't see us ever giving it up because we get so much out of it* (line 83))
　　E　(*I don't think the thrill I get out of this business will ever wear off* (line 101))
10 C　(*it wouldn't tie me down to working shop hours* (line 57))
11 A　(*professionally I had bitten off far more than I could chew* (line 19))
12 E　(*Luckily my father is a devoted art lover …* (line 96))
13 A　(*I invested in a comprehensive business course …* (line 23))
14 D　(*Peter and I have always shared the same dream … I couldn't have managed it without him* (line 80))
15 E　(*Mark, my business partner, … said 'Just because … potential'* (line 91))
16 C　(*to my amazement, several took me up on my offer* (line 63))
17 B　(*in order to succeed … we had to muck in with the others … we all shared the responsibility* (line 40))
18 A　(*The rent I was paying was astronomical and I began to feel very exposed* (line 20))
19 C　(*I didn't go into this to make a fortune* (line 66))
5 1 g　2 c　3 d　4 a　5 h　6 e　7 f　8 b

Writing p.82

1b 1 without any warning　5 It was unsuccessful
　6 reverse their decision　7 In the first place
　9 opposed the idea
1c *Suggested answers*
　2 to come to terms with the proposal　3 it is not sensible
　4 impossible to implement　8 followed the rules
　10 they lost the majority of their customers immediately
　11 I might find myself unemployed
　12 it might be an idea to encourage managers
2 1 concerned　2 implemented　3 explain　4 attempted
　5 introduce　6 appear
3 I am writing to complain about the proposed ban on smoking in public places. I work in Café Noir, a well-known restaurant popular with visitors in the centre of town.
I am very concerned about this proposal, for a number of reasons. Firstly, I don't understand why this is being implemented without any warning, and why there has been no discussion – there is no time for anyone to come to terms with the proposal. And secondly, it is not sensible to suggest it in outdoor bars and restaurants – such an idea is impossible to implement.
To support my argument against the proposed ban, I would like to explain what happened when the authorities tried to enforce a ban on smoking in my home town. It was unsuccessful, and the politicians had to reverse their decision. In the first place, few people followed the rules. Of course, most businesses opposed the idea. A small number of restaurants tried to implement a no-smoking policy, but they lost the majority of their customers immediately. If the same thing happened here, I might find myself unemployed.
As a suggestion, it might be an idea to encourage managers to introduce specific non-smoking areas instead? This would appear to be a better solution.
4 Sorry not to have replied to your email before – I can give you a hand with your articles, so let me know what you have in mind. I will drop a line to the authorities and tell them about my home town – I'll spell out the effects of a smoking ban on businesses generally. I'll let you know what happens.

Module 8

English in Use p.83

2 1 reliable   2 tendency   3 easily   4 response   5 unpredictable
6 representation   7 nostalgic

4 8 widely   9 addition   10 absence   11 unsightly   12 outset
13 commonest   14 trial   15 subscribers

> ### Language development
>
> *easily* needs a spelling change

Language development p.84

1 1 I will   2 will I   3 do I   4 I get   5 I have   6 have I
7 could I   8 I could   9 had she   10 She had

2 1 Under no circumstances will the company give a refund
   without a receipt.
   2 Not only is the new computer system safer, it is also more
   reliable.
   3 Not since we visited Nepal some years ago had we been
   anywhere so interesting.
   4 Rarely do we come across such a hard-working student these
   days.
   5 Hardly had we started dinner when/than she suddenly said
   she had to leave
   6 Only now do I realise how dishonest she is.
   7 Not a penny did we spend on food all the time we were there.
   8 No way will I work on the afternoon of the Cup Final.

3 1 Years it took to complete the building of the tunnel.
   2 This I'm going to enjoy!
   3 Weeks we waited with no news from them.
   4 Jerry's going to run a marathon? That I'd like to see!
   5 They say the health service is improving? That I find very
   difficult to believe.

4 1 The door opened and in came Stella.
   2 ... and off he ran as fast as his legs would carry him.
   3 ... and out sprang a black dog.
   4 ... and up flew the balloon into the treetops.
   5 There was an outhouse behind the main building; in front,
   there was an old well.

5 1 So tired was he that he could hardly walk.
   2 Such danger was there in the streets that we dared not go out.
   3 Such was their anxiety that they did not sleep at all for three
   days.
   4 So confident were they of victory that they planned the
   celebrations before the election had taken place.
   5 Such was his ability on the football field that no one could
   stop him scoring goals.

English in Use p.85

1 1 a website
   2 You make a bid, and the highest bidder is able to buy the
   goods.

2 1 B (*goes + by the name*)
   2 D (*widely regarded* = collocation)
   3 A (*alter the course* = collocation)
   4 D (*appear on a website*)
   5 B (= *in fact*)
   6 C (*to make a bid*)
   7 A (*to turn out to be*)
   8 A (*the proud owner* = collocation)

9 D (*on + offer*)
10 B (*to be based on*)
11 C (*lies in the fact that* is a fixed expression)
12 D (*word-of-mouth recommendations* = collocation)
13 A (*sense* = non-personal)
14 D (*appeals + to*)
15 B (summarises the argument)

> ### Language development
>
> Not only has the company gone …
>
> Rarely do you find people …

Language development p.86

1 1 actually,   2 Not surprisingly,   3 honestly,   4 Annoyingly,
5 Obviously   6 Naturally,   7 arguably   8 presumably

2 1 funnily   2 Indeed   3 Worryingly   4 surely   5 frankly
6 understandably   7 of course   8 Granted

3 1 Generally   2 considered   3 whole   4 large   5 rule   6 main

4 1 speaking   2 Believe   3 honest   4 far   5 truth   6 Judging
7 afraid   8 turned

5 **Suggested answers**
   1 Generally speaking / By and large   2 as far as I know
   3 Obviously / Of course / Granted / Admittedly   4 As a matter
   of fact / Indeed   5 Strictly speaking   6 As it turned out
   7 surprisingly/funnily enough   8 Worryingly   9 Surely

Listening p.87

2 1 D   (*I now have to leave home at six to avoid the jams … it's
      nose-to-tail all the way back*)
   2 G   (*sitting in front of a screen … I use it for … keeping in
      touch with the children*)
   3 A   (*dinnertime, when I like to catch up with the news on the
      satellite channel … she says … mealtimes should be a time
      for conversation*)
   4 C   (*usually pick up a snack on the way home … that stuff's
      getting so popular*)
   5 E   (*I was making calls … I'd be popping out to see if I had a
      message*)
   6 F   (*I'm feeling run-down*)
   7 B   (*it's a lot cheaper than calling them on their mobiles*)
   8 E   (*Mum objects, though … she's not convinced*)
   9 C   (*otherwise people would never fit in everything they wanted
      to do*)
   10 H   (*the bill came … I started to plan my expenditure*)

Tapescript

Speaker 1

I used to get out for a run at least three mornings a week –
cheaper than the gym and it kept me fit and set me up for the day.
But those days are over, I'm afraid, because I now have to leave
home at six to avoid the jams, and I still get held up – it's worse
each year. Thank goodness my office hours are flexible – that's
one advantage of doing everything on screen. Then it's nose-to-
tail all the way back. It's no wonder I'm feeling run down because
when I get in, there's no chance to do anything except eat
whatever my wife's left for me to pop in the microwave, then
collapse in front of the TV.

Speaker 2

I used to think it was a strange thing to do – sitting in front of a
screen when you could actually be talking to someone. But my
husband's away a lot, works irregular hours, so it comes in   →

terribly handy – you can see why it's caught on the way it has. The main thing <u>I use it for is keeping in touch with the children</u> now they're away at university. They'd never normally put pen to paper, but this way they reply within hours sometimes, and <u>it's a lot cheaper than calling them on their mobiles</u>. They were never much into computer games as kids – though all their friends had them, of course – but that hasn't held them back, really.

Speaker 3

I can't wait to get to university – I'll have my own study-bedroom, with a link to the computer network, so it'll be much easier to plan my work schedule, and no more arguments. At the moment, at home, I spend three hours a night studying, and the only time I have to relax is <u>dinnertime, when I like to catch up with the news on the satellite channel</u>. <u>Mum objects, though</u> – <u>she says</u> it's unhealthy because <u>mealtimes should be a time for conversation</u>, but I've no idea what she wants me to talk about! I keep telling her we need to keep up-to-date with current affairs, and everyone does it, so I can't miss out – but <u>she's not convinced</u>.

Speaker 4

My boyfriend goes jogging every lunchtime, but in my job I can never manage to get away for long enough. My hours are so unpredictable, it makes planning anything difficult. I do yoga two evenings a week – which is much more relaxing. Those nights, I <u>usually pick up a snack on the way home</u>, eat it quickly, then dash out again. He says that kind of diet isn't good for me, but you can see why <u>that stuff's getting so popular</u>, because <u>otherwise people would never fit in everything they wanted to do</u>. I'm always careful to pick something that's low in fat, though, like they tell you to on TV – and I keep fairly fit.

Speaker 5

When they put up the rent on my flat, I thought if I gave up my gym membership, I'd manage it. But the gym wasn't the problem. I drive a lot in my job, so like everyone these days, <u>I was making calls</u> whenever I was held up in traffic – I mean, you've got to keep tabs on your friends, haven't you? Even in the office where they're prohibited, <u>I'd be popping out to see if I had a message</u>. Then <u>the bill came</u> – talk about a shock! Luckily my father bailed me out – on condition that <u>I started to plan my expenditure</u>. He was OK about it, but reminded me how email's much more cost-effective, so I've gone over to that.

Vocabulary p.88

1 1 joyriding   2 armed robbery   3 drunk driving
  4 drug dealing   5 computer hacking   6 shoplifting
2 1 slander   2 arson   3 burglary   4 shoplifting
  5 manslaughter   6 joyriding   7 hacking   8 forgery
3 1 mugging   2 mugger   3 burgle   4 burglar   5 murder
  6 murderer   7 arsonist   8 stealing/theft   9 thief   10 forge
  11 forger   12 robbery   13 robber   14 joyride   15 joyrider
4a 1 search   2 fight   3 maintain   4 scene   5 acting
  6 commit   7 detect   8 catch   9 liaise
4b 1 amnesty   2 schemes   3 tackle   4 anonymity   5 arrest
  6 come forward   7 penalty   8 clamp down

Language development p.89

1 1 Nirvana are still my ~~most~~ favourite band of all time.
  2 James is slightly taller ~~as~~ **than** his brother.
  3 Life is ~~a great much~~ **much / a great deal** noisier nowadays.
  4 This is easily the ~~worse~~ **worst** murder we have ever had to deal with in this city.
  5 The job now is nothing like **as** dangerous as it was.

6 Some people think that shoplifting is not such **a** serious crime as burglary.
7 Murder is by far ~~a~~ **the** most serious crime anyone can commit.
8 He is one of the most experienced **officers** in the police force.
2 1 The trial was so complex that it went on for weeks. / It was such a complex trial that it went on for weeks.
  2 The cost of legal proceedings can be so high that some people cannot afford it.
  3 Lawyers earn such a lot of money / so much money that many people want to become one.
  4 Some laws are so outdated (that) they need to be rewritten.
  5 The evidence was so strong / Such was the strength of the evidence / The strength of the evidence was such that the jury reached a decision very quickly.
  6 After the trial, there were so many people outside the court (that) we couldn't see anything.
3 1 The police arrived too late to catch the criminals.
  2 There were not enough officers on duty to control the crowd.
  3 The crime was too serious to ignore.
  4 There was enough evidence against him for the police to charge him.
  5 Too many crimes are committed for the police to solve (all of them).
  6 The joyrider drove too fast for the police cars to catch him. / The police cars couldn't go fast enough to catch the joyrider.
4 1 The sooner they change the law, the better it will be.
  2 Prisons are becoming more and more overcrowded.
  3 The more police officers we have on the street, the safer we will feel.
  4 More and more police officers would like to carry a gun.
  5 The more serious the crime, the tougher the penalty.
  6 In some places, criminal gangs are becoming more and more violent.
5 1 As   2 like   3 like   4 as   5 like   6 as

English in Use p.90

1 The information sheet is formal.
2a individual = their own personal; where anyone could see them = on display; checking = patrol; the gardens = grounds
2b 1 c   2 b
3 1 arrival   2 produce   3 proof   4 (kept) with   5 item/article
  of   6 to memory   7 disclosed / divulged / given / passed on
  8 of value / valuable   9 deposited/placed   10 located
  11 a regular   12 observant/vigilant/alert   13 chance

Language development

Comparison: *one of the <u>most popular</u> ways*

Double comparison: *tighter and tighter*

Writing p.91

1 You should say what the problem is and ask for suggestions.
2 1 as   2 As you all know   3 obviously   4 in this way
  5 In spite of   6 As a result   7 now   8 after that   9 Naturally
3a Paragraph A   Background information
  Paragraph B   Initial suggestions
  Paragraph C   Your input
3b Paragraph B
  ● a regular disco on Friday evenings, which would not interfere with studies

- longer hours for the campus shop – preferably 24-hour opening
- inter-college sports activities on a regular basis.

4 1 a bad effect on their work 2 like to know what you think
3 the amount of money we have 4 put forward your ideas

5 *Suggested answers*
As you all know …
Many of you have told us …
… you have said how much …
… take this opportunity …
… it's over to you!
What you do is …
Complete model answer
To: all students
From: Student Union Committee
Date: May 24th
Subject: Campus life
This is a message from your Student Union, as we need your help!
Background information
As you all know, the campus is very quiet in the evenings and weekends. We feel that it's time that the college joined the 24-hour society, and obviously we would welcome your input into this. Many of you have responded to questionnaires before and told us how much you have appreciated the chance to provide feedback in this way. So, take this opportunity to influence what happens in your college.
Initial suggestions
In spite of the feeling among some students that there could be a negative impact on their studies, we feel that there needs to be some fresh approach to activities on campus. As a result, we have come up with the following ideas:
- a regular disco on Friday evenings, which would not interfere with studies
- longer hours for the campus shop – preferably 24-hour opening
- inter-college sports activities on a regular basis.

Your input
They are our suggestions – but now it's over to you! What you do is send your ideas in to us at the office, and after that we will consider them all, together with the budget we have to spend. Naturally, we want to come up with a clear porposal that can be presented at the mext meeting of the Committee with the principal.
Thanks – and we're looking forward to hearing from you all!

Reading pp.92–93

1 **Suggested answers**
1 A 'young offender' is a criminal in Britain who is not yet an adult in the eyes of the law.
2 Some may see them as a waste of time, while others may welcome them as a distraction from their everyday routine.

2 1 Nathan – a young offender
2 Sally Brookes – the theatre company's Programme Director
3 Lou Heywood – the theatre company's Touring Director

5 1 A (*depending on a 'front' … I felt I had to be the "tough" guy or the "cool" guy to survive … you just carry on pretending that you're a particular kind of person* (line 2))
2 D (*his willingness to admit this … the result of an innovative drama course … extended to young offenders to help them examine their reactions to things* (line 16))
3 D (*the audience … calls out for the character to lift the mask and explain … how he might find ways to act on that feeling, rather than according to the front* (line 34))

4 A (*we work from the premise that each person can nonetheless make active choices and has a responsibility for their actions* (line 52))
5 C (*they get to explore behaviour patterns one step removed … they themselves don't end up feeling judged or interrogated* (line 60))
6 B (*Lou believes that each workshop must be tailor-made to the needs of a particular group* (line 75))

6 1 c 2 g 3 i 4 h 5 a 6 f 7 e 8 d 9 b

Module 9

English in Use p.94

1 Repeats what people say to him, invents his own sentences and own words, remembers things he has done, asks for things.

2 1 B (*describe + as*)
2 D (*close companions* = collocation)
3 C (*repeat + back*)
4 A (adverb of contrast)
5 D (*in return for* is a fixed expression)
6 B (*to run to a total*)
7 C (*in + context*)
8 A (*particularly impressive* = collocation)
9 D (*comment + on*)
10 B (= *remembers*, transitive verb)
11 C (links to *pesters*)
12 A (*life expectancy* = collocation)
13 B (logical follow-on from previous sentence)
14 C (*high hopes* = collocation)
15 D (intransitive verb)

Language development

So successful has she been that N'Kisi is now the world's most talked-about talking bird. (The verb is inverted.)

Language development pp.95–96

1 1 John reported that sales had increased by 20 per cent.
2 Dave announced that the new campaign started / would start three days later.
3 Adam told them that they were getting a lot of positive feedback from consumers.
4 Jenny said that she had met the clients the day before and she was sure they didn't have any worries.
5 Adam confessed that he hadn't seen the new posters yet.
6 Dave admitted that unfortunately he didn't have them with him, but he promised that he would get everyone a copy the next day.
7 Jenny encouraged everyone to keep up the good work and reminded everyone that she would see them all there again at the same time the following week.

2 The interviewer asked me:
1 where I had worked before.
2 why I wanted to work for this/that company.
3 if I had ever worked in marketing before.
4 what my favourite advertising slogan is/was.
5 if I am/was a good communicator.
6 where I thought I would be in ten years' time.
7 if/whether I worked better on my own or as part of a team.
8 what I least liked about my old job.

9 what impression I had when I went in there this/that morning.

10 if/whether I could start next/the following Monday.

3 1 Harvey explained that he might not be here/there tomorrow/the next day.

2 Amanda said that she shouldn't have said what she did.

3 The shop assistant promised that he/they could get it for me by the following Tuesday.

4 My neighbour said that he/she could help if I needed a hand.

5 I told the class they didn't need to do any more; they had done enough.

6 The teacher explained that he/she wouldn't be there next / the following week because he/she would be on holiday.

7 Rachel asked if she should put the lights on, as it was getting dark.

8 The critic admitted that it is/was a great film.

4 1 A   2 B   3 B   4 A   5 C   6 B   7 A   8 C

5 1 My classmate advised me to ask him to speak more slowly.

2 Dad promised that he would get a film on the way home.

3 My colleague refused to help me tonight.

4 My brother denied reading my private diary.

5 My secretary reminded me that I had an appointment at 4 p.m.

6 Anne's friend begged her to tell her where she got that shirt.

7 The driver thanked me for helping him/her change the wheel.

8 Julie blamed Gerald for getting lost.

6 1 Fake CDs are known to be widely available.
It is well known that fake CDs are widely available.

2 It has been announced that the police have made a major arrest.

3 It is reported that 100,000 CDs have been confiscated.
A hundred thousand CDs are reported to have been confiscated.

4 It is believed that the fake CDs were made abroad.
The fake CDs are believed to have been made abroad.

5 It is thought that the CDs were smuggled into the country in boats
The CDs are thought to have been smuggled into the country in boats.

6 The man arrested is suspected of being the ringleader of an international gang.

7 He is reputed to have made millions of dollars from crime.
It is reputed that he has made millions of dollars from crime.

8 He is rumoured to have homes on five continents.
It is rumoured that he has homes on five continents.

9 It has been suggested that fewer people would buy fake CDs if genuine ones were not so expensive.

10 The industry is said to be looking at new ways to prevent illegal copying.

English in Use p.97

2 1 D   2 F   3 B   4 H   5 I   6 A

Language development

Abley asks how a minority language can compete …

He also points out that where such a language does survive …

But Abley insists that it is not their complexity …

The present tense is used because the author is talking generally about things that are still true now.

Listening p.98

2 1 A   (*I just wished she'd put on a pair of jeans like the other mums, rather than showing us up all the time*)

---

2 D   (*I never knew what Mum thought … she was so bound up in her own career that she didn't make much of it*)

3 A   (*as a student, you're always struggling to make ends meet*)

4 C   (*I'm determined to give them the confidence to go off and lead their own lives*)

5 A   (*reflect on my own upbringing … All that will inform my writing*)

6 B   (*I was never keen on the whole celebrity thing, but I'll have to see how I feel as all that fades away*)

3a 1 make   2 take   3 catch   4 attract

3b 1 c   2 d   3 a   4 b

Tapescript

Int. = Interviewer, JH = Jessica Hanson

Int.: Jessica Hanson's been a top model in the fashion industry for over ten years. But she's recently retired from the catwalk, and is here in the studio with me today. I suppose it's every little girl's dream, Jessica, to be a fashion model. Was this something you always wanted to do?

JH: When I was a child, my mother was the editor of a fashion magazine, so I was surrounded by that world from an early age – but it somehow just failed to catch my imagination at that stage. My mother had dealings with all the top designers so, you know, she'd come to meet us from school wearing all sorts of outrageous outfits – attracting a lot of attention at the school gate. <u>I just wished she'd put on a pair of jeans like the other mums, rather than showing us up all the time</u>. My sister, always the confident, sociable one, just used to laugh it off – but I used to take it to heart if I thought we were being giggled about.

Int.: But your mother had a strong influence on you, though?

JH: When I was going through school, she was very tough, very strict with us – we didn't get much praise – though I wouldn't call her critical or unkind. But, like, if I won a prize at school, my father would be thrilled – but <u>I never knew what Mum thought</u>. I was the first person in the family to get to university, but <u>she was so bound up in her own career that she didn't make much of it</u>. I think I must've inherited my drive from her – and in the fashion industry, that certainly comes in useful.

Int.: So how was it that you ending up in modelling?

JH: I did English literature at university – I wasn't doing that badly, but it wasn't really my scene exactly either. Then I met someone at a party who turned out to be an agent. He had no idea I was my mother's daughter, but offered me the chance to do some modelling. I jumped at it, not least because, <u>as a student, you're always struggling to make ends meet</u>. And things took off from there – I wasn't trying to make a point or anything, but after that, I was offered several more modelling jobs. At the end of the course, much to my parents' amazement, I decided to take it up professionally.

Int.: And now you're retiring. Why's that?

JH: It's mainly because of the children. I've got twin girls, and I was given the opportunity to write a book – which, as an occupation, is more conducive to family life. I want my children to know I'm there for them if they want to talk to me – being on the end of a telephone line's not enough. <u>I'm determined to give them the confidence to go off and lead their own lives</u>, as I did – I want them to feel supported, but not pushed – so it's up to them exactly what they end up doing. I'm not going to be breathing down their necks.

Int.: Tell us about the book.

JH: While I was at university, I wrote short stories, though I never managed to get anything published – and at the back of my mind was the idea that I'd like to be a novelist one day. And that's stayed with me – although it's something I've kept very much to myself. So much so that my friends don't quite know what to make of it – you know, they assume it's some kind of publishing gimmick. But I think I do have something to say – I'm not just jumping on the bandwagon. I've seen a bit of the world since I wrote those rather naive short stories and, of course, had time to <u>reflect on my own upbringing</u> and the ups and downs of family life. <u>All that will inform my writing</u>, but it's not going to be a novel about a model.

Int.: So, will this book be the first of many?

JH: I'll need to see how well it does before deciding, I think. But I don't regret closing the door on the superficiality of the fashion world. My life will be less stressful now, and I can't see myself going back. I hope people don't forget me, but I don't crave publicity either – <u>I was never keen on the whole celebrity thing, but I'll have to see how I feel as all that fades away.</u> Actually, I'm not doing the writing for the money, but I do need to have a career because I don't want the girls to be the only thing in my life – that would be no good for them. I suppose I am rather like my mother in some ways.

Int.: Well, we wish you every success with it.

JH: Thank you.

Vocabulary p.99

1a cloth – U – neutral
clothes – C (plural) – neutral
clothing – U – formal
dress/attire – U – formal
garment – C – formal
kit – C/U – informal
outfit – C – formal
wardrobe – C (usually singular) – neutral
wear – U – formal

1b 1 wardrobe 2 cloth 3 garments 4 clothes 5 clothing
6 kit 7 wear 8 dress 9 outfit

2 1 style 2 label 3 design 4 brand 5 logo 6 pattern

3a 1 let out / take in 2 let down / take up 3 dress up / dress down 4 change into / out of 5 wrap up 6 slip on / off
7 do/zip up 8 grow into / out of

3b 1 change out of; (slip) into 2 dress up 3 grew out of
4 wrap up 5 slipped on 6 let out 7 turn; up 8 Do; up

4 1 in 2 height 3 style 4 catch 5 comeback 6 statement
7 victim

Language development p.100

1

noun [C/U]	desire
verb [T]	desire
adjective (describing something you desire)	desirable
negative adjective	undesirable
adverb (from adjective)	desirably
noun [U] (from adjective)	desirability
negative noun [C] (someone/something that isn't wanted)	undesirable
adjective (from past participle)	desired

1 desirable 2 undesirable 3 undesirables 4 desired
5 desirability

2

noun [C]	origin
plural noun	origins
adjective	original
negative adjective	unoriginal
adverb	originally
verb [I, T]	originate
noun [C] (thing or person)	original
noun [U] (from adjective)	originality

1 origin 2 original 3 unoriginal 4 original 5 originally
6 origins 7 originality 8 originates

3

adjective	secure
negative adjective	insecure
adverb	securely
negative adverb	insecurely
noun [U]	security
negative noun [C, U]	insecurity
verb [T]	secure

1 security 2 insecure 3 securely 4 secure 5 secure
6 insecurities 7 secure 8 insecurely

4

adjective	popular
negative adjective	unpopular
noun [U]	popularity
negative noun [U]	unpopularity
adverb	popularly
verb [T]	popularise
noun [U] (from verb)	popularisation

1 popular 2 popularity 3 popularise 4 unpopular
5 unpopularity 6 popularly 7 popularisation

English in Use p.101

1 b) and c)

2 1 best-selling 2 ✔ 3 marketing 4 What's 5 ✔
6 product's 7 families 8 buying decisions 9 ✔ 10 sector
11 premium,' says 12 Institute 13 behaviour 14 degree
15 ✔ 16 tins

Language development

family – families, strategy – strategies, toy – toys,

holiday – holidays

Reading pp.102–103

1 a Hamish Pringle is the author of a book on the subject.
   b David Graham is an expert in TV audience data.
   c Michael Winner is a celebrity who appears in an advertisement.
   d £100 = cost of attending the function
   e 200,000 years ago = these attitudes were formed
   f 150 = size of groups in which humans lived then

3 1 D (*new book* (line 6) links to *the author*; *the effectiveness … shrewdness of the casting* (line 9) links to *the most successful celebrity … the actress Prunella Scales*)

   2 B (*So eliminating … a well-known name ... is not easy* (line 14) links to *Nonetheless, if we all agree …*; *Can we bottle it?* links to the response *And here another expert thinks he may be on to something* (line 17))

   3 G (*He thinks …* links with *According to Graham, academic evolutionary psychologists believe we may be …* (line 23))

   4 F (*foraging bands of 150 or so …* (line 29) links with *To be successful in such a social grouping …*)

   5 E (*What intrigues Graham … finding practical applications …* (line 39) links with *He proposes, if he can find partners or clients willing to sponsor a study …*; *… whether they connect up with the theory of evolutionary psychology* links with *… in due course, the same theoretical framework …* (line 43))

   6 A (*soap operas are 'fast food for the brain' …* links with *The analogy here is with our taste for sweet and fattening treats* (line 51))

5a 1 d   2 f   3 e   4 a   5 c   6 b
5b 1 c   2 d   3 e   4 f   5 a   6 b

Writing p.104

1b–e Proposal suggesting ways of raising the profile of the Adventure Centre to increase bookings

Introduction

The aim of this Proposal ~~are~~ **is** to suggest ways of promoting the Adventure Centre to increase bookings, and make recommendations for ~~action~~ ~~it is~~ **action. It is** based on information ~~gatherd~~ **gathered** from customer feedback and feedback from colleagues.

Results of feedback

It is clear from customer feedback that the Centre is ~~generaly~~ **generally** popular with those who come, but there is a problem with general publicity. Some said that they ~~have not~~ **had not** heard of the Centre until a friend told them about ~~them,~~ **it,** and others complained that they could not find the website. This last point was <u>supported</u> by comments from staff.

Suggestions and recommendations

In order to deal with the problems ~~identefied~~ **identified** in the feedback and to increase ~~bookings; we~~ **bookings, we** recommend the following measures.

1 To address the problem of publicity:
   ● journalists should be invited to special Open Days so that features on the Centre can be run in the press
   ● brochures and eye-catching posters should be designed for display in Tourist Information Centres
   ● a specialist should be <u>employed</u> to redesign the website, to

make it faster, user-friendly and more ~~accesible~~ **accessible** to Internet browsers
   ● the promotional ~~Budget~~ **budget** should be increased to pay for these measures

2 To attract more bookings:
   ● introduce a series of special ~~offer's,~~ **offers,** including <u>cut prices outside high season</u>, and special packages for school parties.

Conclusion

Implementing the measures above should lead to ~~the~~ **a** general increase in awareness of the Centre and a subsequent increase in bookings. If the Centre is to <u>thrive</u>, we urge the directors to put them in place immediately.

2 *Suggested answers*

Task A

Proposal suggesting ways in which publicity for the Adventure Centre could be improved

Introduction

The aim of this proposal is to suggest ways in which publicity for the Adventure Centre could be improved. It is based on information from feedback provided by visitors to the Centre and observations made by staff.

Results of feedback

Clearly, many people find it difficult to navigate round the website and are often directed to the wrong part of the site. Some claim that brochures ordered via the website have taken a long time to arrive, partly because a second-class stamp has been used. The brochures themselves have also been criticised for being unclear and containing incorrect information – the telephone number is an old one. Many said that they only found out about the Centre from friends.

Suggestions and recommendations

In order to improve publicity, we recommend taking the following measures.
   • it is vital to take on a computer specialist to deal with the website problems; it must be redesigned to be faster, more user-friendly and more accessible to Internet browsers
   • brochures should be updated regularly so that information is current; they should also be redesigned to be clearer and more eye-catching
   • publicity should always be sent out by first-class post, so that it arrives the next day
   • the Centre needs a higher media profile; there should be Open Days with organised events and specially invited journalists who would run follow-up features on the Centre
   • the budget for publicity should be increased.

Conclusion

The suggestions above should result in a great improvement in publicity for the Centre.

Task B

Report on problems with publicity for the Adventure Centre with recommendations for change

Introduction

The aim of this report is to explain problems associated with current publicity for the Centre, and suggest ways in which it could be improved. It is based on complaints made by visitors to the Centre, and observations made by staff.

Background information

There have been a lot of complaints about the difficulty of finding out information about the Centre. It seems as though word of mouth is the only way that some people hear of it. The Internet should be an effective way of advertising, but many people find the Centre website very complicated and hard to navigate. This puts many people off, and they go elsewhere for their holiday. Some claim that brochures ordered via the website have taken a long time to arrive, partly because a second-class stamp has been used. The brochures themselves have also been criticised for being unclear and containing incorrect information – the telephone number is an old one, and the pictures are old and uninspiring.

Suggestions and recommendations

In order to improve publicity, we recommend making the following changes.

- take on a computer specialist to redesign the website so that it is faster, more user-friendly and more accessible to Internet browsers
- update brochures regularly so that information is current and presented more effectively
- use first-class post at all times.

Conclusion

The publicity must be improved, as it is the first point of contact for our visitors and will result in a loss of custom if the recommendations are not implemented.

Module 10

English in Use p.105

2 1 amusing   2 belief   3 apparently   4 beneficial   5 impression   6 infectious   7 uncontrollable

4 8 suspicious   9 charmingly   10 documentary   11 unavoidable   12 painful   13 necessarily   14 depressing   15 helpless

> **Language development**
> unnecessary, unnecessarily, necessitate, necessity

Language development pp.106–107

1 1 I kept calling the box office because I was trying to get tickets.
2 When I had bought my popcorn, I settled down to enjoy the film.
3 We stood at the back of the concert hall and tried to see what was happening.
4 Just as I arrived at the theatre, I realised that I had left the tickets behind.
5 The lights went out, and as a result, the audience was left in total darkness.

2 1 Growing up in Los Angeles, she dreams of becoming an actress.
2 Brad has had a busy year, starring in three films.
3 Living in London, it is easy for me to get to the theatre.
4 Reading the review, I realised that I had seen the film before.
5 Holding a top hat in one hand and a cane in the other, he performed an amazing tap dance routine.
6 Not being able to swim, he had to rely on other actors to do all his swimming stunts for him.

3 1 Being an art lover, she was very keen to go and see the exhibition.
2 Having packed / After packing the car up, we set off.
3 Never having been to Italy before, I was feeling slightly nervous.
4 Despite being pleased to be in New York, I missed my old friends.

5 Putting the phone down / Having put the phone down, I grabbed my suitcase and ran.
6 Not having performed on the stage before, I didn't know quite what to expect.

4 1 Once the cast had been chosen, they could start the rehearsals.
2 Because the show is booked solid for weeks, it is hard to get into.
3 If the chase scenes are carefully edited, they could look spectacular.

5 1 Bored, I fell asleep in the second act.
2 Given the right coaching, Claudia could become a great soprano one day.
3 Rated by the critics as a 'must see' show, it should be pretty good.
4 Poorly constructed, the set was starting to collapse.
5 Better publicised, the show would have been more successful.
6 Once properly advertised, the show started to do better.

6 1 I bought a programme so that I could see who else was in the show.
2 I sat down and started watching, and then realised I had seen the film before.
3 I've seen the Rocky Horror show a lot of times, and as a result I have learnt most of the words.
4 If you heard her sing, you'd never believe she was totally untrained.

7 1 We got seats at the front to have a better view.
2 They sold enough tickets for the production to be a financial success.
3 To hear her talk, you'd think she was a great actress herself.
4 We arrived at the theatre only to discover that the lead actor was sick.
5 I had had enough rehearsals to be confident in the role.
6 To be successful, a new musical needs to have at least three great tunes.

8 1 The plan was for the show **to be** transferred to Broadway after a few months in London.
2 The children jumped up, ~~to shout~~, **shouting** 'He's behind you!' when the villain appeared.
3 Not ~~to have~~ **having** a ticket, I couldn't get into the concert.
4 Unsuccessfully, I searched the Internet ~~finding~~ **to find** the soundtrack.
5 I enjoyed the show, ~~laughed~~ **laughing** all the way through.
6 Julie was the first person ~~playing~~ **to play** the role in the theatre.
7 ~~Walking on stage the audience greeted the singer with a loud cheer.~~ **As the singer walked on stage, the audience greeted him/her with a loud cheer.** *(subject of both clauses must be the same)*
8 I'm very disappointed not **to** have seen Elvis perform live.
9 She walked on stage only ~~realising~~ **to realise** she had forgotten her words.
10 ~~Rising to their feet, the soloist bowed to the ecstatic audience.~~ **The soloist bowed to the ecstatic audience, who rose to their feet.** *(subject of both clauses must be the same)*

9 1 having (been) closed down   2 being   3 Having persuaded   4 to renovate   5 restore   6 Helped   7 welcoming   8 staging

English in Use p.108

1 sorts/kinds of   2 as well   3 up for   4 go at   5 charge of   6 show   7 us making   8 better   9 point   10 the chance   11 open air   12 laid   13 advised

Language development

… participants can enrol on workshops, trying their hand at …

Workshops are very popular, led by professional musicians …

The festival continues for the whole weekend, culminating in …

Held in the park, the outdoor concert …

Listening p.109

2 1 20,000   2 playback singer   3 silent (films)   4 225   5 range
6 shocking   7 restaurants   8 notes

3 1 musical   2 characters   3 screen   4 recorded   5 released
6 soundtrack

Tapescript

If I were to ask you who you think is the most recorded singer in history, you'd probably come up with names like the Beatles, Elvis Presley, Madonna – but you'd be completely wrong. In fact, you'd be thinking of the wrong continent entirely. For the holder of that record lives and works in India. Her name is Asha Bhosle, and she has recorded more than 20,000 songs in more than a dozen languages.

Asha has been working in the Indian film industry ever since the late 1950s. She is what is called a 'playback singer'. In Indian films, many of which are musicals, the actors you see on the screen do not actually sing the songs. These are recorded by playback singers, and the actors just move their lips as if they were singing. The Indian film industry – 'Bollywood' as it's sometimes called – is huge, producing many more films a year than Hollywood, with an enormous worldwide audience, and Asha Bhosle is one of its biggest names.

Asha was born in the 1930s and grew up at a time when cinema was the main form of public entertainment in India. Until 1931, all films were silent films, which meant that they could reach an enormous audience, because there was no need to translate them into local languages. The introduction of what are known as 'talkies' – films with a soundtrack – complicated the issue in a multilingual country like India, where there were at least 225 different languages being spoken at the time. The industry responded by concentrating on making musical films of a type unique to India, where the story is really told through the medium of song – much more accessible than dialogue.

What made Asha Bhosle into such a big star was her vocal range. She was able to sing all sorts of parts, from young heroine to world-weary older woman, and this range was what made the films successful because the more expressive the singing, the easier it was for the actress on screen to bring the character to life. Another reason why Asha became well known was that many of the roles she sang were regarded as rather shocking in 1960s India – although they do not shock at all by today's standards! And despite being well over retirement age, Asha is still working, and not just in the world of film. She is currently planning to open a chain of restaurants across India. It's not hard to guess what music diners will hear as they tuck into their meal. She has also been involved in bringing her music to an even wider audience. A new CD featuring the voice of Asha Bhosle has just been released in Europe, and she has helped with both the choice of songs to be included and with the notes that give the background to the songs for those of us less familiar with the conventions of Indian cinema. As well as the notes, there are also some pictures of Asha and shots from the films on the sleeve. So, let's now hear a bit from the CD …

Vocabulary p.110

1 D   2 B   3 B   4 A   5 C   6 B   7 A   8 D   9 A   10 D   11 C
12 B   13 A   14 C

Language development p.111

1 1 A, B   2 B, C   3 B, C   4 B   5 A, B   6 C   7 A   8 B, C
2a 1 for   2 over   3 about   4 in   5 of   6 against
2b 1 rude   2 annoyed   3 perfect   4 deficient   5 pleased
6 scared
3 1 of   2 from   3 for   4 for   5 with   6 from   7 for   8 for
9 for   10 at   11 from   12 with   13 at   14 of   15 of   16 for
17 about   18 about

English in Use p.112

1 Some people do not approve of singers like Hayley because they believe that classical music should not be made popular in this way.

2 1 some/every   2 what   3 which   4 such   5 as   6 of   7 that
8 taken   9 would   10 been/become/got   11 if
12 may/could/might   13 had   14 for   15 unless

Language development

dismissive of   interested in

Writing p.113

2 1 Having recently tried out two games, I had mixed reactions.
2 Although I enjoy playing computer games, I want to be challenged by them.
3 In my opinion, this game was not challenging enough.
4 In spite of the (excellent) graphics, they did not make up for the rather boring game.

3 1 The second game, called *Demons on the Loose*, was considerably more interesting.
2 The game involved attacking villains and demons which are hidden among the very realistic graphics.
3 In my opinion, this game is better than *Castle Raider*, not only because it is much more difficult to find the demons but also because the levels are difficult to get through.

4 Number 1 is the best conclusion.

5 *Complete model answer*
I appreciate it when new games come on the market, but unfortunately not all of them are equally good. Having recently tried out two new games, I had mixed reactions to them.
The first game is called *Castle Raider*, and is a 'search and rescue' game. Although I enjoy playing computer games, I want to be challenged by them. In my opinion, this game was not challenging enough. There are 16 levels, **and the idea is to find a person who is trapped in the castle and rescue them from dangerous situations.** Each level is more complex than the last, but I found they were easy to get through and took very little time. In spite of the excellent graphics, **which include colourful settings within the castle,** they did not make up for the rather boring game. **Children might enjoy it, but it is not very sophisticated.**
The second game, called *Demons on the Loose*, was considerably more interesting. The game involved **finding hidden treasure by** attacking villains and demons which are hidden among the very realistic graphics. In my opinion, this game is better than *Castle Raider*, not only because it is much more difficult to find the demons, but also because the levels are difficult to get through.

Imagine a game which takes four hours to complete a level! The game gives you value for money, **and anyone who likes a challenge will really enjoy it.**

All in all, if you're looking for fast fun, challenge and value for money, then *Demons on the Loose* fits the bill.

Reading p.114–115

4 1 D (*the raw intensity of the music here makes up for the lack of studio polish* (line 50))

2/3/4 A (*and their own compositions* (line 10))
C (*eight self-composed tracks* (line 34))
E (*Manu's melodic tunes* (line 63))

5 F (*he is in fact owner of, and inspiration behind, popular restaurants in London and Paris* (line 72))

6 B (*singers less well-known outside the Arab-speaking world* (line 26))

7 F (*While most compilations sound … is an entity in its own right* (line 74))

8 E (*reflecting his mixed ethnic background* (line 56))

9 B (*backed up by intelligent sleeve notes* (line 19))

10 A (*was praised in the British music press* (line 3))

11 D (*formidable reputation as a live act … goes some way to showing why* (line 38))

12 F (*sublime offerings from unfamiliar names* (line 81))

13 C (*trained as a teacher in Havana* (line 29))

14 D (*a non-stop musical maelstrom* (line 41))

15 A (*the unlikely but successful addition of accordion, trumpet and slide guitar* (line 12))

16 D (*Ironically, after a decade of international success, these concerts were the first in the city* (line 44))

17 C (*a fast-developing talent; someone to keep a close eye on* (line 36))

5 1 e 2 d 3 a 4 g 5 c 6 b 7 f

Practice exam

Reading
Paper 1 Parts 1–4

1 C (*Yet no portrait … is candid, and none of its documentary aims to reveal the truth* (line 43))

2 A (*this retrospective tribute* (line 8))

3 F (*We all know that he's been one of the best of our travel writers* (line 86))

4 B (*100 photographs, one for each year of the 20th century* (line 30))

5 E (*a real curiosity … classical musicians and writers* (line 78))

6 C (*They are posed, hi-tech and ingeniously constructed* (line 42))

7 A (*multi-authored study … by virtue of its diversity* (line 2))

8 D (*mistitled* The Art of Seeing *… the most dramatic of them looks staged* (line 49))

9 F (*photographic autobiography … his skills with a camera lens complement his personal journeys* (line 85))

10 E (*The use of black and white … 1960s photography … turn their backs on the colour technology to remind us of the swinging days* (line 66))

11 B (*the book's commentary makes a connection between the examination of the body and wider cultural issues* (line 32))

12 D (*photographers … heroes of the profession* (line 58))

13 E (*full of detail and are often of domestic contexts* (line 76))

14 B (*useful introductions aimed at novices and students of photography* (line 26))

15 C (*There are plenty of pictures of women … misleading* (line 38))

16 E (*surely he was at the peak of his professional career during his 14-year association with* Queen *magazine* (line 73))

17 D (*favourite shots by two dozen staff photographers … the long-established news agency* (line 50))

18 A (*his camera lens transformed … composition* (line 18))

19 F (*catching fish on four different channels* (line 10) links with *On each of these …*)

20 C (*a whole range of products … financial services* (line 18) links with *you can acquire celebrity status through frequent appearances on the back of biscuit cartons*)

21 A (*due to its tendency to fly out of the water* (line 28) links with *As a result, … you can buy leaping fish T-shirts*)

22 G (*they swing them into the boat with as little ado as possible* (line 42) links with *To compensate for these visual shortcomings, …; such a well-orchestrated spectacle* (line 45) also links back to paragraph G)

23 B (*the fishermen use the very latest technology to assist them* links with *Despite all this* (line 53))

24 D (*the 175 entrants have been gradually whittled down to just ten finalists* (line 59) links with *I watch the anglers standing apprehensively on the central stage*; the story of a keen amateur fisherman contrasts with a more recent fishing story about Darren Nixon (line 62))

25 D (*I hadn't thought about who would want to be led by me, but it was a perplexing and humbling question.* (line 11))

26 A (*the course was going to force me to ask questions of myself that I wasn't sure I wanted the answers to … my fear of exploring my own weaknesses* (line 21))

27 B (*the quiet leaders are often overlooked and underdeveloped … the most competent leaders are not always the ones that are obvious to us* (line 40))

28 A (*Leadership is all around us … the leaders all around us contribute to our everyday lives* (line 54))

29 C (*Evaluate the leadership skills that you demonstrate and concentrate on building them* (line 80))

30 D (*there's probably a parallel to be drawn between the complexity of Mahler's orchestration and the technical wizardry of the modern car* (line 67))

31 F (*why should young people suddenly relate to classical music? 'It's a trend …* (line 97))

32 C (*it may also be significant … suggestive of confectionary* (line 51))

33 B (*advertising teams are rarely made up of musical connoisseurs* (line 20))

34/35 D (*a winner for marketing luxury cars* (line 57))
E (*giving a decidedly budget product an improved marketing image* (line 82))

36 D (*Adverts for cars often tend to use classical music in a very clichéd way* (line 61))

37 B (*it often comes down to gut instinct … It's so subjective – everyone's opinion … is clouded by their emotional attachment to a piece of music* (line 22))

38 F (*You've got to be conscious of not alienating people* (line 102))

39 C (*employ composers to create the music to complement a specific ad in production* (line 40))

40/41 C (*in ads mainly targeted at women* (line 44))
D (*ads which are aimed at male consumers* (line 55))

42 F (*Who knows what it may have done for the sales figures of Puccini and Handel* (line 110))

43/44 A (*a well-known piece of music … creates a mental link* (line 8))

E (*thanks to the footballing associations of the piece* (line 84))

45 D (*dreaming up visions of far-flung, exotic places* (line 76))

46 A (*they have gained favour through being an integral part of a certain advert* (line 12))

47 E (*the same music has been selected by polar opposites in the retail world* (line 87))

48 B (*the juxtaposition of images … a very different one* (line 27))

Paper 2 Writing

Part 1

Suggested answer

Report on the visit to the UK

This report is based on personal experiences during last year's UK trip, plus information gathered from fellow students.

Programme

The trip involved a considerable amount of travelling, and some people found this excessive. For instance, travelling overnight to the UK was a tiring start to the trip, and the train journey from London to Edinburgh was felt to take too long compared to the very quick flight back. Another unpopular aspect of the programme was the early start time for the language classes, although these were successful in all other respects.

Accommodation

The London hotel, with its busy staff, provided little opportunity for students to practise their English. In contrast, staying with the very welcoming families in Scotland gave us ample opportunity to do so. The hotel in Scotland was in a lovely location, but unfortunately it is a cold place at this time of year.

Sightseeing

The bus tour around London was very informative, but should have been in English rather than our own language. Younger students found the museum visits a little dull, and older students mentioned a lack of organised evening entertainment in London. In Scotland, there was an excellent tour around Edinburgh, and everyone enjoyed the wonderful dancing display in the evening.

Recommendations

Overall, this trip was a success, but we have some improvements to suggest. Firstly, a longer stay with local families would give more scope for language improvement. Rethinking the travel arrangements could make the trip less tiring. Finally, students should be advised to pack warm clothing for the Scottish part of the trip.

Part 2

Suggested answers

2 Speaking around the world

I wonder how many people reading this article are trying to learn another language? Probably most of you! Whether you are studying alone or in a class, language learning has never been so easy.

Twenty years ago, in the country where I was brought up, language teaching was done using very traditional methods; students had only textbooks, a cassette player and a teacher to help them make progress. There was nothing wrong with these methods, but we have many more resources available to us today.

Indeed, we can choose from a huge range of language-learning methods, and each student can select the method and timescale that suits him or her best. For example, switch on the TV and

you can get access to programmes in a variety of languages, or you might choose to follow a language course on video. You can also use your home computer to study languages on the Internet according to your own personal timetable. Even if you find it easier to learn with a group of other students, you can take a classroom-based course which makes use of all this language-learning technology.

But what will advances in technology have to offer us in the future? Will we be practising our speaking in the virtual reality of a foreign country? What about the boredom of learning endless vocabulary? Maybe this will become a thing of the past? But whatever the future holds, I know I'm glad to be a language student now, rather than 20 years ago!

3 Reference for Alexandre Henderson

To whom it may concern

I have known Alexandre for the last ten years and worked with her on several occasions. She is a cheerful, optimistic person, and her warm and sensitive personality, makes her an ideal person to work with young people. She is used to caring for children, as she comes from a large family and she has frequently been a reliable babysitter for me, looking after my two children aged seven and ten.

Alexandre has always been an enthusiastic sportswoman and is one of the leading members of our local tennis club. She has also recently competed in a national athletics event, winning trophies in both long-distance running races and the high jump. She shows great determination and follows a regular personal training programme to maintain a good all-round fitness level. Alexandre has been a colleague of mine, working on a part-time basis as a personal trainer at our local gym for the last two years. I have watched her working with clients of all ages, encouraging them to achieve their personal goals. She shows great patience and kindness towards those who are not used to exercise, and she is able to motivate the best athletes to excel at their particular sport. She has recently completed a six-month course on sports technology in order to bring her technical knowledge up to date.

Alexandre is a person who is extremely honest and also totally trustworthy. I have no hesitation in recommending her for this position.

4 A proposal for the International Cultural Exhibition

France is a country of endless variety. Each city and department has its own character and history. As you travel through the country, you can see the ever-changing scenery, from the wide flowing rivers in the Loire to the beauty of the high Alps in the Savoie. I suggest that an exhibition featuring France should illustrate the full range of its geography and culture through the medium of colour photography and video film.

Historical cities

The beauty of the capital city, Paris, is well known worldwide, but there are historical towns and cities throughout France which should be included in the display. The history of France goes back centuries, and this is reflected in the style of the architecture as you visit cities such as Bordeaux in the west, Beaune in the east and Montpellier in the south.

Art and culture

No exhibition of France would be complete without some of the wonderful works of art which have been produced by French artists. There could be a small art exhibition for visitors to see, perhaps with French jazz music playing in the background to help to create a truly French atmosphere.

Food and wine

French cuisine enjoys worldwide renown, and there are fine cheeses and wines produced in all the various regions. A range of these different foods could be made available for visitors to the exhibition to taste.

I consider that all these suggestions would give a good impression of the most important aspects of the French culture.

5 Letter of complaint

Dear Sir/ Madam,

Over the past year, this company has been holding business meetings at your hotel, and we have frequently booked overnight accommodation with you for our overseas clients. Unfortunately, a number of problems regarding the facilities and services offered by the hotel have been brought to our attention, and we are writing to make you aware of these.

Firstly, when booking a room for our business seminars, we request various facilities to be available in the room. On the last two occasions, we ordered a video player for use during the seminar, but on the day none was available.

We also order coffee to be served in the meeting room prior to the start of the meeting. Unfortunately, twice in the last month this wasn't provided on time, and on one occasion it didn't appear for an hour.

Given the length of our meetings, it is essential that the seating is comfortable. We have had several complaints from colleagues who feel that the quality of the furniture should be improved. Furthermore, several of our important clients have been unhappy with the level of cleanliness in the bedrooms and have commented on the limited choice of food offered on the restaurant menu.

I hope that you are able to take our comments on board and that some improvements can be made in the quality of the service we and our clients receive. Otherwise we will be forced to search for an alternative location for our business seminars.

I look forward to receiving your early reply,

Yours faithfully

Paper 3 English in Use

Part 1

1 D   (*rapid advances in* = collocation)
2 B   (*composition of a population*)
3 A   (*attractive option* = collocation)
4 C   (*in the vicinity of* = set phrase)
5 D   (*to take advantage of*)
6 C   (*to fit in with*)
7 A   (*to grow in popularity*)
8 D   (either *worry* or *concern* would link to *feared that*, but *worry* is too strong here)
9 B   (*to be deprived of*)
10 B   (*an important aspect of* = collocation)
11 A   (*to become evident that*)
12 B   (*readily accessible* = collocation)
13 C   (*lively exchange* = collocation)
14 D   (*a wide audience* = collocation)
15 B   (*to be provided with*)

Part 2

16 took   17 only   18 such   19 grew   20 because/as/since
21 found   22 up   23 a   24 with   25 ought/needed/had
26 could   27 what   28 to   29 fact   30 which

Part 3

31 so 32 when   33 ✔   34 because   35 what   36 such   37 ✔
38 to   39 with   40 and   41 it   42 ✔   43 ✔   44 also
45 not   46 of

Part 4

47 surrounding   48 strength   49 downpour   50 equipment
51 tropical   52 muddy   53 composure   54 entertainment

55 daily   56 limitless/unlimited   57 operations   58 irrelevant
59 potential   60 layout   61 irritating

Part 5

62 if/though it   63 inform   64 intend   65 By all   66 at least
67 reminder   68 at all   69 (very) dull/tedious/uninteresting
70 Take your   71 a bad/poor/negative
72 exceeding / going over   73 draw/bring   74 a word

Part 6

75 E   76 I   77 B   78 H   79 F   80 C

Paper 4 Listening

Part 1

1 docks   2 life jacket   3 platform   4 hand(s)   5 smooth
6 clapping; cheering   7 exciting   8 stress   9 135 dollars / $135

Part 2

10 7th–9th (of) July   11 *Summertime*   12 Africa   13 carrot(s)
14 (highest/best/top/good) quality   15 organic   16 dry
17 soup

Part 3

18 B   (*A friend of mine said that I'd never make a living as a painter and suggested I learnt to do something more useful*)
19 C   (*lecturers … putting you down*)
20 C   (*I was also very focused and willing to push myself forward*)
21 B   (*So I went in the opposite direction*)
22 A   (*I have a go at all manner of things*)
23 B   (*a desperation on the part of the designers to show how original they are being*)
24 D   (*If you want superb detail, you won't get it by scribbling something on the back of an envelope*)

Part 4

25 G   (*he was so passionate about what he was trying to explain*)
26 D   (*made me think about things from his point of view*)
27 H   (*everyone just wrote me off as a failure. But he found the time to talk to me, to find out what the problem was*)
28 B   (*you've got to be prepared to stick your neck out*)
29 E   (*that made me realise I was messing up my own life*)
30 D   (*I wouldn't have got my degree at all*)
31 B   (*I've met loads of people, and we've all got something in common*)
32 G   (*I hope to start out in my own business soon*)
33 A   (*I say to the people on my team, 'Come on – let's give it a try'*)
34 E   (*I dreamed of being in a rock group ... We're releasing our first album next week*)

Tapescript

PART 1

Hello and welcome to the Travel Programme with me, Hilary Barrington. I'm just back from the island of Bermuda, where I've been visiting an attraction that goes by the name Dolphin Quest, based in Bermuda's disused navy <u>docks</u>. As the name suggests, this is a place where you can find dolphins, those famously endearing sea animals. But at Dolphin Quest, you do more than just watch them swimming around performing tricks – because, if you want, you can get in the water and swim round with them, and as everyone has to wear a <u>life jacket</u>, you don't even have to be a swimmer to join in!

For the less adventurous visitor, though, there is a shallow area where you can sit on a <u>platform</u> which lies just under the water, and you can get close to the dolphins that way, even if you're not a swimmer. Then there's a deeper area for keener swimmers and those who want to go snorkelling.   →

Not many people know this, but there is a proper protocol for meeting a dolphin. You should introduce yourself gradually – even a little formally – keeping to the edge of the water with your arms by your sides until the animals get used to you. After a while, you give them <u>hand</u> signals to prepare them for the fact that you're about to enter their personal space, and then you can start to come closer. After that, you can feed them fish, swim with them or even touch them. They love to be touched – their skin is <u>smooth</u> – and to play. People hug them, stroke them, even kiss them. It's one of the few opportunities you'll get to be a kid again.

What you do have to do in return, though, is show appreciation – <u>clapping</u> and <u>cheering</u> are welcomed by dolphins, and even the most cynical person would be hard pressed not to appreciate the animals themselves, especially when they are appear to be so pleased to see you. As you arrive, they jump, whistle and click to attract your attention. The dolphins just love the attention, and I got the impression that they find being around people very <u>exciting</u>. So you don't get the feeling that they're being exploited particularly.

And hugging a dolphin, it seems, is good for you, too – according to experts, it's an excellent activity for lowering your <u>stress</u> levels and increasing your feeling of well-being. Many people end up in tears; others are elated, even euphoric. As one of my fellow visitors remarked, it made her look at life in a different way.

At <u>$135</u> for 30 minutes, it may seem like a rather expensive hug. Nevertheless, swimming with dolphins was at the top of the wish list when 20,000 Britons took part in a survey call 'Your Top 20 Thrills', saying that swimming with dolphins was the thing that they most wanted to try just once in their lives.

If you'd like to find out more about swimming with dolphins …

PART 2

If you're a fan of experimental music, then there's a real treat in store for you at the Henley Music Festival, which is taking place between the <u>7th and 9th of July</u> at Henley, near London. Because that's where you'll get a chance to see the Vienna Vegetable Orchestra in action – yes, that's right, I said 'Vegetable' Orchestra.

Now this is not a joke; the orchestra really exists, and they'll be playing a variety of pieces, ranging from traditional folk music to opera favourites like Gershwin's *Summertime* – and all the music will be performed not on traditional musical instruments, but on instruments made completely out of fresh vegetables.

The inspiration behind the orchestra lies in the simple concept that it's possible to make musical sounds with anything. As is well known, in <u>Africa</u> and elsewhere, musicians make their own very effective instruments out of recycled materials such as bits of old cars and discarded cooking utensils, so why not food? Well, one reason is that vegetables are not particularly noisy as a rule, but unlike their African counterparts, the musicians in the orchestra will have the benefit of amplification to make sure the audience catches each tiny sound.

In the Vienna Orchestra, for example, there'll be drums made out of pumpkins, a flute that started life as a <u>carrot</u>, and a violin where two leeks are rubbed together to create a sound. Easiest to make are the carrot flutes, apparently, so there's something you might all like to try at home! But beware: I'm assured by members of the orchestra that only vegetables of the <u>highest quality</u> should be used. They make their instruments freshly an hour before each concert, as they tend to deteriorate after that, as does the quality

of the sound. Another interesting fact I gleaned from the orchestra was that vegetables in Britain tend to be larger than those back home in Vienna.

To get round this, they've had to order <u>organic</u> produce when they're performing there, which tends to be more the size they're used to dealing with at home.

On the day of the concert, around 40 kilos of vegetables are delivered to the venue. Once made, the instruments have to be stored very carefully, as the sound is impaired if they get too <u>dry</u> – so humid conditions are needed – which is an issue in some concert venues, especially in the winter when there is central heating.

And in case you're thinking that this is all a bit of a waste of food, let me assure you that nothing gets thrown away. After the performance, the musicians wash the remaining vegetables, chop them up and serve them to the audience as <u>soup</u> at the end of the evening. And in the cool of the evening, what could be nicer – let's hope these vegetables taste as good as they sound!

If you're interested in seeing the Vienna Vegetable Orchestra perform …

PART 3

Int. = Interviewer, JB = Jocelyn Burton

Int.: My guest today is Jocelyn Burton, an artist working in precious metals. She's been creating jewellery and other beautiful objects out of silver and gold for the last 30 years. Jocelyn, was it always your intention to go into this sort of work?

JB: My first love was painting – that's why I went to art college. But in those days, there were really very few first-rate women painters around, and that was a bit discouraging. <u>A friend of mine said that I'd never earn my living as a painter and suggested I learnt to do something more useful</u> by enrolling in a crafts course. He was teaching in the silver and jewellery department, so that was the course I went for – it was pure chance, really. But, once I started, I realised that it was a completely blank canvas and a new world in which few artists had done anything much.

Int.: But did you enjoy the fine art classes?

JB: I always had the feeling that, when we were drawing, the <u>lecturers would bend over backwards to admire the work of certain students; but, if you happened to be a woman, they would say, 'I detect the influence of so-and-so' – putting you down</u> when you'd put so much into your work. It was deeply discouraging. Then, at the end of my second year, I won an international design award for a diamond necklace I'd made on my crafts course. Everybody said I should use the opportunity to start professionally, so I went to the college principal and asked for one day off a week to do it. He refused, so I walked out

Int.: That was a brave move.

JB: I was catapulted into the real world. My first job was with a company in London which was manufacturing really very ordinary engagement rings. Although I never wanted to be a jeweller as such, it did give me a great deal of experience that was very useful when I started on my own as a silversmith. I *was* lucky, but <u>I was also very focused and willing to push myself forward</u>, too. It was through working there that I met the managing director of a smart London shop. I showed him samples of my work. When he commissioned a collection of objects in silver from me, that meant I could resign and set up my own studio.

Int.: So, how did you make your mark – what was it in your studio's work that caught people's eye?

JB: When I first started, things made out of silver tended to be extremely heavy and masculine. Silversmiths were mostly busy making objects that wealthy businessmen would want sitting on their desks. So I went in the opposite direction and made pretty objects for the dressing table and romantic pens. I know that a lot of silversmiths didn't take my work very seriously, but, in the end, when I was successful, they had to sit up and take notice. That was very satisfying.

Int.: But you've now moved away from that particular style?

JB: I'm extremely unusual in that I have a go at all manner of things. Nearly everyone else in the trade sticks entirely to one style. I love the diversity – I'm passionately interested in making things, and it doesn't matter what the metal is, although the objects created must be beautiful. They must justify their existence by being either attractive or very usable.

Int.: Or both?

JB: Well, it depends. Sometimes, there's a desperation on the part of designers to show how original they are being. I saw a strange silver teapot in a catalogue the other day which would be virtually unusable given the shape of the handle. Though it was a contemporary piece, it reminded me of 1970s architecture, all heavy and square. I mean, why make that in silver? Make it in stainless steel, perhaps, so that lots of people can buy it. But it beats me why you should use a beautiful precious metal like silver to make something that is ugly.

Int.: And when clients ask you to make something for them, how do you know you're getting it right?

JB: Well, you have to flexible and adapt your ideas constantly. But if, for example, I'm making a big, elaborate light fitting for somebody, they get a life-sized drawing so that they can hang it up and see if it is the right size. If you want superb detail, you won't get it by scribbling something on the back of an envelope. Actually, I used to let clients keep these drawings, but now I tend to hang on to them as works of art in their own right! I hang them on my studio walls. I'm very fortunate in what I do – it's all great fun. Not many people can say that about their work.

Int.: That's very true, Jocelyn. Thank you for joining me today.

JB: Thank you.

PART 4

Speaker 1

My parents were both very artistic, so I followed the same path. I really struggled with science subjects – I had a kind of mental block against technology, but he showed me that engineering could be creative. His lessons were fun, he involved the whole class – he was so passionate about what he was trying to explain, he'd even use the classroom furniture to demonstrate his point! If it wasn't for him, I wouldn't have got my degree at all, because I used to think university was a waste of time, but I've just been offered a job with a construction company in South America – how about that!

Speaker 2

My parents lived abroad, and I was lonely at boarding school, so I just kept my head down in class, wrapped up in my own problems. He said, 'Imagine how I feel, putting so much effort into a lesson, and all you do is stare at the floor.' It really brought me out of myself – made me think about things from his point of view. It's through him I'm so into amateur dramatics now – I've met loads of people, and we've all got something in common. He pushed me into it and said, 'Why don't you get into the school play?' On stage, I relax – I become the character I'm playing.

Speaker 3

I was always in trouble at school, and my attendance record was awful. I kept playing truant, because I was being bullied a lot. I didn't dare tell anyone – not even my parents. My results were bad, so everyone just wrote me off as a failure. But he found the time to talk to me, to find out what the problem was. He even gave me extra tuition, so I did pass Maths and Geography. I'm training to be a plumber and I hope to start out in my own business soon, so I'll be making serious money – way ahead of all my friends who are going through university now.

Speaker 4

Most of the teachers were very strict, but he was different, he looked like your conventional middle-aged teacher, but he wasn't at all. I had this really weird idea for a science project, and I never thought I'd get it approved, but he said, 'I hadn't thought of that – go for it.' I ended up getting a science prize! I realised that, if you believe in something, you've got to be prepared to stick your neck out and see it through. I work as a graphic designer now, in advertising, and if we've got a winning idea, I say to the people on my team, 'Come on – let's give it a try!' It's the only way to succeed.

Speaker 5

I was disruptive at school, and my parents never disciplined me. Playing the drums was all I cared about, I dreamed of being in a rock group. I had no interest in other subjects, and took my frustrations out on the teachers. He threatened to expel me from school if I didn't control my anger – that made me realise I was messing up my own life. So I asked him for extra help in Maths and, in return, he encouraged me to practise my drumming. It was through his contacts that I started working in a recording studio, which led to me being the drummer in a band. We're releasing our first album next week.

Pearson Education Limited
Edinburgh Gate
Harlow
Essex CM20 2JE
England
and Associated Companies throughout the world.

www.longman.com

© Pearson Education Limited 2004

First published 2005

Third impression 2006

ISBN-13: 978-0-582-82401-0 (Book with key and CD pack)
ISBN-13: 978-0-582-82398-3 (Book with key for pack)
ISBN-13: 978-0-582-82399-0 (Book with key)

Set in Minion 12pt

Printed in Spain by Mateu Cromo

Designed by Roarr Design

Page layout by eMC Design, www.emcdesign.org.uk

Illustrated by Colin Brown, Beehive Illustration

Picture research by Sally Coles

Project managed by Catriona Watson-Brown

Acknowledgements

Drew would like to thank his family – Annie, Louis and Freya – for their patience and for all the cups of tea, and his colleagues for their support.

Nick would like to thank Peter Sunderland for his help in the early stages of the project.

Photo acknowledgements

Action Plus/M. Greene p.61; Advertising Archive p.102; Alamy/Sir S. Marsden p.26, R. Chapple/Thinkstock Royalty Free p.23, P. Tweedie p.37, Image State p.41, S. Moudavaris p.43, D. Wall p.53, H. Sykes p.64, G. Palmer p.87, R. Morris p.94, A. King p.105, C. Anania, D. Hallinan p.138 (ml), Photolibrary Wales p.139 (tl), J. Smalley p.139 (ml), Mediacolor's p.138 (bl), Greydon Photography p.138 (tr); foybles p.139 (tr); Clare Kendall p.46; Chronicle Books p.50; Corbis/M. Keller p.44, R. Nowitz p.55, P. Schermeister p.83, S. Cardinale p.98, K. Fleming, H. King p.140 (tr), W. Stone p.138 (mr); Digital Vision Royalty Free p.140 (ml); © ebay p.85; EMAP/Trail Magazine p.58; Empics/EPA p.56; Europics p.24; Getty Images p.30, p.76, B. Vincent p.6, B. Guay p.7, Time Life Pictures p.19, P. Harris p.29, D. Hogan p.48, S. Cohen p.54, Colour Day Production p.57, C. Sanders p.72, J. Haeusler p.79, C. Allegri p.112, A. Mo p.140 (mr); Image Source Royalty Free p.10; John Cole p.101; Justin Slee p.138 (tl); Ken Hunt p.109; Kobal Collection/Los Hooligans/Columbia p.20; National Portrait Gallery/S. Idriss p.39; Natural History Museum p.71; Panos Pictures/P. Tweedie p.97, M. Henley p.139 (bl); Photofusion/M. Murray p.140 (tl), J. Chapman p.140 (br); Punchstock/Photodisc Royalty Free p.138 (br), Brand X Royalty Free p.139 (mr); Rex Features p.35, R. Tang p.32, Sipa press p.139 (br); Sal Idriss/National Portrait Gallery p.39; Science Photo Library/ P. Hayson p.63, A. Bluesky/Society for Complementary Medicine p.66; Topfoto/A. Carey p.140 (bl).

Every effort has been made to trace the copyright holders and we apologise in advance for any unintentional omissions. We would be pleased to insert the appropriate acknowledgement in any subsequent edition of this publication.

The publishers are grateful to the following for permission to reproduce copyright material:

BBC Music Magazine for an extract from 'Consumer Classics' by Catherine Nelson published in *BBC Music Magazine* March 2004; Jocelyn Burton and Vanessa Berridge for details from an interview taken from 'Shining examples' published in *The Lady Magazine* 10th to 16th June 2003 © Vanessa Berridge; Chronicle Books LLC for an extract from *The Pleasures of Slow Food* by Corby Kummer © 2002 www.ChronicleBooks.com; Classic FM Plc for an extract adapted from 'A step-by-step guide to making your own instrument' published in *Classic FM Magazine* August 2004; Design Week and Adrian Shaughnessy for an extract adapted from 'Balance the books' by Adrian Shaughnessy published in *Design Week* 15th April 2004; EMAP for an extract from 'The art of persuasion' by Maria del Carmen Clegg published in *Trail Magazine* October 2002 © emap active; The Financial Times Ltd for extracts adapted from 'The power behind the throne' by Edwin Heathcote published in *Financial Times Magazine* 13th September 2003, 'You are feeling … prosperous?' by John-Paul Fintoff published in *Financial Times Magazine* 29th November 2003 and review of 'The Rise of the Indian Rope Trick by Peter Lamont' by Michael Glover published in *Financial Times Magazine* 24th January 2004 © FT Ltd; Geographical and Christopher Winney at ATG Oxford for details from an interview with Christopher Winney published in *Geographical Magazine* January 2004; Guardian News Service Limited for an extract adapted from 'A map through the moral maze' by Katie Splevins published in *The Guardian* 24th January 2004; Allan Hall for an extract adapted from 'World's luckiest man wins the lottery'; New Scientist for an extract adapted from 'Little house of horrors' published in *New Scientist* 26th July 2003; Richard Henson for an extract adapted from 'The first lady of space' published in *The Lady Magazine* June 2003 © Richard Henson; Nick Higham for an extract adapted from 'In celebrities we trust, in gossip we act on instinct' published in *Marketing Week* 18th March 2004 © Nick Higham; Kate Hilpern for an extract adapted from 'Facing facts' published in *The Guardian* 11th April 2001 © Kate Hilpern; Independent Newspapers for an extract adapted from 'Christmas books' by Tim Hilton published in *The Independent* 13th December 2000 © Independent 2000; John Brown Citrus Publishing, Sankha Guha and The Roseman Organisation for details adapted from 'A bit of rough' published in *Up Magazine* Summer 2001; Metro-Free London Paper for extracts adapted from 'Iron men let off steam' by David Fickling published in *Metro* 20th July 2001 and 'Hallee: why vanity ops are insane' by Georgina LittleJohn published in *Metro* 3rd August 2004 © Metro; Origin Publishing Ltd for extracts from 'I liked digging in the dirt when I was a kid' by Sally Palmer published in *Focus Magazine* November 2003 and 'Feats of endurance' published in *Focus Magazine* June 2004; Pearson Education Limited for extracts from *Brilliant Selection Test Results* by Hodgson © Pearson Education Limited 2003; Pride Media for an extract from 'A view from the top' by India Gary-Jenkins published in *Pride Magazine* March 2004; Dame Anita Roddick, Founder of The Body Shop and Times Newspapers Limited for details from an interview taken from 'The lost art of kindness' by Heather Nicholson published in *The Times* 26th November 2002; Anna Selby for an extract from 'Pampering pleasure: Endorphins and dolphins' published in *The FT Magazine* 20th March 2004 © Anna Selby; Solo Syndication Ltd for an extract from 'Scientists find clue to keeping us young' by Mark Prigg published in *The Evening Standard* 29th April 2004; The Telegraph Group Limited for extracts from 'Manual labour, the latest spectator sport' by Jeff Howell published in *The Telegraph* 2nd July 2000, 'What are friends for' by Tim Dowling published in *The Telegraph* June 2003, 'Stella takes a stand' by Tim Walker published in *The Telegraph* 18th January 2004, 'No one speaks the language' by Nicholas Bagnall published in *The Telegraph* 8th February 2004 and 'Taking the bait' by Richard Grant published in *The Telegraph* 14th April 2004 © Telegraph Group Limited 2000, 2003, 2004; Times Newspapers Limited for articles adapted from 'Same difference' by Candida Crewe published in *The Times* 24th May 2003 and 'Upsetting the odds' by Paul Connolly published in *The Times* 6–12th September 2003 © The Times 2003; Wanderlust Magazine for extracts adapted from 'World Music Reviews' published in *Wanderlust Magazine* August/September and October/November 2001 and an 'interview with Yann Arthus-Bartrand' published in *Wanderlust Magazine* April/May 2003; and World Music Network (UK) Ltd for an extract from 'The Rough Guide to Bollywood Legends: Asha Bhosle' by Ken Hunt published on www.worldmusic.net.

In some instances we have been unable to contact the owners of copyright material and we would appreciate any information that would enable us to do so.